Lecture Notes in Computer Science 11846

Dajiang Zhu · Jingwen Yan ·
Heng Huang · Li Shen ·
Paul M. Thompson · Carl-Fredrik Westin ·
Xavier Pennec · Sarang Joshi ·
Mads Nielsen · Tom Fletcher ·
Stanley Durrleman · Stefan Sommer (Eds.)

Multimodal Brain Image Analysis and Mathematical Foundations of Computational Anatomy

4th International Workshop, MBIA 2019
and 7th International Workshop, MFCA 2019
Held in Conjunction with MICCAI 2019
Shenzhen, China, October 17, 2019
Proceedings

 Springer

Editors
Dajiang Zhu
The University of Texas at Arlington
Arlington, TX, USA

Heng Huang
University of Pittsburgh
Pittsburgh, PA, USA

Paul M. Thompson
University of Southern California
Marina Del Rey, CA, USA

Xavier Pennec
Inria Sophia-Antipolis
Sophia-Antipolis, France

Mads Nielsen
University of Copenhagen
Copenhagen, Denmark

Stanley Durrleman
Inria
Paris, France

Jingwen Yan
Indiana University – Purdue
University Indianapolis
Indianapolis, IN, USA

Li Shen
University of Pennsylvania
Philadelphia, PA, USA

Carl-Fredrik Westin
Harvard Medical School
Boston, MA, USA

Sarang Joshi
University of Utah
Salt Lake City, UT, USA

Tom Fletcher
University of Virginia
Charlottesville, VA, USA

Stefan Sommer
University of Copenhagen
Copenhagen, Denmark

ISSN 0302-9743   ISSN 1611-3349   (electronic)
Lecture Notes in Computer Science
ISBN 978-3-030-33225-9   ISBN 978-3-030-33226-6   (eBook)
https://doi.org/10.1007/978-3-030-33226-6

LNCS Sublibrary: SL6 – Image Processing, Computer Vision, Pattern Recognition, and Graphics

This Springer imprint is published by the registered company Springer Nature Switzerland AG
The registered company address is: Gewerbestrasse 11, 6330 Cham, Switzerland

Additional Workshop Editors

Satellite Events Chair

Kenji Suzuki
Tokyo Institute of Technology
Yokohama, Japan

Workshop Chairs

Hongen Liao
Tsinghua University
Beijing, China

Hayit Greenspan
Tel Aviv University
Tel Aviv, Israel

Challenge Chairs

Qian Wang
Shanghai Jiaotong University
Shanghai, China

Bram van Ginneken
Radboud University
Nijmegen, The Netherlands

Tutorial Chair

Luping Zhou
University of Sydney
Sydney, Australia

Preface

Multimodal Brain Image Analysis (MBIA)

The 4th International Workshop on Multimodal Brain Image Analysis (MBIA 2019) was held on October 17, 2019, in conjunction with the 22nd International Conference on Medical Image Computing and Computer Assisted Intervention (MICCAI 2019) in Shenzhen, China. This workshop, which focuses on brain image analysis employing information from multiple modalities, has been well received when previously held in 2011 (Toronto), 2012 (Nice), and 2013 (Nagoya).

Multimodal brain imaging technologies, including structural MRI, perfusion MRI, diffusion MRI, functional MRI, PET, SPECT, CT, EEG, and MEG can provide distinctive yet complementary knowledge that is critical to the understanding of brain structure, function, and their relationship. The objective of MBIA is to exchange the ideas, methodologies, algorithms, software systems, validation approaches, benchmark datasets, and neuroscience/clinical applications in multimodal brain image analysis among researchers worldwide.

The MBIA 2019 proceedings contain 16 high-quality papers of 8 to 10 pages, and all papers underwent a rigorous double-blind peer-review process. Each submission was reviewed by at least 2 members of the Program Committee, comprising 15 experts in the brain imaging field. Among these 16 accepted papers, 5 of them were selected for oral presentations and the others were selected for poster presentations.

We are grateful to all the MBIA 2019 authors for their participation, the members of the Program Committee for evaluating the papers, the presenters for their inspiring presentations, and all who supported MBIA 2019 by attending the workshop.

August 2019

Dajiang Zhu
Jingwen Yan
Heng Huang
Li Shen
Paul M. Thompson
Carl-Fredrik Westin

Organization

Organizing Committee

Dajiang Zhu	University of Texas at Arlington, USA
Jingwen Yan	Indiana University-Purdue University Indianapolis, USA
Heng Huang	University of Pittsburgh, USA
Li Shen	University of Pennsylvania, USA
Paul M. Thompson	University of Southern California, USA
Carl-Fredrik Westin	Brigham and Women's Hospital, USA

Program Committee

Liana Apostolova	Indiana University School of Medicine, USA
Moo K. Chung	University of Wisconsin-Madison, USA
Junzhou Huang	University of Texas at Arlington, USA
Neda Jahanshad	University of Southern California, USA
Xi Jiang	University of Electronic Science and Technology of China, China
Xiang Li	Harvard Medical School and Massachusetts General Hospital, USA
Jinglei Lv	University of Melbourne, Australia
Franco Pestilli	Indiana University Bloomington, USA
Shannon L. Risacher	Indiana University School of Medicine, USA
Andrew J. Saykin	Indiana University School of Medicine, USA
Li Su	University of Cambridge, UK
Li Wang	University of Texas at Arlington, USA
Yixuan Yuan	City University of Hong Kong, Hong Kong, China
Liang Zhan	University of Pittsburgh, USA
Tuo Zhang	Northwestern Polytechnical University, China

Preface

Mathematical Foundations of Computational Anatomy (MFCA)

This volume contains the proceedings of the 7th International Workshop on Mathematical Foundations of Computational Anatomy (MFCA 2019), which was held on October 17, 2019, in conjunction with the 22nd International Conference on Medical Image Computing and Computer Assisted Intervention (MICCAI 2019) in Shenzhen, China. The first workshop in the MFCA series was held in 2006 in Copenhagen, Denmark. This was followed by workshops in New York, USA, in 2008; Toronto, Canada, in 2011; Nagoya, Japan, in 2013; Munich, Germany, in 2015; and Quebec City, Canada, in 2017.

The goal of computational anatomy is to analyze and to statistically model the anatomy of organs in different subjects. Computational anatomic methods are generally based on the extraction of anatomical features or manifolds which are then statistically analyzed, often through a non-linear registration. There are nowadays a growing number of methods that can faithfully deal with the underlying biomechanical behavior of intra-subject deformations. However, it is more difficult to relate the anatomies of different subjects. In the absence of any justified physical model, diffeomorphisms provide the most general mathematical framework for enforcing topological consistency. However, working with this infinite dimensional space raises some deep computational and mathematical problems, in particular, for doing statistics. Likewise, modeling the variability of surfaces leads to relying on shape spaces that are much more complex than for curves. To cope with these, different methodological and computational frameworks have been proposed (e.g., using smooth left-invariant metrics, focusing on well-behaved subspaces of diffeomorphisms, or modeling surfaces using currents, etc.). The goal of the MFCA workshop is to foster interaction between researchers investigating the combination of geometry and statistics in non-linear image and surface registration in the context of computational anatomy from different points of view. A special emphasis is put on theoretical developments, with applications and results being welcomed as illustrations.

The seven papers presented in this volume were carefully selected from a number of very high-quality submissions following a thorough peer-review process. All of the papers were presented as oral presentations, with ample time for in-depth discussions. We would like to thank the authors of the papers and the members of the Program Committee for their efforts in making a strong program for MFCA 2019.

October 2019

Xavier Pennec
Sarang Joshi
Mads Nielsen
Tom Fletcher
Stanley Durrleman
Stefan Sommer

Organization

Organizing Committee

Xavier Pennec	Inria Sophia-Antipolis, France
Sarang Joshi	University of Utah, USA
Mads Nielsen	University of Copenhagen, Denmark
Tom Fletcher	University of Virginia, USA
Stanley Durrleman	Inria, Brain and Spine Institute ICM, France
Stefan Sommer	University of Copenhagen, Denmark

Program Committee

Alexandre Bône	Inria, Brain and Spine Institute ICM, France
Ian Dryden	University of Nottingham, UK
Guido Gerig	New York University, USA
Darryl Holm	Imperial College London, UK
Marc Niethammer	University of North Carolina at Chapel Hill, USA
Kaleem Siddiqi	McGill University, Canada

Contents

MFCA

MBIA

Non-rigid Registration of White Matter Tractography Using Coherent Point Drift Algorithm

Wenjuan Wang[1,2], Jin Liu[1,3], Tengfei Wang[3,4], Zongtao Hu[3,4],
Li Xia[3,4], Hongzhi Wang[3,4], Lizhuang Yang[3,4(✉)],
Stephen T.C. Wong[5], Xiaochu Zhang[1], and Hai Li[3,4(✉)]

[1] University of Science and Technology of China, Hefei 230027, China
[2] School of Science, Anhui Agricultural University, Hefei 230036, China
[3] Anhui Province Key Laboratory of Medical Physics and Technology, Center of Medical Physics and Technology, Hefei Institutes of Physical Science, Chinese Academy of Sciences, Hefei 230031, China
lzyang@ustc.edu.cn, hli@cmpt.ac.cn
[4] Cancer Hospital, Chinese Academy of Sciences, Hefei 230031, China
[5] Department of Systems Medicine and Bioengineering, Houston Methodist Cancer Center, Weill Cornell Medicine, Houston, TX 77030, USA

Abstract. Axonal fibers in the white matter are in charge of bio-signal delivery and relate information between neurons within the nervous system and between neurons and peripheral target tissues. Tract-based analysis (TBA) can directly bridge white matter and its connected cerebral cortex to achieve a joint analysis of the brain's structure and function. However, the accuracy of TBA is highly dependent on the quality of spatial registration of fiber bundles of different individuals to the standard space. In this paper, a non-rigid point registration, Coherent Point Drift (CPD), is applied for registration of fiber bundles. Both the fiber features and the registration accuracy are evaluated to determine the correspondence among fiber bundles. Experiment results on twelve real data showed higher registration accuracy of the proposed method on mean nearest neighbor distance and fractional anisotropy (FA) profiles than traditional registration methods, such as affine, elastic and Iterative Closest Point (ICP).

Keywords: DTI · Tract-based analysis · Registration · CPD

1 Introduction

There are three approaches to analyze the fiber bundles, namely, ROI-based analysis (RBA) [1], voxel-based morphometry (VBM) [2, 3], and tract-based analysis (TBA) [4–6]. The ROI-based analysis identifies the differences about the region of interest based on the brain map. Voxel-based morphometry searches local changes in the grey matter density according to the T1-weighted structural MRI brain images.

Wenjuan Wang and Jin Liu contributed equally to this work.

© Springer Nature Switzerland AG 2019
D. Zhu et al. (Eds.): MBIA 2019/MFCA 2019, LNCS 11846, pp. 3–11, 2019.
https://doi.org/10.1007/978-3-030-33226-6_1

Although the two aforementioned approaches have been widely used, there is insufficient information about fiber bundles contained, thus making it difficult to correlate fibers directly with the specific brain function [7]. To detect more fiber features, quantitative analysis of DTI data along the white matter tracts is presented and is known as tract-based analysis. Furthermore, tract-based spatial statistics (TBSS) [8] is created combining VBM and TBA for estimating a group mean FA skeleton which represents the centers of all fiber bundles. It is more sensitive to the FA value than VBM, but the FA skeleton is easily break off at the crossing fiber bundles which generates an inexact result. Spatial registration and analysis at the fiber level is a promising research diretion to overcome the disadvantage of TBSS.

Registration on fiber bundles is essential to compare and analyze fibers from different subjects directly. The reliability of the quantitative analysis relies on the accuracy of registration. During the past three decades, a large amount of studies have been conducted on the registration of fibers. Consequently, three registration methods are evolved, namely, scalar registration, tensor-based registration, and fiber-based registration. Based on the previous studies [9], the transformation matrix of registration is calculated based on one or more channels of the scalar DTI images, such as FA and B0. There are certain limitations of the scalar or vector registration for lacking the information of orientation, only based on the intensity message. Tensor-based registration methods take the directional signal into account in contrast to the scalar registration as mentioned [10–12]. However, tensor reorientation may introduce extra errors for tractography, thus restricting the application of tensor-based methods. Direct fiber registration is also proposed in [13, 14], where each fiber is projected into a high dimensional feature space leading to model and target feature points sets. The paper utilized the Coherent point drift (CPD) [15] algorithm to perform a non-rigid registration in order to make a point-to-point correspondence along the fiber tract. According to the CPD algorithm, every point on the fiber bundles is treated as a normal distribution while the optimal matching is completed by the optimization procedure [16].

2 Methods

2.1 Overview and Preprocessing

The main steps of the proposed method for registration of fibers are presented in Fig. 1. Preprocessing includes eddy current correction, tensor calculation, channel image generation and tractography by Diffusion toolkit (DTK) [17]. In tractography, the FA threshold is set as 0.15, and the turn angle threshold is set as $35°$. After preprocessing, automated fiber tract clustering is applied to obtain a set of reliable and compact fiber tracts. Meanwhile, the central fiber for each fiber tract is extracted to represent the whole bundle. Then, the center fibers are registered to establish the correspondence among bundles for tract-based analysis. Each step is described in detail in the following subsections.

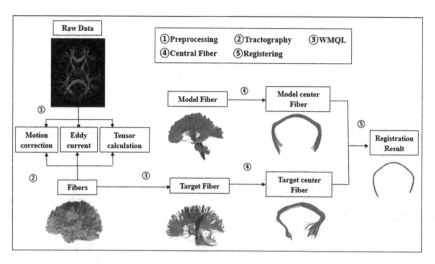

Fig. 1. Main steps of the proposed method.

2.2 Clustering and Central Fiber Extracting

Here, using the white matter query language method described in [18], we extract the corpus callosum (CC) connecting left/right frontal lobe, the uncinate fasciculus (UNC), and the superior longitudinal fasciculus (SLF) for analysis. The model fibers and reference fibers are described as point sets in 3D coordinates.

After clustering, the center fiber for each fiber bundle is extracted. The center fiber f_c of the fiber bundle F is defined as the fiber with the smallest average distance from all other fibers in F, where the distance is measured by Hausdorff distance. The Hausdorff distance refers to the maximum distance between one point set and the nearest point set of another. $d_{m,n}$ is the Hausdorff distance of fiber m and fiber n.

$$d_{m,n} = max_{p_k \subset F_m} min_{p_l \subset F_n} \|p_k - p_l\| \tag{1}$$

where p_k and p_l are two point sets belong to fiber m and fiber n, respectively.

$$f_c = Arg \min d(f) \tag{2}$$

Figure 2 shows the fiber tract clustering and central fiber extracting results for the SLF, UNC, and CC connecting left/right frontal lobe are showed, and the red line represents the central fiber for each bundle.

2.3 Non-rigid Registration

CPD is a non-rigid matching algorithm based on a uniform velocity field, which uses the calculus of variations to register the maximum likelihood estimation after normalization [15]. The basic idea of the proposed registration method is to measure the correlation between two fiber sets by considering their continuous approximations.

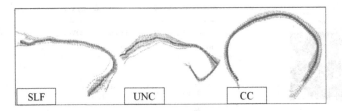

Fig. 2. Results of the central fiber extracting, red lines represent the central fibers. (Color figure online)

To solve the flexible deformation and relative relation of the fiber point set data, we use Gaussian mixture model (GMM) to fit the fiber point sets to get a probability distribution. Then the EM (Expectation Maximization) algorithm is used to optimize the parameters with the theory of the maximum likelihood estimation. The transformation is derived after several terms of optimal iteration. Specifically, CPD not only can achieve the registration of non-linear and non-rigid point sets, but also has an accurate result in case of large noise and frequent changes.

We assume the point set of the model central fiber $M_{\xi * i} = (M_1, ..., M_i)^T$ as the kernel of GMM and the point set of the target central fiber data $T_{\xi * j} = (T_1, ..., T_j)^T$ as the data set of GMM. The starting point of the model fiber is $Y = v(M_0) + M_0$.

$$p(t) = \omega \frac{1}{j} + (1 - \omega) \sum_{x=1}^{i} \frac{1}{i} p(t|x) \tag{3}$$

$$p(t|x) = \frac{1}{(2\pi\sigma^2)^{\frac{\xi}{2}}} exp\left(-\frac{\|t - M_i\|^2}{2\sigma^2}\right) \tag{4}$$

The formula above is the probability density of GMM. $\omega \in (0, 1)$ is a weighting parameter of spill points, redundant points and noise points. ξ represents the dimension of the point set, which in this article is 1. The p(t) expresses the probability that t, the data point, is generated by M GMM centers (including the influence of noise). After setting the parameters of the model, EM algorithm is used to optimize the calculation to get the transforming relationship between two point sets.

The centroid position of the point set Tj is adjusted by a series of transformation parameters that can be estimated by minimizing the following negative log likelihood function below.

$$E(\theta, \sigma 2) = -\sum_{n=1}^{N} log \sum_{m=1}^{M} p(x)p(t|x) \tag{5}$$

EM Algorithm is used to calculate θ and σ^2. E step establishes the target function Q which represents the upper bound of the negative log-likelihood function (5). Based on the Gaussian mixture model clustering and EM algorithm, E-step can be derived as foll-ows:

$$Q(W) = \sum_{m=1}^{M} \sum_{n=1}^{N} p(m|x_n) \times \left\| \frac{x_n - y_m - G(m,R)W}{\sigma} \right\|^2 / 2\sigma^2 + D \qquad (6)$$

$$P_{mn} = exp\left(-\frac{1}{2}\left\|\frac{y_m - x_n}{\sigma}\right\|^2\right) / \sum_{m=1}^{M} exp\left(-\frac{1}{2}\left\|\frac{y_m - x_n}{\sigma}\right\|^2\right) \qquad (7)$$

The posterior probability P can be obtained by calculating the parameter values, where G is the matrix, m and R are the rows and columns of the matrix. By calculating the partial derivative of W for the above equation, we can obtain Eq. (7) above.

3   Experiment and Results

3.1   Registration Based on CPD

All studies were obtained on 1.5T MR units (Siemens, Sonata, VA25 operating system). Twelve DT imaging data were acquired by using a single-shot, echo-planar imaging sequence with sensitivity encoding and a parallel imaging factor of 2.0. The imaging matrix was 96×96 with a field of view of 240×240 mm. Diffusion weighting was encoded along 30 independent orientations and the b-value was 700 s/mm^2 [19]. Three kinds of fiber bundles are selected to make the registration based on CPD, namely, CC, UNC and SLF. The registration results are showed in Fig. 3. The blue line presents the model set while the red line shows the target. In order to verify the reliability and superiority of the proposed tract-based registration method, we chose three other classical registration methods for comparison, namely Affine [20], Rigid [21], and ICP [22].

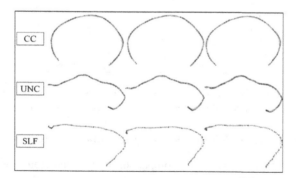

Fig. 3. Results of fiber registration based on CPD

3.2   Evaluation Based on Distance Between Fiber Tracts

We choose to implement the mean of the closest distances since it provides an estimate that uses all the available data. It is more discriminative than the minimum of the closest distances. We use K-means algorithm to find the nearest point of the target fiber set to the model set which is defined to be the mean nearest distance as the evaluation based on the distance between fiber tracts. Here, Mean Nearest Neighbor Distance (MND) is defined to be the index. The Euclidean distance is used to measure the distance of two samples where N_i represent the nearest point of the registered fibers from the model fiber point set M_i as Eq. (8) shows.

$$MND = \frac{1}{n} \sum_{i=1}^{n} \|N_i - M_i\| \qquad (8)$$

Figure 4 shows the Mean Nearest Neighbor Distance between model fibers and the reference fibers of twelve subjects. Smaller values of MND show a better registration because it indicates the difference levels after registration between each subject and the model. As we can see, CPD shows the lowest value while the other three methods exhibits a higher result, indicating the CPD registration algorithm stands out among the registration methods evaluated.

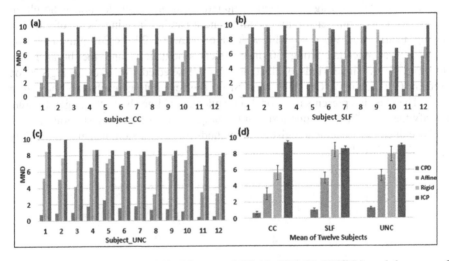

Fig. 4. The Mean Nearest Neighbor Distance of CC (a), SLF (b), UNC (c), and the mean of twelve subjects with the Standard deviation (d) on four registration methods

3.3   Evaluation Based on FA Profile Along the Fiber Tracts

A key function of registration is for comparison among individual images. So the registration assessment performance also should be the measurement of anatomical structures. A profile metric based on the normative correlation is calculated along each fiber. The FA value is obtained on the corresponding points captured from template for each registered subject. Figure 5 show the FA profile of three selected fibers from 12 subjects using different tract-based registration methods. In these figures, the x-coordinate represents the arc length of the fiber bundles, and the y-coordinate is the value of FA. According to the FA distribution, the mean FA distribution of CPD algorithm has the highest degree of template fitting and almost coincides. However, the distribution of other algorithms is not as high as the FA distribution of template fiber bundles, which indicates that CPD algorithm guarantees the distribution of fiber bundles' characteristic parameters to the greatest extent while ensuring the registration accuracy. Therefore, the application of CPD algorithm in fiber bundle registration enables more accurate results to be obtained in subsequent analysis.

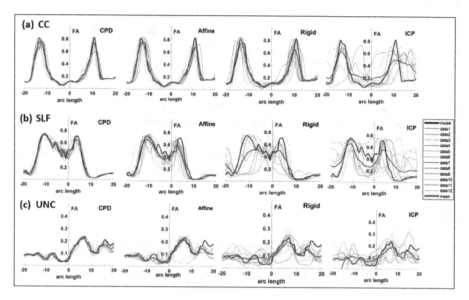

Fig. 5. FA profiles of the CC (a), SLF (b), UNC (c) for the four registration methods.

On the basis of the automatic clustering and marking of fiber bundles, it is possible to find the landmarks whose shape features are stable according to the shape information of the fiber bundles. The feature points are described by maximum curvature along the fiber bundles and the landmark is also defined to be the origin of the FA profile. p_l is the landmark point where the cosine value is the maximum. Figure 6 is the schematic diagram of fiber landmark where the deeper the red is, the greater curvature it shows.

$$p_l = Arg\,max\,cos\left(p_i, p_j\right) \tag{9}$$

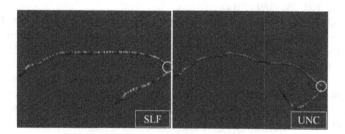

Fig. 6. The schematic diagram of fiber landmark.

4   Conclusion

In this paper, we proposed a novel tract-based analysis method based on the CPD non-linear registration algorithm. CPD algorithm is applicable to multi-dimensional point set registration under rigid and non-rigid transformation, it has strong robustness to the influence of noise, out of line point and missing point. To evaluate the performance of the proposed method, the mean nearest neighbor distance and the FA profile were calculated and the comparison with three traditional registration methods was conducted. The results support the superiority of CPD over the existing methods. Thus, the tract-based analysis based on the new CPD non-linear registration poses an exciting research direction for brain mapping.

Acknowledgements. This work was supported by the National Key R&D Program of China (2017YFB1300204), Hefei Foreign Cooperation Project (ZR201801020002), Director's Fund of Hefei Cancer Hospital of CAS (YZJJ2019C14, YZJJ2019A04), the Key R&D Program of Anhui Province (201904a07020104), the Natural Science Fund of Anhui Province (1708085MF141), as well as John S Dunn Research Foundation and TT and WF Chao Foundation (STCW).

References

1. Tong, Y., et al.: Seeking optimal Region-Of-Interest (ROI) single-value summary measures for fMRI studies in imaging genetics. PLoS ONE **11**(3), e0151391 (2016)
2. Scarpazza, C., De Simone, M.: Voxel-based morphometry: current perspectives. Neurosci. Neuroecon. **5**, 19–35 (2016)
3. Ceccarelli, A., et al.: The impact of lesion in-painting and registration methods on voxel-based morphometry in detecting regional cerebral gray matter atrophy in multiple sclerosis. Am. J. Neuroradiol. **33**(8), 1579–1585 (2012)
4. Zhang, Y.J., et al.: Atlas-guided tract reconstruction for automated and comprehensive examination of the white matter anatomy. Neuroimage **52**(4), 1289–1301 (2010)
5. Lee, S.-H., et al.: Tract-based analysis of white matter degeneration in Alzheimer's disease. Neuroscience **301**, 79–89 (2015)
6. Chen, Y.J., et al.: Automatic whole brain tract-based analysis using predefined tracts in a diffusion spectrum imaging template and an accurate registration strategy. Hum. Brain Mapp. **36**(9), 3441–3458 (2015)
7. Rath, Y., et al.: Statistical analysis of fiber bundles using multi-tensor tractography: application to first-episode schizophrenia. Magn. Reson. Imaging **29**(4), 507–515 (2011)
8. Bach, M., et al.: Methodological Considerations on tract-based spatial statistics (TBSS). Neuroimage **100**, 358–369 (2014)
9. Forsberg, D., Rathi, Y., Bouix, S., Wassermann, D., Knutsson, H., Westin, C.-F.: Improving registration using multi-channel diffeomorphic demons combined with certainty maps. In: Liu, T., Shen, D., Ibanez, L., Tao, X. (eds.) MBIA 2011. LNCS, vol. 7012, pp. 19–26. Springer, Heidelberg (2011). https://doi.org/10.1007/978-3-642-24446-9_3
10. Li, J., Shi, Y., Tran, G., Dinov, I., Wang, D.J.J., Toga, A.W.: Fast diffusion tensor registration with exact reorientation and regularization. In: Ayache, N., Delingette, H., Golland, P., Mori, K. (eds.) MICCAI 2012. LNCS, vol. 7511, pp. 138–145. Springer, Heidelberg (2012). https://doi.org/10.1007/978-3-642-33418-4_18

11. Pai, D., Soltanian-Zadeh, H., Hua, J.: Evaluation of fiber bundles across subjects through brain mapping and registration of diffusion tensor data. Neuroimage **54**, S165–S175 (2011)
12. Wang, Y., Shen, Y., Liu, D., et al.: Evaluations of diffusion tensor image registration based on fiber tractography. BioMed. Eng. OnLine **16**, 9 (2017). https://doi.org/10.1186/s12938-016-0299-2
13. Xue, Z., Wong, S.T.C.: Simultaneous tensor and fiber registration (STFR) for diffusion tensor images of the brain. In: Liao, H., Linte, C.A., Masamune, K., Peters, T.M., Zheng, G. (eds.) AE-CAI/MIAR -2013. LNCS, vol. 8090, pp. 1–8. Springer, Heidelberg (2013). https://doi.org/10.1007/978-3-642-40843-4_1
14. Mayer, A., et al.: A supervised framework for the registration and segmentation of white matter fiber tracts. IEEE Trans. Med. Imaging **30**(1), 131–145 (2011)
15. Myronenko, A., Song, X.B.: Point set registration: coherent point drift. IEEE Trans. Pattern Anal. Mach. Intell. **32**(12), 2262–2275 (2010)
16. Caan, M.W.A., et al.: Nonrigid point set matching of white matter tracts for diffusion tensor image analysis. IEEE Trans. Biomed. Eng. **58**(9), 2431–2440 (2011)
17. Wang, R., Benner, T., Sorensen, A.G., Wedeen, V.J.: Diffusion toolkit: a software package for diffusion imaging data processing and tractography. Proc. Intl. Soc. Mag. Reson. Med. **15**, 3720 (2007)
18. Wassermann, D., Makris, N., Rathi, Y., et al.: The white matter query language: a novel approach for describing human white matter anatomy. Brain Struct. Funct. **221**(9), 4705–4721 (2016)
19. Anna, V., et al.: Development of a high angular resolution diffusion imaging human brain template. Neuroimage **91**, 177–186 (2014)
20. Leemans, A., Sijbers, J., Backer, S.D., Vandervliet, E., Parizelet, P.M.: Affine coregistration of diffusion tensor magnetic resonance images using mutual information. Adv. Concepts Intel Vis. Syst. **3708**, 523–530 (2005)
21. Studholme, C., Hill, D.L.G., Hawkes, D.J.: An overlap invariant entropy measure of 3D medical image alignment. Pattern Recogn. **32**(1), 71–86 (1999)
22. Sharp, G.C., Lee, S.W., Wehe, D.K.: Icp registration using invariant features. IEEE Trans. Pattern Anal. Mach. Intell. **24**(1), 90–102 (2002)

An Edge Enhanced SRGAN for MRI Super Resolution in Slice-Selection Direction

Jia Liu[1], Fang Chen[2], Xianyu Wang[1], and Hongen Liao[1(✉)]

[1] Department of Biomedical Engineering, School of Medicine,
Tsinghua University, Beijing, China
liao@tsinghua.edu.cn
[2] Department of Computer Science and Engineering,
Nanjing University of Aeronautics and Astronautics, Nanjing, China

Abstract. The low resolution MRI in slice-select direction will lead to information loss and artifacts in 2D multi-slices MRI, which is not conducive to the diagnosis and treatment of diseases. Therefore, we proposed an edge enhanced super-resolution generative adversarial networks (EE-SRGAN) for MRI super resolution in slice-select direction. Firstly, a two-stage super-resolution generator network (TSSR) for solving the problem that the down-sampling ratio of MRI resolution in single direction reached 12 times. In addition, in order to overcome the problem of image smoothness caused by high peak signal-to-noise ratio (PSNR) and improve the visual reality of reconstruction image, we construct a generative adversarial networks based on TSSR. Finally, in order to achieve more texture details, we proposed an edge enhanced loss function to optimize the generator network. From the experimental results, we find that our TSSR is better (increased 1.78 dB PSNR), EE-SRGAN provides more satisfactory visual effect and beneficial to segmentation task (increased 2.14% Dice index) than state-of-art super-resolution network.

Keywords: MRI Slice-Selection · Two-Stage Super-Resolution · Edge enhanced

1 Introduction

Magnetic resonance imaging (MRI) is a medical imaging technique for producing images of parts of the human widely used in hospitals and clinics for medical diagnosis. Considering that conventional 3D imaging usually leads to infeasible scan times, 2D multi-slice imaging is used instead for clinical diagnosis in most hospitals. Due to hardware induced limitations on gradient strength, requirements on signal-to-noise ratio (SNR), and other factors, the 2D multi-slices are usually relatively thick and resolution that is high in-plane and is low in the slice-select direction, especially some undesirable artifacts are observed due to the resolution reduction in the slice-select direction. Such anisotropy negatively affects tissue segmentation, visualization and disease diagnosis.

The isotropy and resolution of 2D multi-slice images can be improved by super-resolution reconstruction (SRR) methods [1]. Super-resolution reconstruction algorithm

© Springer Nature Switzerland AG 2019
D. Zhu et al. (Eds.): MBIA 2019/MFCA 2019, LNCS 11846, pp. 12–20, 2019.
https://doi.org/10.1007/978-3-030-33226-6_2

can effectively balance the resolution, signal-to-noise ratio and scanning time of MR images, which has important practical value and significance. Many studies and substantial advances have been studied in SRR methods. Early methods mainly focus on interpolation technology such as bicubic interpolation and Lanczos resampling [2]. Interpolation method is very fast, but usually fails to recover the high-frequency image information on an overly smooth solution. Sparse coding [3] methods use a learned compact dictionary based on sparse signal representation to address the task of SISR.

In recent years, with the development of deep learning (DL), especially convolutional neural network (CNN). Various network structure design and training strategies have continuously improved SR performance for natural images field, especially peak signal-to-noise ratio (PSNR) [4]. However, these PSNR-oriented methods tend to output too smooth results without enough high-frequency details, because the PSNR measurement is basically inconsistent with the subjective evaluation of human observers. Furthermore, the research on super-resolution reconstruction of medical images is relatively few, while SRR processing of natural images does not take into account the special characteristics of 2D Multi-Slice MR images, that is, the direction of low resolution is only one-dimensional and the difference of resolution is greater than that of natural images. Therefore, there are still many shortcomings and difficulties in the research of super-resolution reconstruction algorithm in 2D Multi-Slice MR images.

In this study, we proposed an edge enhanced super-resolution generative adversarial networks (EE-SRGAN) for MRI super resolution reconstruction in slice-selection direction. Our contributions are as follow: Firstly, a two-stage super-resolution generation network (TSSR) for the phenomenon that single direction resolution of MRI down-sampling ratio reached 12 times. In addition, in order to overcome the problem of image smoothness caused by high PSNR and improve the visual reality of reconstructed image, we construct a generative adversarial networks based on TSSR, and the Wasserstein distance is used as the loss function of discriminator to ensure the stability of network training. Finally, in order to make the reconstruction MRI with more texture details, we proposed an edge enhanced loss function to optimize the generator network. From the experimental results, we find that our TSSR is better in state-of-art super-resolution network, the edge enhanced loss function provides a sharper edge and a more satisfactory visual effect.

2 Method

Our super resolution reconstruction goal is to train a generator G, which estimates the corresponding SR images for the given LR input image. To achieve this, we train a generator network, which is a feed-forward CNN G_{θ_G} with parameter θ_G. Here, $\theta_G = \{W_{1:L}; b_{1:L}\}$ represents the weights and deviations of L layer networks and can be obtained by optimizing specific loss function L_{SR}. Given training image I_n^{HR}, $n = 1, \cdots, N$ and corresponding I_n^{LR}, the parameter θ_G is solved by minimizing the loss function as follows:

$$\widehat{\theta}_G = \operatorname*{argmin}_{\theta_G} \frac{1}{N} \sum_{n=1}^{N} L_{SR}\left(G_{\theta_G}\left(I_n^{LR}\right), I_n^{HR}\right) \tag{1}$$

In this work, we have design a hybrid loss function L_{SR} for edge enhancement, which will be described in detail in Sect. 2.3. Our Edge Enhanced Super-Resolution Generative Adversarial Networks consists of three parts (see Fig. 1), including generator network, discriminator network and edge enhancement hybrid loss function, which will be described in detail below.

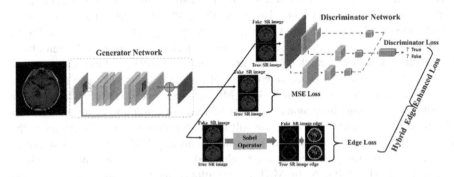

Fig. 1. The network structure diagram of super-resolution reconstruction generator network. It consists of two stages, the first stage is basic reconstruction network, and the second stage is denoising and refinement network.

2.1 Two-Stage Super-Resolution Generator Network

Considering that the difference between low-resolution and high-resolution images of medical images is only in one direction, and the difference is greater than that of natural images, we designed a two-stage super-resolution generator network. Since VDSR network has achieved good results in the field of super-resolution reconstruction, we used VDSR network as the basic module to obtain the details of high-resolution images. Most super-resolution reconstruction networks added the input (low-resolution image) to the last layer of the reconstruction network to supplement the basic texture information of the reconstruction image. However, information loss problem of the slice-select direction low-resolution image of medical image is more serious than natural images. The network with the input addition will introduce a lot of artifact information. Therefore, we designed the two-stage module to further supplement the high-frequency detail information of the reconstruction image, and to reduce volume artifact brought by the basic reconstruction network importantly. The network structure of two-stage SR Generator is shown in Fig. 2.

(1) Basic Reconstruction Network. Using the idea of VDSR in reference [5], we built an initial reconstruction network to learn the difference between high-resolution and low-resolution images. We used stack small filters to obtain a large receptive, it can effectively help us to reconstruct super-resolution images. A global residual

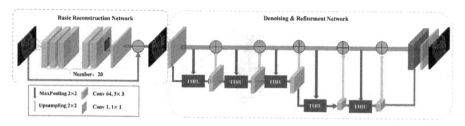

Fig. 2. The network structure diagram of super-resolution generator network. It consists of two stages, the first stage is basic reconstruction network, and the second stage is denoising and refinement network.

connection is used to solve the gradient problem caused by deepening the network and make network converge faster. The configuration is outlined in Fig. 2. The number of convolution layers used is 20, except the first and last layers. These convolution layers have same type: 64 convolution filters with kernel size of 3×3, and each convolution layer uses ReLU activation function. The first layer is the input image. The last layer is used for image reconstruction, and consists of a convolution filter with a kernel size of 3×3. Then, an addition operation is performed with the input low-resolution image to obtain the reconstruction high-resolution image.

(2) Denoising and Refinement Network. Although the basic reconstruction network can learn a lot of image details, but most of the supplemented information is low-level feature information, the fine structure of the image is less, and the reconstruction image is still blur. Therefore, inspired by two information flows in FRRN [6], we design a new residual unit, two information residual unit (TIRU). We use five TIRUs to construct our denoising and refinement network. The network consists of two information streams. This network combines high-low level features: one steam is residual information, which is calculated by adding continuous residual, which is low-level features, while the other information steam is pooling information, which is the result of a series of convolution and pooling operations applied to input, which is high-level features. Therefore, we use this structure after the initial reconstruction network to supplement more high-low level features of the image (shown in Fig. 2).

TIRU is the modification of residual element (shown in Fig. 3(a)). Each TIRU has two inputs (R_{n-1} and P_{n-1}) and two outputs (R_n and P_n), running simultaneously. Let R_{n-1} be the residual input of the n-th TIRU and P_{n-1} be the concatenation input, then the output is calculated as follows:

$$R_n = R_{n-1} + HP_{n-1}, R_{n-1}; W_n \tag{2}$$

$$P_n = G(P_{n-1}, R_{n-1}; W_n) \tag{3}$$

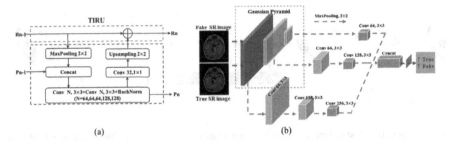

Fig. 3. Illustration of two information residual unit (TIRU) and multi-scale discriminator network. (a) Illustration of TIRU, Total 5 TIRUs in refinement network, N = 64, 64, 64,128,128 is the number of convolution filter. (b) Illustration of multi-scale discriminator network.

2.2 Discriminator Network

Because multi-scale structure is the essence and attribute of image, different observation scales are very meaningful for image assessment. Therefore, Gaussian pyramid multi-scale extraction method was first used to estimate three different scales images of the input image of discriminator. Then three different scales of images are as three new input images into different feature extraction layers. Finally, three feature extraction layers are guaranteed to get the same size of features. After the concatenation of three features extraction results, a global pooling layer is connected to compress the features. Finally, a full connection layer (output dimension is 1) are connected to get the classification results of images (True high resolution image or Fake high resolution image). As shown in Fig. 3(b), all convolution layers except the last layer use LeakyRelu activation.

2.3 Edge Enhanced Hybrid Loss Function

The definition of loss function is very important to the performance of our generator network and whole super resolution reconstruction network. Although most super-resolution reconstruction networks are modeled based on mean square error (MSE), SRGAN [7] designed a hybrid loss function, which includes a MSE and total variation (TV) combined content loss, an adversarial loss and a perceptual loss. However, the input of the perceptual loss function is extracted by the feature extractor obtained from the training of natural images. After our experimental demonstration, we find that this perceptual loss is not applicable to medical images and will produce many spot-like artifacts. The total variation loss will cause the image to be too smooth. In addition, the loss function based on MSE will also result in blurred images and obscure edges between different tissues because of the serious information loss and partial volume artifacts in medical images. Therefore, in order to solve these problems, we proposed a edge enhanced hybrid loss function L_{SR}, and it consists of MSE, adversarial loss and edge loss, which are defined as follows:

$$\mathcal{L}_{MSE}^{SR} = \frac{1}{WH} \sum_{x=1}^{W} \sum_{y=1}^{H} \left(I_{x,y}^{HR} - G\left(I_{x,y}^{LR} \right) \right)^2 \tag{4}$$

$$\mathcal{L}_{Adv}^{SR} = \min_{\theta_G} \max_{\theta_D} \mathbb{E}_{X_r}[D_{\theta_D}(X_r)] - \mathbb{E}_{X_f}\left[D_{\theta_D}\left(X_f\right)\right] \tag{5}$$

$$p_t = \begin{cases} p & if \ y = 1 \\ 1 - p & otherwise, \end{cases} \tag{6}$$

$$\mathcal{L}_{Edge}^{SR} = -\alpha_t(1 - p_t)^\gamma log(p_t) + \left(1 - \frac{2p * y}{p + y - p * y} \right) * 10 \tag{7}$$

$$L_{SR} = \mathcal{L}_{MSE}^{SR} + \mathcal{L}_{Adv}^{SR} + \mathcal{L}_{Edge}^{SR} \tag{8}$$

Where, $G()$ presents the generator network, $D_{\theta_D}()$ presents the discriminator network, p is the pixel of $E\left(G\left(I_{x,y}^{LR}\right)\right)$, y is the pixel of $E\left(I_{x,y}^{HR}\right)$, $E()$ presents Sobel operator edge extractor and threshold proceeding (threshold = 85% percentile), X_r presents true high-resolution image, X_f presents reconstruction fake high resolution image.

3 Experiment and Result

3.1 Dataset and Training Detail

The medical images used in this study were all from Neurosurgery Department of Beijing Tiantan Hospital, Capital Medical University in China. With the approval of the Ethics Committee, a total of 150 groups of 2D Multi-Slice preoperative T1-weighted MR images were collected. The acquisition equipment was GE Discovery MR750, and the standard MR imaging protocol was non-enhanced axial T1-weighted (TR, 2031 ms; TE, 19.536 ms; slice thickness: 6.0–6.25 mm). The FOV is 24 cm, the image size in-plane direction is 512×512 pixels, the pixel resolution is 0.46875 * 0.46875 mm, the image size of slice-selection direction is $512 \times (23/24)$ pixel.

The data of 150 patients were randomly divided into 130 groups and 20 groups, which were used as training and testing set respectively. We use the in-plane direction high-resolution image I_{HR} as the ground truth, apply the Gauss filter to I_{HR}, and then use the down-sampling factor R in the y direction of the 2D image and then use linear interpolation to obtain simulated large-thickness low-resolution MR slice-selection images I_{LR} with the same size of high-resolution images. In addition, considering that there are 23/24 slices axial images for each patient in the original data, in order to achieve data augmentation of training set, we interpolate the original $512 \times 512 \times 24$ Multi-Slice data using MATLAB bicubic kernel function to obtain $512 \times 512 \times (138–150)$ images, and then take many 512×512 images at intervals of 2 in slice direction. Finally, training set includes 9316 images and testing set includes 1585 images. The low resolution image input and the high resolution output of our network are 512×512 pixel images. Our model training is divided into two stages. In the first stage, the generator network is trained, the learning rate is 10^{-4}, the loss function is Eq. (4) + (7), and the Adam optimizer is used to optimize 50,000 iterations. In the second stage, the model weights obtained from the first stage pre-training are used as the initialization parameter model in the second stage, which can avoid undesirable local optimum phenomena. In the second stage, the training of discriminator and the generator are updated alternately. Both the discriminator and the generator adopt Adam optimizer. The learning rate of the discriminator is 10^{-4}, and the loss function is Eq. (5). The learning rate of generator network is 10^{-4}, and the loss function is Eq. (8). The number of iterations in the second stage is 50,000. Keras-tensorflow framework and an NVIDIA GTX 1080Ti GPU are used.

3.2 Results

Firstly, in order to verify the performance of our proposed two-stage super-resolution reconstruction generator network, we quantitatively compared our method with some state-of-art methods (including SRCNN, the pioneer of deep learning super-resolution reconstruction field, VDSR is excellent MSE-based reconstruction method and ESR-GAN [8] is the advanced SRGAN-based reconstruction method). The quantitatively comparison results are shown in Tables 1 and 2. We evaluated the performance of the super resolution reconstruction network on training set and testing set respectively. From the Tables 1 and 2, it can be seen that our TSSR network outperforms the generators VDSR and ESRGAN in the evaluation index of PSNR and SSIM. In addition, in order to prove the advantages of our method, HR images of training set were used to establish a tumor segmentation model, and the reconstructed images by different methods were tested. The segmentation results are shown in Table 2, which proves that our method is also better than other methods in segmentation task.

Table 1. Quantitative comparison results of different reconstruction methods on training set

Indexes	Method					
	Bicubic	SRCNN	VDSR	ESRGAN	TSSR	EE-SRGAN
PSNR (dB)	26.84	28.17	29.92	28.54	31.70	**31.88**
SSIM	0.8720	0.8848	0.9025	0.8842	0.9187	**0.9207**

In order to further demonstrate the performance of our algorithm, we qualitatively compared the reconstruction results of our method and other methods. As can be seen from the Fig. 4, partial volume artifacts are very serious in the image obtained by "bicubic" method. Compared with other CNN methods, SRCNN method achieves the worst results and very blur images. VDSR has better reconstruction results than SRCNN and ESRGAN. The main reason is that SRCNN network is too simple, and ESRGAN used several dense blocks with input information cascades, while low-resolution medical images with large thickness as input not only contain texture

Table 2. Quantitative comparison results of different reconstruction methods on testing set

Indexs	Method					
	Bicubic	SRCNN	VDSR	ESRGAN	TSSR	EE-SRGAN
PSNR(dB)	26.99	28.45	30.31	28.84	31.75	**31.85**
SSIM	0.8777	0.8913	0.9088	0.8907	0.9238	**0.9251**
Dice	0.7490	0.7222	0.7355	0.7196	0.7522	**0.7569**

information, but also it contains serious partial volume artifacts, which results in poor quality of reconstructed images, as shown in the Fig. 4. From the Fig. 4, we can see that the super-resolution image reconstructed by the EE-SRGAN using hybrid edge enhanced loss function is more realistic than the image reconstructed by TTSR.

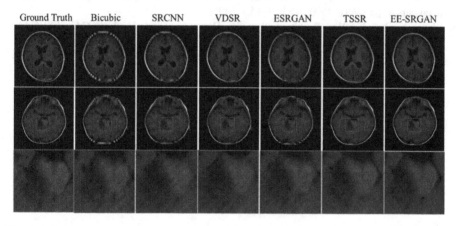

Fig. 4. Illustration of two information residual unit (TIRU) and multi-scale discriminator network. (a) Illustration of TIRU, Total 5 TIRUs in refinement network, N = 64, 64, 64,128,128 is the Number of convolution filter. (b) Illustration of multi-scale discriminator network.

4   Conclusion

We have proposed a two-stage super-resolution generator network for the phenomenon that down-sampling ratio of MRI resolution in single direction is very large. We have proposed an edge enhanced hybrid loss for MRI-SR to achieve more image details. Our EE-SRGAN achieved better experimental results for MRI slice-selection super resolution reconstruction than state-of-art models. Our method is significant to reduce scanning time under the image quality assurance for clinical application.

References

1. Greenspan, H., Oz, G., Kiryati, N., et al.: MRI inter-slice reconstruction using super-resolution. Magn. Reson. Imaging **20**(5), 437–446 (2002)

2. Duchon, C.E.: Lanczos filtering in one and two dimensions. J. Appl. Meteorol. **18**(8), 1016–1022 (1979)
3. Yang, J., Wright, J., Huang, T.S., et al.: Image super-resolution via sparse representation. IEEE Trans. Image Process. **19**(11), 2861–2873 (2010)
4. Lai, W.S., Huang, J.B., Ahuja, N., et al.: Deep laplacian pyramid networks for fast and accurate super-resolution. In: Proceedings - 30th IEEE Conference on Computer Vision and Pattern Recognition, pp. 5835–5843. IEEE, USA (2017)
5. Kim, J., Kwon Lee, J., Mu Lee, K.: Accurate image super-resolution using very deep convolutional networks. In: Proceedings of the IEEE Conference on Computer Vision and Pattern Recognition, pp. 1646–1654. IEEE, USA (2016)
6. Pohlen, T., Hermans, A., Mathias, M., Leibe, B.: Full-resolution residual networks for semantic segmentation in street scenes. In: Proceedings of the IEEE Conference on Computer Vision and Pattern Recognition, pp. 4151–4160. IEEE, USA (2017)
7. Ledig, C., et al.: Photo-realistic single image super-resolution using a generative adversarial network. In: Proceedings of the IEEE Conference on Computer Vision and Pattern Recognition, pp. 4681–4690. IEEE, USA (2017)
8. Wang, X., Yu, K., Wu, S., Gu, J., Liu, Y., Dong, C., Qiao, Y., Loy, C.C.: ESRGAN: Enhanced Super-Resolution Generative Adversarial Networks. In: Leal-Taixé, L., Roth, S. (eds.) ECCV 2018. LNCS, vol. 11133, pp. 63–79. Springer, Cham (2019). https://doi.org/10.1007/978-3-030-11021-5_5

Exploring Functional Connectivity Biomarker in Autism Using Group-Wise Sparse Representation

Yudan Ren[1(✉)] and Shuai Wang[2]

[1] School of Information Science and Technology,
Northwest University, Xi'an, China
nwpuryd@163.com
[2] School of Automation, Northwestern Polytechnical University, Xi'an, China

Abstract. Exploring the brain as a complex, networked system and inferring the dysfunction of diseased brains by abnormal functional connectivity has received great attention in recent years. One critical problem in brain network analysis is how to identify functionally homogeneous brain regions as network nodes. Inspired by the nature of sparse population coding of the human brain, we propose a novel data-driven method to identify whole-brain network nodes based on group-wise sparse representation (gSR) algorithm. Using a publicly available autism dataset as test-bed, we evaluate our method and compare it with group-wise independent components analysis (gICA). The experimental results demonstrate that the brain ROIs identified by our method are more functionally homogeneous and thus may improve the sensitivity and accuracy of functional connectivity biomarkers in differentiating autism and healthy controls.

Keywords: Resting-state fMRI · Brain network · Functional connectivity · Sparse representation · Autism

1 Introduction

Identifying functional connectivity biomarkers to characterize dysfunction in diseased brains have been drawing greater interest [1–4]. The common pipeline towards brain network studies involves two steps. The first step is identifying isolated brain regions of interest (ROIs) as network nodes. The second step is measuring functional connectivities using functional magnetic resonance imaging (fMRI). In this pipeline, identifying nodes as the structural substrate for connectivity mapping is a critical problem. It is typically expected that a node should be functionally homogeneous [1, 2].

Independent component analysis (ICA) is a widely-used approach in brain network studies. ICA aims at a blind separation of independent sources from the complex mixture of signal resulting from different sources [1]. Despite the successful applications of ICA, it has been recognized that sparse population coding of a set of neurons is likely to be more effective than independent exploration, that is, a sparse set of neurons encode specific concepts rather than responding to the input stimuli independently [5]. Therefore, growing interest has been directed to fMRI analysis approaches by taking

D. Zhu et al. (Eds.): MBIA 2019/MFCA 2019, LNCS 11846, pp. 21–29, 2019.
https://doi.org/10.1007/978-3-030-33226-6_3

the intrinsic sparsity of human brain into consideration. For example, Lv et al. demonstrated that both task-evoked and resting-state brain networks can be robustly identified in normal brains using sparse representation (SR) [6, 7]. Lv et al. performed SR on task-fMRI data for each subject separately, while the correspondence of the components across subjects cannot be automatically established, which makes assessing group differences of functional brain activities difficult. However, in [6, 7], only the correspondence for the components related to task paradigm was established by time-frequency analysis, which does not work for rsfMRI. Also, the advantages of SR-based fMRI data analysis in identifying functional connectivity biomarkers in diseased brains have rarely been explored.

In this study, we propose a new framework and a comparative study to assess the performance of SR-based resting-state fMRI (rsfMRI) data analysis in identifying functional connectivity biomarkers by taking autism spectrum disorder (ASD) as a test-bed. To establish the correspondence across subjects, we adopt a group-wise sparse representation method, and extract a dictionary matrix and a common coefficient matrix for all the subjects. Our experimental results on both simulated fMRI data and ASD rsfMRI data demonstrated that brain regions with improved functional homogeneity can be identified by our method, and consequently, the sensitivity and accuracy of functional connectivity biomarkers can be improved compared with ICA-based method. While there have been several studies mainly focusing on default mode network using rsfMRI in clinical analysis [8–10], in this paper, we use gSR to explore the functional connectivity biomarkers in autism among the whole-brain. The identified ASD biomarkers in our study not only cover those well documented brain regions in the literature such as precuneus, angular and right temporal lobe [8–10], but also cover some novel brain regions such as insular.

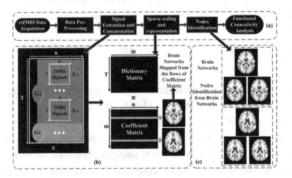

Fig. 1. The computational framework of group-wise sparse representation (gSR) of whole-brain fMRI signals from two groups of subjects (G_A: Autism, G_C: Healthy control)

2   Materials and Methods

2.1   Overview

Figure 1(a) shows the overview of our study. RsfMRI data for subjects in 2 groups (G_A: Autism, G_C: Healthy control) are concatenated (Fig. 1(b)), which is then decomposed into representative signal patterns (each column in dictionary **D**) and associated spatial maps (each row in coefficient matrix **A**) by sparse representation (Fig. 1(b)). Then, brain ROIs are localized using the spatial maps and are used as common brain network nodes for functional connectivity analysis (Fig. 1(c)). We examine the performance of functional connectivity biomarkers for ASD in differentiating autism patients from health controls using a support vector machine classifier, and compare our method with ICA-based method.

2.2   Data Acquisition and Pre-Processing

Simulated fMRI Dataset. Simulated fMRI dataset consists of 20 subjects, each with up to 27 sources, 200 time points, and 136×136 voxels are generated using the toolbox SimTB (http://mialab.mrn.org/software).

Autism Dataset. We used the dataset from Autism Brain Imaging Data Exchange (http://fcon_1000.projects.nitrc.org/indi/abide/NYULangoneMedicalCenter/).   Thirty participants with autism (11.89 ± 3.66) and thirty healthy controls (11.34 ± 2.66) are included in our study. The fMRI data were obtained on a 3T Siemens Allegra scanner. The scanning parameters are TR/TE/FA/FOV of 2000 ms/15 ms/90°/240 mm, voxel size of 3 mm $\times$ 3 mm $\times$ 4 mm, and data matrix of $64 \times 80 \times 33$. The preprocessing of rsfMRI data includes skull removal, motion correction, slice time correction, spatial smoothing, detrend, and band-pass filtering (0.01 Hz–0.1 Hz). A common brain mask is generated to extract whole-brain fMRI signals of all subjects.

2.3   Sparse Representation Theory

Sparse representation could be summarized as [11]:

$$s = \mathbf{D}a = a_1 d_1 + a_2 d_2 + \ldots + a_m d_m \tag{1}$$

where $s = [s_1, s_2, \ldots, s_n]^T$ is input signals. $\mathbf{D} = [d_1, d_2, \ldots, d_m]^T$ is a dictionary with each column d_i representing a basis, and $a = [a_1, a_2, \ldots, a_m]^T$ is the associated coefficient matrix. Equation (1) can be rewritten to account for small representation error by:

$$s = \mathbf{D}a + z \tag{2}$$

where z is the representation error. Equation (2) can be approximately solved by using the L1-norm minimization:

$$\hat{a} = \text{argmin}\|a\|_1 \text{ subject to } \|s - Da_2\| \le \varepsilon \tag{3}$$

where $\|.\|_1$ and $\|.\|_2$ are L1-norm and L2-norm, respectively. $\varepsilon \ge 0$ is the error tolerance.

2.4 Sparse Representation of Whole-Brain FMRI Data

Based on the assumption that the components of each voxel's fMRI signal are sparse and the neural integration of those components is linear [12], the whole-brain sparse representation framework holistically considers the whole-brain signals and can achieve a comprehensive collection of meaningful functional networks [6, 7]. In this framework, the whole-brain fMRI signals of each subject are extracted and stacked into a 2D signal matrix S_x (Fig. 1(b)). Each column in S_x is the fMRI signal for a voxel. Then S_x for all the subjects are concatenated, resulting in a big matrix S (Fig. 1(b)). S consists of two groups of subjects:

$$S = [S_{G_A}; S_{G_c}], S_{G_A} = [S_{A1}; S_{A2}; \ldots; S_{Ak}], S_{G_C} = [S_{C1}; S_{C2}; \ldots; S_{Ck}] \tag{4}$$

We adopt a very effective online dictionary learning method in [13] to optimize D and A, which can train dictionary from very large sets of samples and accelerate convergence and improve the trained dictionary. Both D and A are shared by all the subjects. Each atom in D corresponds to a representative fMRI signal pattern, and each row in A represents a coefficient vector. We project each coefficient vector back to the brain volume space. A classic t-statistic analysis, which converts a coefficient map to a T-statistic spatial map, is used to evaluate the significance of the contribution of the atom in fMRI signal reconstruction. In our gSR-based method, the number of dictionary atoms m is set to be 200 empirically and experimentally.

2.5 Functional Connectivity Analysis

We experimentally use $z = 2.3$ as threshold to finalize the nodes from the spatial maps. fMRI signals for each node are retrieved and averaged. Functional connectivity is calculated as the Pearson correlation coefficient. In addition, gICA was performed using FSL MELODIC (http://www.fmrib.ox.ac.uk/fsl). The number of independent components is automatically estimated. Fifty-one components are extracted for both two groups of subjects. Similar method (including the same z-score threshold) is used to identify network nodes and estimate the functional connectivity.

A t-test with false discovery rate (FDR) correction is performed to identify the connectivity biomarkers in ASD. A support vector machine (SVM) classifier [14] is used to test the performance of the biomarkers. Due to the limited number of samples, a leave-one-out cross-validation (LOO-CV) strategy is adopted in classifier testing.

3 Result

3.1 Node Identification on Simulated Data

Both gSR and gICA are performed on the concatenated simulated data, which can provide ground truth to compare two methods on real fMRI datasets. Thirteen corresponding spatial nodes can be defined by these two methods. We perform a principal component analysis (PCA) on the set of fMRI signals in a ROI to measure the functional homogeneity of the ROI. In brief, the ratio between the first eigenvalue and the sum of all the eigenvalues, which is typically used to evaluate how much information is preserved by the first eigenvector, is used to measure the functional homogeneity. The distribution of the functional homogeneity for each node is shown in Fig. 2(a). A two-sample *t*-test is performed for the comparison of functional homogeneity between gSR and gICA. Eight nodes identified by gSR have higher temporal consistency (as shown in Fig. 2(b)). Functional homogeneity (FH), or spatial coherent, is a critical metric. Lower FH indicates that the candidate ROI locates in the conjunction of multiple functional systems of the brain, which will result in decreased reliability in following functional connectivity analysis. It is seen that the nodes identified by gSR-based method are more functionally homogeneous, which indicates its increased reliability in functional connectivity analysis.

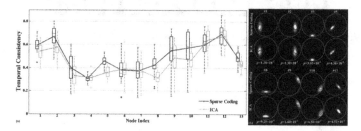

Fig. 2. (a) The temporal consistency of simulated signals in thirteen corresponding common nodes, (b) eight nodes with higher values of temporal consistency identified by our method

3.2 Node Identification on ASD Data

As shown in Fig. 3, 74 spatial common nodes are localized in total for all the subjects by gSR. 62 nodes are extracted from gICA, while thirteen spatial common nodes that have correspondence between gSR and gICA are selected to compare temporal consistency. The correspondence of the nodes from gSR and gICA is identified by matching with the AAL template and careful manual inspection. The distribution of the temporal consistency in all 60 subjects for each node is shown in Fig. 4. Ten nodes identified by gSR have significantly higher functional homogeneity (Temporal_Sup_L, Temporal_Sup_R, Cingulum_Mid, ParaHippocampal_L, Occipital_Sup_L, Occipital_Sup_R, Precuneus, Frontal_Mid_Orb_R, Temporal_Mid_R, Precentral_L), indicating that the nodes identified by gSR are more functionally homogeneous.

3.3   Functional Connectivity Biomarkers

For gSR, the functional connections are pairwise among all the 74 nodes. Then two-sample t-tests (significance level 0.05 after FDR correction) are performed to identify twenty connectivity biomarkers ($p < 0.001$), which are used as features for classifier training (as shown in Fig. 5), while only twelve functional connections ($p < 0.005$) are found to be significantly altered in gICA (as shown in Fig. 6). Left-tailed represents that the control group has significantly higher functional connectivity than ASD group. Interestingly, there are five connections commonly detected by both of the methods, which are highlighted in different colors in Figs. 5 and 6. Furthermore, the identified functional connectivity between node pair 64–47 in our method is in line with what has been reported in the literature [8].

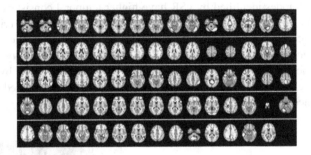

Fig. 3. Visualization of the 74 identified common network nodes by sparse representation

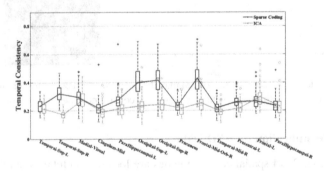

Fig. 4. The temporal consistency of fMRI signals in thirteen corresponding common nodes identified by both methods (The box-plots are in the same order as that in Fig. 2 (a))

3.4   Classification Performance

In LOO-CV, the SVM classifier trained by the connectivity biomarkers resulted from gSR successfully predicted 27 out of 30 autism subjects (90%), and 28 out of 30 controls (93.33%), with a total classification accuracy of 91.67%. In comparison, the SVM classifier trained by the connectivity biomarkers resulted from gICA successfully predicted 23 out of 30 autism subjects (76.66%), and 25 out of 30 control subjects

(83.33%), with a total classification accuracy of 80%. The results demonstrated that the connectivity biomarkers obtained in gSR have better (91.67%) discriminability compared with those in gICA (80%). We speculate that this observation may attribute to the improved functional homogeneity of the brain ROIs identified in gSR.

3.5   Anatomical Locations of Network Nodes

Table 1 lists the anatomical locations of the brain regions shown in Fig. 5. Node 10 and 21 are on the auditory cortex (Temporal_Sup), and node14 and 23 correspond to primary motor cortex (Precentral gyrus). Tempral_Inf (node 2 and 69) is associated with visual object recognition and receiving processed visual information. Node 15 (Occipital_Mid) is responsible for higher order visual processing. Node 64 and node 37 correspond to precuneus that is the core node of default mode network and angular respectively. Parahippocampal (node 62) is involved in memory encoding and retrieval. Among the brain regions above, precuneus, angular and right temporal lobe have been reported to be related to autism. Furthermore, the brain region such as insular is also associated with the functional connectivity biomarkers identified by our method, which may provide new clues for autism study. Overall, more biomarkers with higher discriminability have been detected by sparse representation-based method, compared with that in ICA-based method, which perform much better in discriminating healthy control and autism patients.

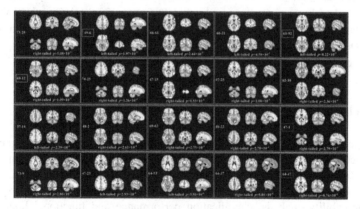

Fig. 5. Connectivity biomarkers detected by our method (sorted by p-value in ascending order)

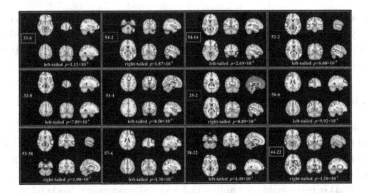

Fig. 6. Connectivity biomarkers detected by ICA-based method.

Table 1. The anatomical locations of the brain regions in Fig. 5

Node index	Brain region	Node index	Brain region	Node index	Brain region
1	Cerebelum_Crus_R	22	Parietal_Inf_L	61	Temporal_Mid_L
2	Temporal_Inf_R	23	Precentral_R	62	ParaHippocampal_L
6	Frontal_Mid_Orb_R	25	Cerebelum_Crus_L	64	Parietal_Mid
9	Cerebelum	37	Angular_R	66	Frontal_Inf_R
10	Temporal_Sup_R	47	Temporal_Mid_R	69	Temporal_Inf_L
12	Caudate_R	48	Lingual_R	73	Cingulum_Mid
14	Precentral_L	49	Parietal_R	74	SupraMarginal_R
15	Occipital_Mid	52	Insula_R		
21	Temporal_Sup_L	53	Frontal_Orb_L		

4   Conclusion

In this paper, we presented a novel framework and a comparative study to evaluate the performance of group-wise sparse representation-based fMRI data analysis for exploring functional connectivity biomarkers in ASD. In our experiments, we took ASD as test-bed, and compared our method with ICA-based method. Our experiment on discriminability analysis, classification performance and functional homogeneity analysis demonstrated the feasibility and superiority of sparse representation-based method in exploring functional connectivity biomarkers in brain diseases.

References

1. Beckmann, C.F., et al.: Investigations into resting-state connectivity using independent component analysis. Philos. Trans. Roy. Soc. B: Biol. Sci. **360**, 1001–1013 (2005)

2. De Luca, M., Beckmann, C., De Stefano, N., et al.: fMRI resting state networks define distinct modes of long-distance interactions in the human brain. Neuroimage **29**, 1359–1367 (2006)
3. Zhou, J., Greicius, M.D., et al.: Divergent network connectivity changes in behavioural variant frontotemporal dementia and Alzheimer's disease. Brain **133**, 13-152 (2010)
4. Fair, D.A., Posner, J., Nagel, B.J., et al.: Atypical default network connectivity in youth with attention-deficit/hyperactivity disorder. Biol. Psychiat. **68**, 1084–1091 (2010)
5. Daubechies, I., Roussos, E., Takerkart, S., et al.: Independent component analysis for brain fMRI does not select for independence. PNAS **106**, 10415–10422 (2009)
6. Lv, J., Jiang, X., Li, X., et al.: Sparse representation of whole-brain FMRI signals for identification of functional networks. Med. Image Anal. **20**(1), 112–134 (2014)
7. Lv, J., Jiang, X., Li, X., et al.: Holistic atlases of functional networks and interactions reveal reciprocal organizational architecture of cortical function. IEEE Trans. Biomed. Eng. **62**(4), 1120–1131 (2014)
8. Monk, C.S., Peltier, S.J., et al.: Abnormalities of intrinsic functional connectivity in autism spectrum disorders. Neuroimage **47**, 764–772 (2009)
9. Cherkassky, V.L., Kana, R.K., Keller, T.A., et al.: Functional connectivity in a baseline resting-state network in autism. NeuroReport **17**, 1687–1690 (2006)
10. Kennedy, D.P., Courchesne, E.: The intrinsic functional organization of the brain is altered in autism. Neuroimage **39**, 1877–1885 (2008)
11. Chen, S.S., Donoho, D.L., Saunders, M.A.: Atomic decomposition by basis pursuit. SIAM J. Sci. Comput. **20**, 33–61 (1998)
12. Li, Y., Long, J., He, L., et al.: A sparse representation-based algorithm for pattern localization in brain imaging data analysis. PLoS ONE **7**, e50332 (2012)
13. Mairal, J., Bach, F., Ponce, J., et al.: Online learning for matrix factorization and sparse coding. J. Mach. Learn. Res. **11**, 19–60 (2010)
14. Chang, C.-C., Lin, C.-J.: LIBSVM: a library for support vector machines. ACM Trans. Intell. Syst. Technol. (TIST) **2**, 27 (2011)

Classifying Stages of Mild Cognitive Impairment via Augmented Graph Embedding

Haoteng Tang[1], Lei Guo[1], Emily Dennis[2], Paul M. Thompson[3],
Heng Huang[1], Olusola Ajilore[4], Alex D. Leow[4], and Liang Zhan[1(✉)]

[1] Department of Electrical and Computer Engineering, University of Pittsburgh,
Pittsburgh, USA
liang.zhan@pitt.edu
[2] Harvard Medical School, Harvard University, Boston, USA
[3] Institute for Neuroimaging and Informatics, University of Southern California,
Los Angeles, USA
[4] Department of Psychiatry, University of Illinois at Chicago, Chicago, USA

Abstract. Mild Cognitive Impairment (MCI) is a clinically intermediate stage in the course of Alzheimer's disease (AD). MCI does not always lead to dementia. Some MCI patients may stay in the MCI status for the rest of their life, while others will develop AD eventually. Therefore, classification methods that help to distinguish MCI from earlier or later stages of the disease are important to understand the progression of AD. In this paper, we propose a novel computational framework - named Augmented Graph Embedding, or AGE - to tackle this challenge. In this new AGE framework, the random walk approach is first applied to brain structural networks derived from diffusion-weighted MRI to extract nodal feature vectors. A technique adapted from natural language processing is used to analyze these nodal feature vectors, and a multimodal augmentation procedure is adopted to improve classification accuracy. We validated this new AGE framework on data from the Alzheimer's Disease Neuroimaging Initiative (ADNI). Results show advantages of the proposed framework, compared to a range of existing methods.

Keywords: Mild Cognitive Impairment · Brain structural network · Graph embedding · Random walk · Natural Language Processing · Data augmentation

1 Introduction

Alzheimer's Disease (AD) is the leading cause of dementia and there are approximately 50 million people living with AD. Treatment options for AD remain limited, and there is no known cure. It is well known that AD causes progressive cell death in the brain, but the pattern and rate of brain changes differs to some degree across individuals, and the degenerative processes in two AD patients can follow very different trajectories. Mild Cognitive Impairment (MCI), a clinically intermediate state between normal aging and AD, can cause cognitive changes that are severe enough to be noticed by the individuals experiencing them or by other people, but the changes are not severe

© Springer Nature Switzerland AG 2019
D. Zhu et al. (Eds.): MBIA 2019/MFCA 2019, LNCS 11846, pp. 30–38, 2019.
https://doi.org/10.1007/978-3-030-33226-6_4

enough to interfere with daily life or independent function [1]. Approximately 15 to 20 percent of people aged 65 or older have MCI. MCI patients, especially MCI involving memory problems, are more likely to develop AD or other dementias than people without MCI. However, MCI does not always lead to AD. Some MCI patients will stay in the MCI status for the rest of their life while others develop AD eventually [2, 3]. In order to better understand MCI, the Alzheimer's Disease Neuroimaging Initiative (ADNI) divided MCI into early (EMCI) and late (LMCI) stages based on the severity of memory impairment [4, 5]. Accurately classifying the stages of MCI – and features that help to distinguish them - will significantly benefit clinical research on MCI and AD and may offer insight into factors that affect disease progression.

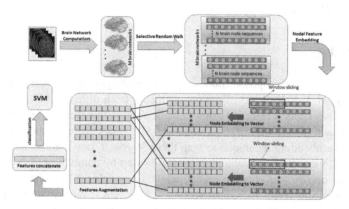

Fig. 1. The proposed Augmented Graph Embedding (AGE) framework.

A typical approach for disease classification tasks is to extract features from brain imaging data (such as MRI or PET) and use these features to classify EMCI and LMCI, prior to identifying potential biomarkers for MCI staging [6–11]. For example, Shashank Tripathi et al. proposed to use hippocampal and sub-cortical morphological features to classify EMCI and LMCI, yielding a classification accuracy of 70.95% [12]. In [13], the authors proposed a pipeline using learned features from semantically labelled PET images to perform group classification; their results showed a considerable improvement in classification accuracy for EMCI versus LMCI (72.5%), using FDG-PET compared to using PET scans with the AV-45 radiotracer. In work by La Rocca et al., the authors computed several network features (e.g., clustering coefficients) from a 74×74 brain network and then used a support vector machine (SVM) classifier to compare EMCI and LMCI, with a classification accuracy of 70% [14]. Although much effort has been devoted to the comparison of EMCI and LMCI, more advanced techniques may be beneficial to improve classification accuracy for this challenge.

Modeling the brain as a network using a connectome approach allows us to gain systems-level insights into large-scale neuronal communication abnormalities associated with brain diseases (such as AD) and may also yield novel features to assist diagnosis and prognosis. The brain's structural network - derived from a tractography algorithm applied to diffusion-weighted MRI data - can capture global structural changes caused by different brain diseases including Alzheimer's disease [14]. Prior work [15] has shown the potential of analysis of brain structural networks in Alzheimer's research. Though several studies [16–18] have been carried out on MCI staging tasks using brain structural networks, the classification performance is still far from being useful clinically, so more powerful computation techniques are sorely needed. Based on this challenge, this paper proposes a new technique to explore the brain network's intrinsic geometry based on the augmented graph embedding technique. Initial results show a significant improvement, compared to baseline methods. The rest of this paper is organized as follows: Sect. 2 describes the new augmented graph embedding framework, Sect. 3 shows experimental results on the ADNI data, and Sect. 4 concludes the paper.

2   Method

Figure 1 illustrates the proposed framework, named Augmented Graph Embedding or AGE. Firstly, M $N \times N$ networks are reconstructed from diffusion MRI data for each subject; then we apply a selective random walk process to extract a raw nodal feature vector from each $N \times N$ network and obtain M $N \times L$ raw features; the next step is to use a feature embedding technique to map these M $N \times L$ raw features into M $N \times K$ features; next, we conduct a feature augmentation step by combining M $N \times K$ feature matrices into one $N \times K$ feature matrix and train a cubic SVM classifier with the resulting 1D feature vector with dimension of $1 \times (N \times K)$. We will describe the three main steps: feature preparation, feature embedding, and feature augmentation in the following sections.

Table 1. Random walk procedure.

Input: brain network B, control parameters (α, β, θ), sequence length L.
for *starting node* $=$ *Node* 1,2,3…N **do**
first move: select the node that has largest weight connecting to the starting node as the next walk
for *move* $=$ 2,3,4…L **do**
save all the nodes that connects to the current node and the weight between them and current node into a dictionary as $D =$ [*node* : *weight*].
for each node and corresponding weight in D **do**
If *node* $=$ *the previous node in the sequence* **then**
$weight = \alpha \times weight$
else if *node* $\neq$ *the previous node* **And** node connects to the previous node **then**
$weight = \beta \times weight$
else
$weight = \theta \times weight$
end if
end for
Select the node with the maximum weight as the next walk node and move to the next
end for
end for
Output: Node sequence (*length* $= L$)

2.1   Feature Preparation

Usually, the dimension of brain network features can be up to tens of thousands, including hundreds to thousands of nodes and the weighted connections or "edges" connecting the nodes. It is well known - as the 'curse of dimensionality' - that the statistical performance and stability of machine learning algorithms can degrade as the dimension of the input data increases, without steps for dimension reduction. Thus, how to extract the hallmark features from $N \times N$ network can be very challenging. Here we adopted a selective random walk [19] procedure to generate a sequence vector for each node. In the random walk [19], three parameters (α, β, θ) can be set up to assist in determining the next node in the walk from the current node. Basically, any nodes connecting to the current node will be candidates for the next walk node. For each of these next step candidates: **(A)** If it is the node in the random walk immediately prior to the current node, the weight between this candidate and the current node will be multiplied by a factor α. **(B)** If it is one of the nodes that connects to the current node but does not connect to the previous walk node, the weight between this candidate and the current node will be multiplied by a factor β. **(C)** If it is one of the nodes that connects to the current node as well as the previously visited node of the current node, the weight between them will be multiplied by a factor θ. In this way, all weights between each next step candidate and the current node will be multiplied by a parameter (either $\alpha, \beta, or \theta$) to obtain the next walk controller (NWC). Then the candidate node with the largest NWC will be selected as the next walk node and saved in the nodal sequence. The length of each nodal sequence is set to L. Each of the N nodes in the network is set up as a starting point in the nodal sequence. Thereby N L-length nodal sequences can be extracted from the $N \times N$ network. The entire procedure is summarized in Table 1.

Table 2. Feature embedding.

Input: Node sequence $(length = L)$, $window\ size\ = w$.
For pivot node p in node sequences do
$max_f \sum_{p \in s}[Log(Prob(T(p)|f(p)))]$
where $T(p)$ is the target nodes within the window around pivot node p
End for
Output: Nodal embedded feature vector $(dimension = k\ and\ k < L)$.

2.2   Feature Embedding

Inspired by Natural Language Processing, we can treat each node sequence as a sentence encoding the semantics and each node as the word from a vocabulary. Given the node sequences, we adopted a deep neural network model [19] to embed each node into a low dimension vector. To train the model, we first define a window of size w. In each step, we only focus on w nodes within the window. The node in the center of the window is the pivot node p and other nodes beside the pivot node are target nodes, $T(p)$. The window slides from the left of the node sequence to the right, so each node in the sequence will be a pivot node with the nodes beside them as the target nodes.

The objective of this neural network model training is to find an optimal mapping function f^* to map each node in the network into a k-dimensional vector ($k < L$). Given the set of pivot nodes as S, the optimal mapping function f^* may be defined using Eq. (1). This feature embedding procedure is summarized in Table 2.

$$f^* = argmax_f \sum_{p \in S} [Log(Prob(T(p)|f(p)))] \qquad (1)$$

2.3   Feature Augmentation

Once we have the embedded features, we can use a classification algorithm (e.g., SVM) to classify groups. Here, we also propose a new augmentation procedure. Since our framework is based on diffusion MRI-derived brain structural networks, there are many published tractography algorithms that can be used to reconstruct a brain structural network. In theory, different tractography algorithms for mapping structural connections should eventually provide a consistent anatomical description of the brain. However, different tractography algorithms tend to reconstruct different fiber bundles and thus generate very different networks [20]. Prior work has shown that directly averaging multimodal networks may not be beneficial for a classification task [20]; therefore, we propose a multimodal augmentation strategy to combine multiple networks and reduce the possible biases arising from each unimodal network.

Firstly, each unimodal network can generate one nodal embedding vector for each node using the procedures described in the above sections. Then the final feature representation V_i^* for node i from M networks may be defined by: $V_i^* = \sum_{j=1}^{M} W_j V_{ij}$. Here V_{ij} is the k-dimensional vector of node i computed using nodal embedding procedure described in Sect. 2.2 and W_j is the coefficient associated with the j-th network and $\sum_{j=1}^{M} W_j = 1$. Then we concatenate all the nodes' feature representations together into a 1D vector ($dimension = 1 \times (N \times K)$) and then train the SVM classifier on this 1D vector. The optimal feature combination coefficients W^* may be obtained using Eq. (2):

$$W^* = argmin_{W,\lambda} \left[||\lambda^2|| + \sum_i^K max\left(0, 1 - y_i g\left(\lambda \sum_{j=1}^{M} W_j V_j\right)\right) \right] \qquad (2)$$

Here K is the number of subjects, M is the number of networks for each subject, y_i is the label for subject i, λ is the weights of cubic SVM classifier and g is the kernel function of SVM.

3   Experiment

3.1   Data Description, Preprocessing and Network Reconstruction

Data used in this study are publicly available and were obtained from ADNI2, the 2nd stage of the Alzheimer's Disease Neuroimaging Initiative. In our experiments, we analyzed diffusion-weighted MRI and T1-weighted MRI data from 111 subjects, including 72 EMCI (mean age = 71.20 ± 11.59, 47M) and 39 LMCI (mean age = 72.32 ± 5.83, 24M). No significant difference was identified in age between EMCI and LMCI ($P = 0.57$). Details of the data collection protocols for both diffusion MRI and T1-weighted MRI may be found at the ADNI website (http://www.adni-info.org).

FreeSurfer (surfer.nmr.mgh.harvard.edu) and FSL (fsl.fmrib.ox.ac.uk/fsl) were used as the main tools for data preprocessing. For both T1 and diffusion MRI, we first removed the extra-cerebral tissue and then visually inspected 'skull-stripped' volumes, and manually edited them if needed. Skull-stripped T1 MRI then underwent intensity inhomogeneity normalization and was linearly aligned into the Colin27 space and parcellated into 113 ROIs using Harvard-Oxford Cortical and Subcortical Probabilistic atlas. Using the skull-stripped diffusion MRI, we first corrected for head motion and eddy current distortions, and then corrected the gradient table, and later elastically registered to the corresponding preprocessed T1 MRI to correct for echo-planar induced susceptibility artifacts. The preprocessed diffusion MRI and 113 ROIs were used to reconstruct the brain structural networks.

For each subject, we reconstructed four 113 × 113 brain structural networks using four whole brain tractography algorithms, which include two tensor-based deterministic algorithms (TL [21] and SL [22]) and two ODF-based probabilistic algorithms (Hough Voting [23] and PICo [24]). Deterministic tractography was conducted using the Diffusion Toolkit (trackvis.org). Hough voting was performed using code provided by the authorsm and PICo was conducted using Camino (cmic.cs.ucl.ac.uk/camino). All fiber tracking was restricted to regions where fractional anisotropy (FA) >0.2 to avoid GM and cerebrospinal fluid; fiber paths were stopped if the fiber direction encountered a sharp turn (with a critical angle threshold >30°). The network was then defined as the number of detected fibers connecting each pair of ROIs. This matrix is symmetric, by definition, and has a zero diagonal (no self-connections). To avoid computational bias in the experiments, we normalized each brain network by the maximum value in the network, as matrices derived from different tractography methods have different scales and ranges.

No significant group difference was identified on the raw network data, between EMCI and LMCI, for each of these four networks.

3.2 Experimental Settings

To validate the proposed method, we chose four baseline methods from the published literature. The first baseline method was to conduct Principal Components Analysis (PCA) on the original network data, followed by the SVM. The second baseline method was to run SVM classifier directly on the network measures. Here we separately tested two network measures - modularity (MOD) and global efficiency (GLOB) extracted from the brain network data. The last baseline method used LASSO Regression (https://github.com/jiayuzhou/SLEP) to classify the networks.

For the proposed method, the nodal sequence length L was set to 25. We initially set a range for each of the control parameters (α, β, θ) based on our experiences: $\alpha \in [6 \sim 8]$, $\beta \in [1, 2]$ and $\theta \in [0.001, 0.006]$. The results are consistent therefore, we set $\alpha = 8, \beta = 1$ and $\theta = 0.001$. Then we applied our selective random walk procedure to each of the four 113 × 113 brain networks generated in Sect. 3.1, to generate nodal sequences. After that, we then trained a nodal embedding model (or deep neural network) to obtain the node feature vectors (dimension-reduced nodal feature vectors). The input of the neural network is a series of brain nodal sequences. Each node will be embedded into a vector with a length of 16. The learning rate was set to be 10^{-5}. Lastly, we concatenate all 113 nodal vectors into one vector of dimension 1808 (= 113 * 16) as the 1D vector representation for the entire 113×113 brain network. Based on the 1808-parameter representation for each of the four brain networks, we conducted feature augmentation by combining four feature vectors into one final feature vectors using $V^* = \sum_{j=1}^{4} W_j V_j$. Here, V^* is the fused representation; $W = \{W_j | j = 1, 2, 3, 4\}$ is the weighting coefficients for V_j and initially we treated everyone equally. Then the optimal W^* can be derived using Eq. 2. The actual searching procedure for W^* was as follows: first, the entire dataset was divided into two parts: 80% as the training data and 20% as the test data. The training data was further divided into two parts: 80% and 20%. We used 80% of the training data to train the model using the initial value W, and 20% of the training data to verify the classification accuracy. By gradually adjusting W to W^*, we can maximize this classification accuracy. Once W^* is finalized, we can re-train the model on the entire training data and compute the final classification accuracy on the testing data. For the classification, we adopted nonlinear SVM as the classifier; we report the mean and standard deviation of classification accuracy for each method on 5-fold cross-validation.

3.3   Comparison to Other Baseline Methods

In this section, the performances of the proposed method and other baseline methods are assessed. Following the descriptions in the above section, we reported mean and standard deviation of the classification accuracy from the 5-fold cross validation. The classification results are summarized in Table 3, which shows that the graph embedding outperforms all baseline methods. For example, using the Hough-based network, all baseline methods have less than 60% accuracy while the proposed graph embedding can achieve 64.9% accuracy. This trend is the same for all columns in Table 3, which suggests that graph embedding technique is more powerful in preserving the features in the dimension reduction process. Moreover, the multimodal network may not be a good choice for the traditional methods (i.e., PCA+SVM, SL has 64.9% accuracy while AN only has 63.1%). However, for the proposed method (AGE), there was a classification accuracy of 72.4% ± 3.1%, which clearly demonstrates the advantage of graph embedding in exploring the structure of this multimodal dataset.

Table 3. The comparison of the proposed method (GE) to other baseline methods (PCA+SVM, GLOB+SVM, MOD+SVM, LASSO) for the task of classifying EMCI vs. LMCI. Values are mean (standard deviation) of the classification accuracy from 5-fold cross validation. We compared each method using unimodal network (Hough, PICo, TL, SL) and augmented network (AN). For each baseline method, the AN approach combines multimodal networks using the strategy described in Sect. 2.3. It is evident that the graph embedding has a better classification accuracy (highlighted in **bold** in each column) than all baseline methods and the augmented GE (the last column in the last row) has the best performance (72.4% ± 3.1%).

	Hough (%)	PICo (%)	TL (%)	SL (%)	AN (%)
PCA+SVM	56.8 (7.0)	62.4 (0.2)	58.6 (5.4)	64.9 (1.9)	63.1 (8.6)
GLOB+SVM	55.9 (1.8)	58.6 (2.7)	55.9 (2.8)	61.3 (5.2)	58.6 (3.6)
MOD+SVM	59.4 (9.2)	50.5 (8.1)	59.5 (2.7)	50.5 (6.3)	63.1 (6.3)
LASSO	52.7 (18.6)	60.4 (15.2)	58.18 (2.7)	54.5 (25.9)	60.4 (26.7)
GE	**64.9 (10.8)**	**65.6 (1.6)**	**68.0 (3.1)**	**67.6 (4.0)**	**72.4 (3.1)**

4 Conclusion

In this study, we proposed a new graph embedding framework to classify stages of MCI, based on brain structural network data. Initial experiments on the ADNI2 dataset suggest that graph embedding methods share prominent advantages over traditional methods.

References

1. Petersen, R.C., et al.: Current concepts in mild cognitive impairment. Arch. Neurol. **58**(12), 1985–1992 (2001)
2. Dawe, B., Procter, A., Philpot, M.: Concepts of mild memory impairment in the elderly and their relationship to dementia - a review. Int. J. Geriatr. Psychiatry **7**(7), 473–479 (1992)
3. Petersen, R.C.: : Clinical characterization and outcome (vol 56, pg 303, 1999). Arch. Neurol-Chic. **56**(6), 760 (1999)
4. Lee, E.S., et al.: Default mode network functional connectivity in early and late mild cognitive impairment results from the Alzheimer's disease neuroimaging initiative. Alzheimer Dis. Assoc. Disord. **30**(4), 289–296 (2016)
5. Aisen, P.S., et al.: Clinical core of the Alzheimer's disease neuroimaging initiative: progress and plans. Alzheimer's Dement. **6**(3), 239–246 (2010)
6. Goryawala, M., Zhou, Q., Barker, W., Loewenstein, D.A., Duara, R., Adjouadi, M.: Inclusion of neuropsychological scores in atrophy models improves diagnostic classification of alzheimer's disease and mild cognitive impairment. Comput. Intell. Neurosci. **2015**, 865265 (2015)
7. Shakeri, M., Lombaert, H., Tripathi, S., Kadoury, S.: Deep spectral-based shape features for Alzheimer's disease classification. In: Reuter, M., Wachinger, C., Lombaert, H. (eds.) SeSAMI 2016. LNCS, vol. 10126, pp. 15–24. Springer, Cham (2016). https://doi.org/10.1007/978-3-319-51237-2_2

8. Korolev, S., Safiullin, A., Belyaev, M., Dodonova, Y.: Residual and plain convolutional neural networks for 3D brain MRI classification. In: 2017 IEEE 14th International Symposium on Biomedical Imaging (ISBI 2017), pp. 835–838. IEEE (2017)

9. Jessen, F., et al.: AD dementia risk in late MCI, in early MCI, and in subjective memory impairment. Alzheimer's Dement. **10**(1), 76–83 (2014)

10. Hett, K., Ta, V.-T., Giraud, R., Mondino, M., Manjón, José V., Coupé, P.: Patch-based DTI grading: application to Alzheimer's disease classification. In: Wu, G., Coupé, P., Zhan, Y., Munsell, Brent C., Rueckert, D. (eds.) Patch-MI 2016. LNCS, vol. 9993, pp. 76–83. Springer, Cham (2016). https://doi.org/10.1007/978-3-319-47118-1_10

11. Singh, S., et al.: Deep-learning-based classification of FDG-PET data for Alzheimer's disease categories. In: 13th International Conference on Medical Information Processing and Analysis, 2017, vol. 10572, p. 105720 J. International Society for Optics and Photonics (2017)

12. Tripathi, S., Nozadi, S.H., Shakeri, M., Kadoury, S.: Sub-cortical shape morphology and voxel-based features for Alzheimer's disease classification. In: 2017 IEEE 14th International Symposium on Biomedical Imaging (ISBI 2017), pp. 991–994. IEEE (2017)

13. Nozadi, S.H., Kadoury, S., The Alzheimer's Disease Neuroimaging Initiative: Classification of Alzheimer's and MCI patients from semantically parcelled PET images: a comparison between AV45 and FDG-PET. Int. J. Biomed. Imaging **2018**, 1247430 (2018)

14. La Rocca, M., Amoroso, N., Monaco, A., Bellotti, R., Tangaro, S.: A novel approach to brain connectivity reveals early structural changes in Alzheimer's disease. Physiol. Meas. **39** (7), 074005 (2018)

15. Wang, Q., et al.: The added value of diffusion-weighted MRI-derived structural connectome in evaluating mild cognitive impairment: a multi-cohort validation1. J. Alzheimers Dis. **64** (1), 149–169 (2018)

16. Prasad, G., Joshi, S.H., Nir, T.M., Toga, A.W., Thompson, P.M., Alzheimer's Disease Neuroimaging Initiative: Brain connectivity and novel network measures for Alzheimer's disease classification. Neurobiol. Aging **36**(Suppl. 1), S121–S131 (2015)

17. Zhan, L., et al.: Multiple stages classification of Alzheimer's disease based on structural brain networks using generalized low rank approximations (GLRAM). In: O'Donnell, L., Nedjati-Gilani, G., Rathi, Y., Reisert, M., Schneider, T. (eds.) Computational Diffusion MRI. Mathematics and Visualization, pp. 35–44. Springer, Cham (2014). https://doi.org/10.1007/978-3-319-11182-7_4

18. Kurmukov, A., et al.: Classifying phenotypes based on the community structure of human brain networks. In: Cardoso, M.J., et al. (eds.) GRAIL/MFCA/MICGen -2017. LNCS, vol. 10551, pp. 3–11. Springer, Cham (2017). https://doi.org/10.1007/978-3-319-67675-3_1

19. Grover, A., Leskovec, J.: node2vec: scalable feature learning for networks. In: Proceedings of the 22nd ACM SIGKDD International Conference on Knowledge Discovery and Data Mining, pp. 855–864. ACM (2016)

20. Zhan, L., et al.: Comparison of nine tractography algorithms for detecting abnormal structural brain networks in Alzheimer's disease. Front Aging Neurosci. **7**, 48 (2015)

21. Lazar, M., et al.: White matter tractography using diffusion tensor deflection. Hum. Brain Mapp. **18**(4), 306–321 (2003)

22. Conturo, T.E., et al.: Tracking neuronal fiber pathways in the living human brain. Proc. Natl. Acad. Sci. U. S. A. **96**(18), 10422–10427 (1999)

23. Aganj, I., et al.: A Hough transform global probabilistic approach to multiple-subject diffusion MRI tractography. Med. Image Anal. **15**(4), 414–425 (2011)

24. Parker, G.J., Haroon, H.A., Wheeler-Kingshott, C.A.: A framework for a streamline-based probabilistic index of connectivity (PICo) using a structural interpretation of MRI diffusion measurements. J. Magn. Reson. Imaging **18**(2), 242–254 (2003)

Mapping the Spatio-Temporal Functional Coherence in the Resting Brain

Ze Wang$^{(\boxtimes)}$ ⓘD

Department of Diagnostic Radiology and Nuclear Medicine,
University of Maryland School of Medicine, Baltimore, USA
ze.wang@som.umaryland.edu

Abstract. Human brain functions are underlined by spatially and temporally coherent activity. Characterizing the spatio-temporal coherence (STC) of brain activity is then important to understand brain function, which however is still elusive in the literature. In this study, we proposed a new method to measure the spatio-temporal incoherence (STIC) by segmenting the fMRI time series of neighboring voxels into a series of continuous 4-dimensional elements and recording the similarity of every element to all others. STIC was then calculated as the log differential of the similarity sum of all elements and that when the time window is increased by 1 – a process similar to and directly extended from the time-embedding based approximate entropy calculation. Experiment results showed that STIC revealed the correct irregularity difference between random noise and spatio-temporally coherent signal. STIC was less sensitive to noise than a multi-variate entropy measure. When applied to 917 young health subjects' resting-state fMRI, we identified highly replicable STIC maps with very fine cortical structures. Females and more matured brain (older here) had higher STIC. Higher STIC in putamen showed a trend of correlations with better mental examination outcome. These data showed STIC as a potential functional brain marker.

Keywords: Spatio-temporal coherence · Long-range coherence · Brain entropy mapping

1 Introduction

Spatio-temporally coherent activity is fundamental to human brain functions. Reciprocally, characterizing the spatio-temporal coherence of brain activity (STCA) may reveal information critical to the wellbeing or integrity of brain functions. Because of the relatively high spatial and temporal resolution, fMRI has become a major tool for assessing STCA. Over the past two decades, a variety of methods have been developed to characterize STCA from different aspects using fMRI. Biswal et al. first used the seed-based inter-regional temporal correlation analysis to study functional connectivity between spatially distributed regions [1], but the correlational method can't directly infer local brain activity at each voxel. In [2], Kendal-tau was used to characterize spatial correlations of neighboring voxels, but temporal coherence was not considered. Independent component analysis [3] has been adopted to extract distributed brain

D. Zhu et al. (Eds.): MBIA 2019/MFCA 2019, LNCS 11846, pp. 39–48, 2019.
https://doi.org/10.1007/978-3-030-33226-6_5

networks but it lacks clear analytical descriptions for how the spatio-temporal coherence is modeled. Temporal coherence of brain activity at each voxel can be assessed with entropy. For example, approximate entropy such as the approximate negentropy [4] the sample entropy (SampEn) [5] has been used to map the regional brain incoherence [6, 7] but in a univariate manner. To also consider spatial incoherence, Schutze et al. proposed a multivariate entropy measure based on subspace projection of fMRI data [8], but it was based on an assumption of a Gaussian distribution of the data and only provides one value for the entire volume. One approach to quantify the spatio-temporal incoherence at each voxel is to use the multivariate entropy such as SampEn (mSampEn) [9] but those measures often don't consider the spatial correlations among the multiple variables as signals of all neighboring voxels are simply stacked together to form a one-dimensional vector. There still lacks an explicit way to characterize the spatio-temporal coherence or alternatively incoherence of brain activity. To solve this problem, we proposed a new multivariate SampEn which quantifies the regional long-range temporal coherence of brain activity (here rsfMRI signal) by examining the likelihood of that a temporal segment of the timeseries of the neighboring voxels matches the other segments of the timeseries for a given segment length of m and m + 1. Spatial coherence is considered by including the neighboring voxels in the segment matching process. We then used synthetic data to validate the new method as compared to the current multivariate SampEn for differentiating multivariate signals with known spatio-temporal coherence (or incoherence). Large human rsfMRI data were then used to verify the spatio-temporal coherence patterns in normal healthy subjects as well as their relations to age and sex. Contributions of this work include: (1) we proposed a novel method to quantify the long-range spatio-temporal coherence of brain activity; (2) we demonstrated highly replicable STIC maps with fine cortical structures identified from a large dataset; (3) we showed sex and age effects of STIC identified from the large data.

2   Method

2.1   A New Multivariate SampEn and Spatio-Temporal Coherence Mapping (STCM)

In SampEn, temporal coherence (or regularity) of a time series is measured by the "logarithmic likelihood" that a small segment (within a window of a length 'm') of the data "matches" with other segments will still "match" the others if the segment window length increases by 1. "match" is defined by distance < r times standard deviation of the entire time series (r is a constant). For each voxel of the preprocessed fMRI (resting-state fMRI (rsfMRI) in this paper) data, let's denote the signal as $x = [x_1, x_2, \ldots x_N]$, where N is the number of rsfMRI timepoints. A series of data segments (also called the embedding vectors) can be extracted from x: $u_t = [x_t, x_{t+1}, \ldots x_{t+m-1}]$ where t = 1 to N − m + 1. The number of embedded vectors u_j (j = 1 to N − m, and j ≠ t) whose distance from u_t (dist(u_j, u_t)) are less than r is recorded by $B_t^m(r)$. dist(u_j, u_t) is often chosen to be the L-infinity norm of the difference

$u_j - u_t$, i.e., $\max_{l=0\sim m} |u_{jl} - u_{tl}|$ (u_{jl} means the l-th element of u_j). The same procedure is repeated for the dimension m + 1 to get $B_t^{m+1}(r)$. Defining

$$B^m(r) = \frac{1}{(N-m)(N-m-1)} \sum_{t=1}^{N-m} B_t^m(r) \tag{1}$$

$$A^m(r) = \frac{1}{(N-m)(N-m-1)} \sum_{t=1}^{N-m} B_t^{m+1}(r) \tag{2}$$

we can then calculate SampEn as:

$$SampEn(m, r, N, x) = -\ln\left[\frac{A^m(r)}{B^m(r)}\right] \tag{3}$$

While Eq. 3 provides a statistical way to quantify the coherence or order implicit in the itinerant fMRI dynamics over extended periods of time, it doesn't consider the spatial coherence among neighboring voxels. To solve that problem, we introduce a neighborhood S for each voxel and replace the scalar value x_t (t = 1 $\sim$ N − m + 1) with a vector $\bar{x}_t = \forall x_{t,s} \in S$ (all voxels in the neighborhood S of current voxel at current timepoint t). Accordingly, each embedding vector turns into an embedding matrix U_t whose columns indicate the consecutive timepoints and rows indicate the voxel locations in the 3D neighborhood. To compare a pair of embedding matrices, correlation coefficients between the column vectors at each column position from the two matrices are calculated as the column-wise distance: $CC(U_{jl\cdot}, U_{tl\cdot})$ ($U_{jl\cdot}$ indicates the l-th column vector of the embedding matrix U_j). We then defined

$$dist(U_j, U_t) = \max_{l=0\sim m} |1 - CC(U_{jl\cdot}, U_{tl\cdot})| \tag{4}$$

which satisfies the metric function defining properties. In SampEn, the L-infinity norm is compared with r, which however is arbitrarily defined. A large r may produce too many matches and a small r can result in no matches. The corresponding SampEn value will be either very close to 0 or underdefined (in latter situation). Instead of using such a hard-thresholding (a Heaviside function) based embedding vector matching process: defining a "match" if distance is less than r or no "match" otherwise, we calculated 1 − minimum CC of the m columns as the L-infinity norm of the two embedding matrices and recorded the sum of (1 − $CC_{min}(U_j, U_t)$) (j = 1 to N − m, and j ≠ t) as B_t^m and then got $B^m = \frac{1}{(N-m)(N-m-1)} \sum_{t=1}^{N-m} B_t^m \cdot B_t^{m+1}$ and A^m were similarly defined. Finally, we defined the new metric for characterizing the spatio-temporal incoherence (STIC) of fMRI data as:

$$STIC = \ln\left[\frac{A^m}{B^m}\right] \tag{5}$$

We used incoherence rather than coherence as the measure defined in Eq. 5 indicates the irregularity similar to what entropy measures. The advantages as compared to the univariate and multivariate SampEn are: (1) STIC considers both spatial and temporal coherence, (2) STC doesn't need the arbitrary cut-off threshold r, (3) because CC function is independent of the data scale, so does STIC.

STC was implemented in C++ and CUDA (Nvidia). Video cards with graphic processing units (GPU) (Nvidia 1080Ti) were used to accelerate the computing process. In the following, we dubbed the process of calculating STIC at each voxel as STC mapping (STCM).

2.2   Evaluations with Numerical Simulations

Synthetic data were generated to evaluate the proposed new multivariate SampEn – STIC– for differentiating multivariate signal with known irregularity difference as compared to the existing simple data concatenation based mSampEn [9]. Brain activations were generated by convolving a boxcar function with a canonical hemodynamic response function (HRF, provided by SPM (https://www.fil.ion.ucl.ac.uk/spm)) and were assigned to the center voxel of a 5×5 voxel patch. For the other voxels, the synthetic activations were weighted by the inverse distance of the voxel to the center (weights are inversely dependent on the distance). Random noise was generated for each voxel, convolved, and weighted by the voxel's inverse distance to the center. Purely random noise was also generated for the 5×5 voxels as a control dataset. mSampEn was calculated with m = 3, r = 0.3. All 5×5 voxels were used for calculating STIC.

2.3   Evaluations with rsfMRI Data from Human Connectome Project (HCP)

We then applied STIC to preprocessed rsfMRI data from 917 healthy young subjects (age: 22–37 yrs) obtained from HCP [10]. Each subject had 4 resting scans using the same multi-band sequence[11]. The readout direction was left to right (LR) for 2 scans and right to left (RL) for the other 2. Imaging parameters were: TR/TE = 720/33.1 ms, flip angle = 52°, FOV = 208 180 mm, 2 mm isotropic voxels, 72 slices, multiband factor = 8, 1200 TRs, total scan time = 14:33.

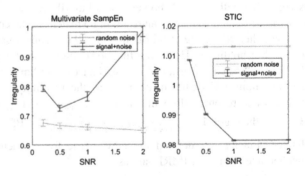

Fig. 1. Irregularity of multivariate noise and signal identified by mSampEn and STIC. Random noise means the HRF-convolved random brain signal + random gaussian noise.

All data were pre-processed by HCP and were registered into the MNI standard space. The final volume size is $91 \times 109 \times 91$. To suppress the residual inter-subject brain structural difference after brain normalization and errors in rsfMRI data introduced by brain normalization, a Gaussian filter with full-width-at-half-maximum (FWHM) = 6 mm was used to smooth the rsfMRI images. To reduce the computation burden, a spherical neighborhood with a radius of 4.1 mm was empirically chosen, resulting in 33 neighboring voxels for each intracranial voxel. 3 computers with totally 7 GPU cards were used to calculate STIC. Mean STIC maps of the first LR and RL scans and the second LR and RL scans were calculated for the following analyses. For SampEn, the parameters were chosen to be m = 3 and r = 0.3 based on literature.

Test-retest stability is an important performance index for any neurophysiological measure. Using the HCP data, we calculated the test-retest stability of STIC using intra-class correlation coefficient (ICC) [12]. STIC maps of the LR and RL from the same subjects were averaged for the first and second scan separately. ICC at each voxel was calculated by ICC = (MSb − MSw)/(MSb + MSw), where MSb represents between-subject variance and MSw means within-subject variance. ICC varies between −1 to 1 with higher value meaning higher stability. ICC > 0.3 is often considered reliable.

Human brain presents significant age and sex effects on both structural and functional measures [13–15]. To examine the potential age and sex effects on STIC, simple regression was performed using SPM to calculate the correlations between STIC at each voxel and age and sex.

3 Results

3.1 Numerical Simulation Results

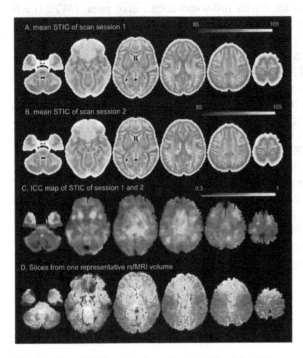

Fig. 2. Mean STIC maps of session 1 and 2 of the 917 young healthy subjects from HCP. C is the ICC map (thresholded at 0.3) of the 917 subjects' test-retest STIC maps. D shows the same slices from a representative rsfMRI image volume.

Figure 1 shows the irregularity calculation results of the synthetic data. Although mSampEn and STIC both differentiated the multivariate correlated brain activation signal (blue line) from the uncorrelated random noise (red line), STIC successfully revealed higher irregularity in the pure noise than that of the noise contaminated signal as it should be. By comparison, mSampEn produced the opposite irregularity (incoherence) contrast: higher irregularity in signal but lower in noise. When SNR increased, STIC of noise didn't change but STIC of signal consistently decreased because of less noise contaminations. mSampEn of noise decreased with SNR though it should not be the case; mSampEn of signal didn't monotonically changed when SNR increased.

3.2 Mean STIC Map and Test-Retest Stability of STIC

Figure 2 shows the mean STIC maps calculated from the 917 healthy subjects recruited in the HCP project. STIC was multiplied by 1000 for the purpose of visualization, meaning that the highest STIC was around 0.1. Highly similar mean STIC maps were observed in the resting scan 1 ((LR + RL)/2) and scan 2 ((LR + RL)/2) (Fig. 2A, 2B). Interestingly, the STIC maps revealed very high structural details of brain gyri and sulci, much finer than what can be seen from the raw rsfMRI image (Fig. 2D). Figure 2C is the ICC map thresholded by ICC >= 0.3. High test-retest stability was found in the entire brain.

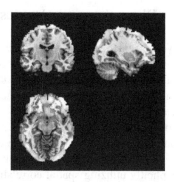

Fig. 3. Women have higher resting STIC (spatio-temporal incoherence) than men. P < 0.05 (FWE corrected).

3.3 Sex Effects on STIC

Nearly identical sex difference of STIC was found in both rsfMRI sessions. For this reason, only the results of session 1 were displayed. Figure 3 shows that women have larger spatio-temporal incoherence of resting brain activity than men in most of cortices and some sub-cortical areas including hippocampus, thalamus, and striatum. The statistical threshold was p < 0.05. Multiple comparison correction was performed using the family-wise error (FWE) based method [16].

3.4 Age Effects on STIC

Nearly identical age effects of STIC was found in both rsfMRI sessions. Figure 4 shows the correlation between age and STIC identified from the 1st rsfMRI session. Significant (p < 0.05 FWE corrected) positive age vs STIC correlation was found in putamen, middle and superior temporal gyri, and cerebellum. To further explore the potential value of STIC for mental health, we examined the correlation between STIC and cognitive impairment as measured by the mini-mental state examination (MMSE) [17]. The bottom right slice in Fig. 4 shows the trend (p < 0.01 uncorrected for multiple comparison) of a positive relationship between STIC and MMSE in putamen.

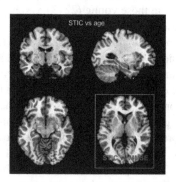

Fig. 4. STIC was positively related to age (P < 0.05 (FWE corrected)). The right bottom slice shows the positive relation between STIC in putamen and MMSE score.

4 Discussion and Conclusion

We presented a new method to measure the regional spatio-temporal incoherence. Evaluations showed that the new STIC measure provided more reasonable incoherence calculation results in terms of stable incoherence for the random brain signal contaminated by different levels of noise; lower incoherence for the pseudo brain activity; stable incoherence for the pseudo brain activity when SNR increases. Applied to 917 young healthy subjects' rsfMRI data, the new STCM method showed high test-retest stability. Significant sex and age effects were observed.

Less sensitivity to noise of our method than the traditional method was a result of explicitly utilizing spatial correlations. Our method yielded lower STIC in signal than in noise as expected. Standard multivariate SampEn produced an opposite irregularity result for the signal and noise mainly because of the ignorance of spatial correlations among neighboring voxels during the sequential signal concatenations. This wrong irregularity contrast (between signal and noise) was not caused by the similarity threshold r involved in SampEn though different r will produce different SampEn. The high ICC in the entire brain suggests STIC as a reliable brain feature, which is consistent with the fine brain sulci structures identified in the whole brain STIC map. Measures derived from function MRI often lack structural details and appear to be blurring. To our best of knowledge, STCM is the first functional brain mapping approach that can reveal brain patterns with high structural details. Females showed high resting brain irregularity, which is consistent with a previous study [18]. Older subjects had higher resting brain incoherence. The regions are mainly located in the motion-related subcortical area (putamen and cerebellum) and memory-related region (temporal gyri). The age effects may indicate a further maturity in the brain so fewer voxels are needed and recruited to facilitate motion and memory function. Interesting, even in those young (22–37 yrs) healthy subjects, STIC in putamen (one of the regions presenting the strongest age effects of STIC) was related to mental health: higher STIC corresponds to better mental state (higher MMSE). Together, the age effects and the trend of a positive STIC vs MMSE suggest a beneficial high incoherence in the resting brain. Although this seems a little counter-intuitive, it may indicate an increased energy use efficiency when the brain is in a better status since coherent activity needs energy to coordinate. Another reason for the beneficial higher STIC is that incoherence (or irregularity) is related to entropy and then information capacity. Higher STIC may then represent a better capability of processing the apparently everywhere information to and from the brain. That may partly explain the high STIC in females too.

The neighborhood size was arbitrarily defined to reduce the computation burden. While different neighborhood sizes may yield different STIC values, that effect should be consistent across subjects and should not affect the cross-subject STIC analysis such as the age and sex association analyses results. To verify that, we ran additional STCM with two different neighborhood sizes: 27 and 83 voxels and observed similar results as we reported in Results.

Acknowledgement. HCP data were provided by the Human Connectome Project, WU-Minn Consortium (Principal Investigators: David Van Essen and Kamil Ugurbil; 1U54MH091657) funded by the 16 NIH Institutes and Centers that support the NIH Blueprint for Neuroscience Research; and by the McDonnell Center for Systems Neuroscience at Washington University.

References

1. Biswal, B., et al.: functional connectivity in the motor cortex of resting human brain using echo-planar MRI. Magn. Reson. Med. **34**(4), 537–541 (1995)
2. Zang, Y., et al.: Regional homogeneity approach to fMRI data analysis. Neuroimage **22**(1), 394–400 (2004)
3. McKeown, M.J., Sejnowski, T.J.: Independent component analysis of fMRI data: examining the assumptions. Hum. Brain Mapp. **6**(5–6), 368–372 (1998)
4. Hyvärinen, A.: New approximations of differential entropy for independent component analysis and projection pursuit. In: Jordan, M.I., Kearns, M.J., Solla, S.A. (eds.) Advances in Neural Information Processing Systems, pp. 273–279. MIT Press, Cambridge (1998)
5. Richman, J.S., Moorman, J.R.: Physiological time-series analysis using approximate entropy and sample entropy. Am. J. Physiol. Hear. Circ. Physiol. **278**(6), H2039–H2049 (2000)
6. Wang, Z.: Characterizing resting brain information using voxel-based brain information mapping (BIM). In: 2012 Annual Meeting of the Organization for Human Brain Mapping, Beijing, China (2012)
7. Ze Wang, A.M., Raichle, M., Childress, A.R., Detre, J.A.: Mapping brain entropy using resting state fMRI. In: 2013 Annual Meeting of International Society of Magnetic Resonance in Medicine, Salt Lake City, USA, p. 4861 (2013)
8. Schütze, H., Martinetz, T., Anders, S., Madany Mamlouk, A.: A multivariate approach to estimate complexity of FMRI time series. In: Villa, A.E.P., Duch, W., Érdi, P., Masulli, F., Palm, G. (eds.) ICANN 2012. LNCS, vol. 7553, pp. 540–547. Springer, Heidelberg (2012). https://doi.org/10.1007/978-3-642-33266-1_67
9. Ahmed, M.U., et al.: Multivariate multiscale entropy for brain consciousness analysis. In: Conference Proceedings of the IEEE Engineering in Medicine and Biology Society 2011, pp. 810–813 (2011)
10. Van Essen, D.C., et al.: The WU-minn human connectome project: an overview. Neuroimage **80**, 62–79 (2013)
11. Moeller, S., et al.: Multiband multislice GE-EPI at 7 tesla, with 16-fold acceleration using partial parallel imaging with application to high spatial and temporal whole-brain fMRI. Magn. Reson. Med. **63**(5), 1144–1153 (2010)
12. Shrout, P., Fleiss, J.: Intraclass correlations: uses in assessing rater reliability. Psychol. Bull. **86**(2), 420–428 (1979)
13. Ingalhalikar, M., et al.: Sex differences in the structural connectome of the human brain. Proc. Natl. Acad. Sci. U. S. A. **111**(2), 823–828 (2014)
14. Gur, R.E., Gur, R.C.: Sex differences in brain and behavior in adolescence: findings from the Philadelphia Neurodevelopmental Cohort. Neurosci. Biobehav. Rev. **70**, 159–170 (2016)
15. Donghui Song, D.C., Zhang, J., Ge, Q., Zang, Y.-F., Wang, Z.: Associations of brain entropy (BEN) to cerebral blood flow and fractional amplitude of low-frequency fluctuations in the resting brain. Brain Imaging Behav. **13**, 1486–1495 (2019)
16. Nichols, T.E., Hayasaka, S.: Controlling the familywise error rate in functional neuroimaging: a comparative review. Stat. Methods Med. Res. **12**, 419–446 (2003)

17. Folstein, M.F., Folstein, S.E., McHugh, P.R.: "Mini-mental state": a practical method for grading the cognitive state of patients for the clinician. J. Psychiatr. Res. **12**(3), 189–198 (1975)
18. Li, Z., et al.: Hyper-resting brain entropy within chronic smokers and its moderation by Sex. Sci. Rep. **6**, 29435 (2016)

Species-Preserved Structural Connections Revealed by Sparse Tensor CCA

Zhibin He[1], Ying Huang[1], Tianming Liu[2], Lei Guo[1], Lei Du[1], and Tuo Zhang[1(✉)]

[1] School of Automation, Northwestern Polytechnical University, Xi'an, China
tuozhang@nwpu.wdu.cn
[2] CorticalArchitecture Imaging and Discovery Lab, Department of Computer Science and Bioimaging Research Center, The University of Georgia, Athens, GA, USA

Abstract. Comparative evolution studies can advance the understating of the brain's functional and structural mechanisms. Efforts have been denoted in the literature to identify structural common connectome preserved between a pair of species, such as macaques and humans. However, very few studies were reported to identify species-preserved structural connections systematically and simultaneously across more than two species at a connectome-scale. In this work, we used diffusion MRI (dMRI) and Brodmann areas as established tools to estimate the whole-brain connectome for three primates: macaque, chimpanzee and human. We designed a sparse tensor canonical correlation analysis (STCCA) algorithm to identify the connective components that are strongly correlated among the three species. Joint analysis of the components can help to identify the white matter pathways preserved among three species. These preserved connections are consistent with the existing neuroscience reports, demonstrating the effectiveness and promise of this framework.

Keywords: Species comparison · Diffusion MRI · Large-scale connectome

1 Introduction

Brain comparison among primates and their evolution has been an intriguing research topic for centuries. It could help understand the mechanisms of higher cognitive function development and the evolution of the underlying structural substrates [1]. It is found in the literature that some white matter axonal bundles or cerebral cortical regions are preserved among macaques, chimpanzees and humans while others are specific to one species, such as the language related Wernicke's area and arcuate fasciculus [1–4]. However, these existing studies mainly focus on a number of specific fasciculus or brain regions, e.g. dorsal prefrontal lobe [1, 3, 5]. Also, most published studies focused only on a pair of species but very few studies are found to provide a comprehensive and systematic comparative method among a group (>=3) of species at a connectome-scale.

In this work, we aim at identifying the structural connectome preserved among three primate species. We adopted diffusion MRI (dMRI) and tractography approaches

© Springer Nature Switzerland AG 2019
D. Zhu et al. (Eds.): MBIA 2019/MFCA 2019, LNCS 11846, pp. 49–56, 2019.
https://doi.org/10.1007/978-3-030-33226-6_6

to estimate the whole-brain connectome based on Brodmann parcellation scheme, which is widely used across primate brains. We then propose a modified data-driven framework based on tensor canonical correlation analysis (TCCA) [6] that is capable of decomposing the most correlated components among more than two views. In this method, we feed the connectome of the three species to obtain the optimized weight vectors so that the connective components associated with large weights are identified, which yield strong correlation among species. Because the connective feature dimension is larger than subject numbers, a constraint is added to TCCA to control sparsity of the weights so that overfitting could be relieved or eliminated. Based on a joint analysis of the weights, we identify the species-preserved connections and the associated white matter fibers. The effectiveness and promise of the framework have been evaluated by cross-validation and the consistency with the reports in the literature.

2   Materials and Methods

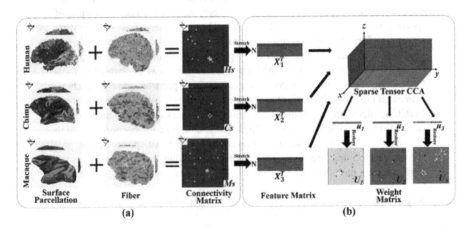

Fig. 1. The flowchart of the framework. (a) Data preprocessing steps. (b) Sparse tensor CCA used to identify species preserved connections.

Generally, as illustrated in Fig. 1, we use T1-weighted MRI and dMRI data to estimate structural connectomes for each of the three species (Hs, Cs and Ms). Then, each connective matrix for a subject is converted to a feature vector, such that the feature vectors for a species compose a feature matrix (X_p, $p = 1 - 3$). Next, the sparse TCCA algorithm is adopted to identify the canonical components that are strongly correlated among the three species. We currently focus on the components with the strongest correlation in this work, and three weight vectors $\mathbf{u}_p$ are consequently yielded, the element of which corresponds to the element of the connectivity matrices. The weight vectors are converted inversely to the matrix format, U_p, which are jointly analyzed. As so, we determine the connectivities co-existed in all weight matrices and extract the corresponding dMRI derived fibers which are suggested to be preserved across species.

2.1   Datasets

Human Brain Imaging

The human brain data is from the Q1 release of WU-Minn Human Connectome Project (HCP) consortium. T1 weighted structural MRI parameters are as follows: voxels with 0.7 mm isotropic, three-dimensional acquisition, TR = 2400 ms, TE = 2.14 ms, flip angle = 8 deg, image matrix = $260 \times 311 \times 260$. The dMRI used in spin-echo EPI sequence, TR = 5520 ms; TE = 89.5 ms; flip angle = 78 deg; refocusing flip angle = 160 deg; Fov = 210×180; matrix = 168×144; spatial resolution = 1.25 mm $\times$ 1.25 mm $\times$ 1.25 mm; echo spacing = 0.78 ms. Diffusion-weighting gradients applied in 90 directions on 3 shells of b = 1000, 2000, 3000 s/mm^2, respectively.

Chimpanzee Brain Imaging

Chimpanzee subjects are from the National Primate Research Center. For T1-weighted MRI data, they optimized at 3T used a TR = 2400 ms, TE = 4.13 ms, flip angle = 8 deg, an image matrix = $256 \times 256 \times 192$, and resolution = $1.0 \times 1.0 \times 0.8$ mm^3. For dMRI data, the spatial resolution is $1.8 \times 1.8 \times 1.8$ mm^3; TR = 5900 ms; TE = 84 ms; Fov = 130×130 mm; diffusion-weighting gradients applied in 60 directions and b value of 1000 s/mm^2.

Macaque Brain Imaging

Macaque subjects are from a publicly available resource at University of California Davis   (http://fcon_on_1000.projects.nitrc.org/indi/indiPRIME.html).   The   dataset includes diffusion MRI and T1 weighted MRI data from 19 macaques. The voxel resolution of T1-weighted structural MRI is $0.3 \times 0.3 \times 0.3$ mm^3, three-dimensional acquisition, TE = 3.65 ms, TR = 2500 ms, TI = 1100 mm, flip angle = 7 deg, image matrix = $480 \times 512 \times 512$. The basic parameters for dMRI data acquisition are: voxel resolution of $1.4 \times 1.4 \times 1.4$ mm^3, TE = 115 ms, TR = 6400 ms, slice gap = 1.4 mm. Diffusion weighted data consisted of 2 shells of b = 800, 1600 s/mm^2 interspersed with an approximately equal number of acquisitions on each shell.

2.2   Data Preprocessing

After data quality control, we select 15 subjects from each species dataset. For T1-weighted MRI of human and chimpanzee, skull removal is performed automatically *via* FSL [7]. For macaque, skull removal is manually conducted. FSL-fast is used to complete tissue segmentation, based on which we reconstruct white matter cortical surface *via* FreeSurfer [8]. To align the surface to dMRI space, T1-weighted MRI image is linearly and nonlinearly warped to b0 map of dMRI *via* FSL-flirt and FSL-fnirt in sequence. The linear transformation matrix and the nonlinear warp field are then applied to the surface. For dMRI data, skull removal and eddy currents are performed *via* FSL. The model-free generalized Q-sampling imaging (GQI) method [9] in DSI Studio is adopted to estimate the density of diffusing water at different orientations. The deterministic streamline tracking algorithm [10] in DSI Studio is used to reconstruct 4×10^4 fiber tracts for each subject using the default fiber tracking parameters (max turning angle = $60°$, streamline length between 30 mm and 300 mm, step length = 1 mm, quantitative anisotropy threshold = 0.2).

2.3 Structural Connective Connectome Construction

DMRI streamline fibers and white matter surfaces are used to construct the structural connectivity matrices (Fig. 1(a)). We use Brodmann areas parcellation scheme as a test bed to develop and evaluate our framework. For human and chimpanzee, template T1-weighted MRI are nonlinearly warped to individual spaces *via* FSL-fnirt [7], such that Brodmann atlas can be warped to individual spaces accordingly and mapped to the white matter surfaces. For macaque data, white matter surfaces are warped to the 'F99' macaque atlas space *via* surface registration method [11]. The Brodmann parcellation is then mapped back to individual surfaces. Because the fibers and the surface with Brodmann atlas are in same space for each individual, we use the Brodmann areas (BAs) as the node to construct structural connective matrix for each individual (Hs, Cs and Ms in Fig. 1(a)). The numbers of fiber tracts connecting two BAs are defined as the connective strength between them. Finally, within each species, the upper triangular part of each individual matrix is converted to a feature vector and those vectors of all subjects comprise a feature matrix (X_p in Fig. 1(b)), which is used in the next section to develop the sparse tensor CCA analysis method.

2.4 Sparse Tensor Canonical Correlation Analysis (STCCA)

As illustrated in Fig. 1(b), the feature matrices for three species are $\{X_p\}_{p=1}^m \cdot X_p = [x_{p1}, x_{p2}, \ldots, x_{pN}]$ is a $d \times N$ matrix. In our problem, $m = 3$, $N = 15$ and each column is a vector converted from the structural connective matrix. The variance matrix for a species is as follows after X_p is centered (zero mean):

$$C_{pp} = X_p X_p^T = \frac{1}{N} \sum_{n=1}^N x_{pn} x_{pn}^T, p = 1, 2, 3 \tag{1}$$

The covariance tensor among all species is as

$$C_{123} = \frac{1}{N} \sum_{n=1}^N x_{1n} \circ x_{2n} \circ x_{3n} \tag{2}$$

where $\circ$ is the tensor (outer) product and C_{123} is a tensor of dimension $d \times d \times d$. Similar to the conventional CCA, the objective of tensor CCA (TCCA) is to maximize the correlation between the canonical variables $z_p = X_p^T h_p$

$$\underset{\{h_p\}}{\text{argmax}} \ \rho = \text{corr}(z_1, z_2, z_3) = (z_1 \odot z_2 \odot z_3)^T e \ s.t. \ z_p^T z_p = 1, p = 1, 2, 3 \tag{3}$$

where h_p is the canonical vector, $\odot$ is the element-wise product of the canonical correlation and e is an identity vector. The optimization problem is demonstrated in [6] to be equivalent to the following one:

$$\underset{\{u_p\}}{\text{argmax}} \ \rho = C_{123} \overline{\times}_1 h_1^T \overline{\times}_2 h_2^T \overline{\times}_3 h_3^T s.t. \ h_p^T C_{pp} h_p = 1, p = 1, 2, 3 \tag{4}$$

where $\overline{\times}_1$ is the p-mode contracted tensor-vector product. To control the model complexity, the regularization term is introduced $\tilde{C}_{pp} = C_{pp} + \in I$, where I is an identity matrix and $\in$ is a trade-off parameter. By using the substitution $\mathcal{M} = C_{123} \times_1 \tilde{C}_{11}^{-1/2} \times_2 \tilde{C}_{22}^{-1/2} \times_3 \tilde{C}_{33}^{-1/2}$ and $\mathbf{u}_p = \tilde{C}_{pp}^{-1/2}\mathbf{h}_p$, the problem is converted to its final form

$$\underset{\{\mathbf{u}_p\}}{\mathrm{argmax}}\, \rho = \mathcal{M} \,\overline{\times}_1\, \mathbf{u}_1^T \,\overline{\times}_2\, \mathbf{u}_2^T \,\overline{\times}_3\, \mathbf{u}_3^T - \sum_{p=1}^{3} \lambda \big|\mathbf{u}_p\big|_1 \quad s.t.\, \mathbf{u}_p^T\mathbf{u}_p = 1, p = 1,2,3 \qquad (5)$$

where the l_1-norm $\lambda|\mathbf{u}_p|_1$ is added to control the sparsity of the canonical vector. The solution to this problem is to find the best rank-1 approximation of $\mathcal{M}$, which is fulfilled by the alternating least square algorithm [12]. Finally, the weight vectors $\{\mathbf{u}_p\}$ are converted inversely to the matrix format $\{U_p\}$(the last column in Fig. 1(b)), which are of the same size of the original connective matrices (Hs, Cs and Ms in Fig. 1(a)).

3   Results

3.1   Cross-Validation

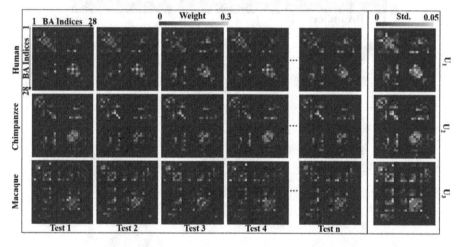

Fig. 2. The weight matrices U_ps of five tests yielded by leave-one-out cross-validation. The standard errors of all U_ps of all leave-one-out tests are shown on the right side.

Currently, only the ipsilateral connections are studied. Contralateral Brodmann areas with the same label are assumed to have the same brain function. Leave-one-out tests are adopted to evaluate the reproducibility of U_ps, where 14 subjects are randomly selected from each species as 'training' samples to yield weight matrices U_ps. This test is repeated for 50 times. In Fig. 2, we show the optimized U_ps from 5 tests. The observable consistency demonstrates U_ps are robust to the inter-individual variability.

In each test, U_ps are also applied to the remaining 'testing' samples to transform them to the canonical space as canonical variables z_p and the Pearson correlation coefficients are computed between them. The averaged correlation coefficient values on the 50 tests are 0.60 ± 0.16, 0.52 ± 0.14 and 0.70 ± 0.15 for human-chimpanzee pair, human-macaque pair and chimpanzee-macaque pair, respectively, suggesting the existence of common connectomes across species and they can be detected by our methods.

The sparsity parameter $\lambda = 2$ is selected from a pool of [0 10] with interval of 0.1. It yields the highest inter-species correlation after X_ps being transformed to the canonical space by u_ps. It is noted that only the 1st canonical component is analyzed in this work.

3.2 DTI Tracts Comparison Between Human and Macaque

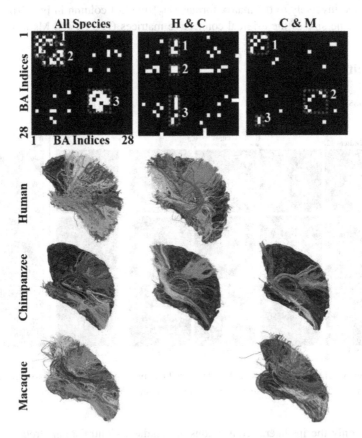

Fig. 3. The preserved connections and DMRI fibers among all the three species (left column), between human and chimpanzee (H&C, middle column) and between chimpanzee and macaque (C&M, right column). In each column, the corresponding fiber bundles across species have the same color. The preserved connections highlighted by numbers are interpreted in the texts.

The mean U_ps are obtained by averaging those from the leave-one-out cross-validation results in Sect. 3.1. Because the connectivity matrices of the three species are constructed on the same parcellation scheme, we can identify the preserved connections among species by overlapping U_ps. The top-left corner of Fig. 3 is the overlapped weight matrix among all the three species (white elements indicate their co-existence on all species). Three clusters on the matrix are observed. Cluster #1 consists of the connections among somatosensory and motor related cortices (BA1–7). Cluster #2 consists of the connections between motor related cortices (BA6–8) and BA9 which is engaged with some higher order functions, such as short term memory [13], attributing intention [14] and etc. There are some scattered off-line connections, such as the ones between motor cortices and superior temporal cortices (BA22). In the middle column, we show the connections that only exist in human and chimpanzee. Most of such connections are linked to anterior prefrontal cortex/orbitofrontal cortex (BA10–11). Cluster #1 consists of the connections between BA10–11 and somatosensory cortices/motor related cortices (BA2–4, 6). Cluster #2 consists of the connections within BA10–11. Cluster #3 consists of the connections between BA10–11 and visual cortices (BA18–19)/temporal lobes (BA20–21). For chimpanzee-macaque pair (the right column), the preserved connections in Cluster #1 consist of connections within somatosensory and motor related cortices (BA1–7). Other scattered connections include those within visual cortices (Cluster #2) and those between motor cortex and cingulate cortex (Cluster #3), which is engaged with functions such as error detection and attention [15].

In summary, the connections preserved among all the three species and those preserved between chimpanzee and macaque are mostly associated to the lower-order cortices, such as somatosensory, motor and visual cortices. This observation is also supported by previous reports, such as [4], where no significant phylogenetic difference was found for BA4. In contrast, those preserved between human and chimpanzee are associated with higher-order cortices, such as anterior prefrontal cortex/orbitofrontal cortex, which is engaged with functions, such as processing rewards, decision making and etc [16, 17]. This observation is in concordance with previous reports, such as [5], where the prefrontal connections to the posterior brain regions were suggested to be enhanced during the course of brain evolution. These comparative results partially reflect the upgrading trend of brain functions from lower primates to higher ones.

4   Conclusion

In this work, the dMRI derived structural connectomes are estimated from brains of three primates. The comparative studies of the connectomes among these three species are performed based on the modified sparse tensor CCA algorithm, based on which the sparse weights which yield strong correlated canonical components among species are jointly analyzed among the three species. Structural connections and white matter fiber bundles preserved across species and along the evolution line are identified and interpreted, which also find supports from previous literature reports, demonstrating the effectiveness and promise of this framework. Our works offer novel insights into the species-preserved organizational architectures of primate brains and their evolution.

References

1. Rilling, J.K., et al.: The evolution of the arcuate fasciculus revealed with comparative DTI. Nat. Neurosci. **11**(4), 426–428 (2008)
2. Jbabdi, S., Lehman, J.F., Haber, S.N., Behrens, T.E.: Human and monkey ventral prefrontal fibers use the same organizational principles to reach their targets: tracing versus tractography. J. Neurosci. **33**(7), 3190–3201 (2013)
3. Li, L.: Mapping putative hubs in human, chimpanzee and rhesus macaque connectomes via diffusion tractography. NeuroImage **80**, 462–474 (2013)
4. Raghanti, M.A., Stimpson, C.D., Marcinkiewicz, J.L., Erwin, J.M., Hof, P.R., Sherwood, C. C.: Cortical dopaminergic innervation among humans, chimpanzees, and macaque monkeys: a comparative study. Neuroscience **155**(1), 203–220 (2008)
5. Sakai, T., et al.: Differential prefrontal white matter development in chimpanzees and humans. Curr. Biol. **21**(16), 1397–1402 (2011)
6. Luo, Y., Tao, D., Ramamohanarao, K., Xu, C., Wen, Y.: Tensor canonical correlation analysis for multi-view dimension reduction. IEEE Trans. Knowl. Data Eng. **27**(11), 3111–3124 (2015)
7. Jenkinson, M., Beckmann, C., Behrens, T.E.J., Woolrich, M.W., Smith, S.M.: FSL. NeuroImage **62**(2), 782–790 (2012)
8. Fischl, B., Liu, A., Dale, A.M.: Automated manifold surgery: constructing geometrically accurate and topologically correct models of the human cerebral cortex. IEEE Trans. Med. Imaging **20**(1), 70–80 (2001)
9. Yeh, F.C., Wedeen, V.J., Tseng, W.I.: Generalized q-sampling imaging. IEEE Trans. Med. Imaging **29**(9), 1626–1635 (2010)
10. Yeh, F.C., Verstynen, T.D., Wang, Y., Fernández-Miranda, J.C., Tseng, W.Y.I.: Deterministic diffusion fiber tracking improved by quantitative anisotropy. PLoS ONE **8**(11), e80713 (2013)
11. Yeo, B.T.T., Sabuncu, M.R., Vercauteren, T., Ayache, N., Fischl, B., Golland, P.: Spherical demons: fast diffeomorphic landmark-free surface registration. IEEE Trans. Med. Imaging **29**(3), 650–668 (2010)
12. Kroonenberg, P.M., de Leeuw, J.: Principal component analysis of three-mode data by means of alternating least squares algorithms. Psychometrika **45**(1), 69–97 (1980)
13. Babiloni, C., et al.: Human cortical responses during one-bit delayed-response tasks: an fMRI study. Brain Res. Bull. **65**(5), 383–390 (2005)
14. Brunet, E., Sarfati, Y., Hardy-Baylé, M.-C., Decety, J.: A PET investigation of the attribution of intentions with a nonverbal task. NeuroImage **11**(2), 157–166 (2000)
15. Weissman, D.H., Gopalakrishnan, A., Hazlett, C.J., Woldorff, M.G.: Dorsal anterior cingulate cortex resolves conflict from distracting stimuli by boosting attention toward relevant events. Cereb. Cortex **15**(2), 229–237 (2005)
16. Rogers, R.D., et al.: Choosing between small, likely rewards and large, unlikely rewards activates inferior and orbital prefrontal cortex. J. Neurosci. **19**(20), 9029 (1999)
17. Kringelbach, M., Rolls, E.: The functional neuroanatomy of the human orbitofrontal cortex: evidence from neuroimaging and neuropsychology. Prog. Neurobiol. **72**(5), 341–372 (2004)

Identification of Abnormal Cortical 3-Hinge Folding Patterns on Autism Spectral Brains

Ying Huang[1], Zhibin He[1], Tianming Liu[2], Lei Guo[1], and Tuo Zhang[1(✉)]

[1] School of Automation, Northwestern Polytechnical University, Xi'an, China
tuozhang@nwpu.edu.cn
[2] Cortical Architecture Imaging and Discovery Lab,
Department of Computer Science and Bioimaging Research Center,
The University of Georgia, Athens, GA, USA

Abstract. Cortical folding has been demonstrated to be correlated with brain connective diagrams and functions. Identifying meaningful cortical folding patterns and landmarks could be valuable for understanding the relation between brain structure and function, the mechanism of brain organization. It also facilitates brain disease studies such as autism spectral disease (ASD), which in turn provides valuable clues to relate the abnormal folding morphology to abnormal brain function. Recently, a novel cortical folding pattern was identified, which is the conjunction of multiple gyri, termed as a gyral hinge. The uniqueness and importance of such a pattern lie in its maximal cortical thickness, axon density and functional complexity. However, the morphology of this pattern is not explicitly studied and related to brain structure and function on either healthy or diseased brains. In this study, we conduct a comparative MRI study between control group and ASD group in their gyral hinge morphology. The identified difference in morphology and spatial distribution is associated with the reported functional and cognitive differences. Our results demonstrate that gyral hinges could be related to brain functions on disease brains and used as potential predictors.

Keywords: Gyral hinge · Autism spectral disease · Cortical morphology

1 Introduction

Cortical folding patterns have been demonstrated to correlate to brain connective structure and function [1, 2]. Quantitative description of folding patterns could help investigate the relationship between brain structure and function [3], and could further facilitate brain disease studies, such as autism spectral disease (ASD), which has cortical structure abnormality resulting from malfunction of a single or a couple of brain developmental processes, and is accompanied by cognitive problem [4]. Such a brain disease in turn provides a valuable chance to study the relation between altered brain structure and function. Along this line, we identify a novel cortical folding pattern, which is located at the conjunction of multiple gyri, term gyral hinges (Fig. 1(c)). It is noted that hinges having more than four arms are rarely seen, and we thus focus on those

© Springer Nature Switzerland AG 2019
D. Zhu et al. (Eds.): MBIA 2019/MFCA 2019, LNCS 11846, pp. 57–65, 2019.
https://doi.org/10.1007/978-3-030-33226-6_7

with three arms and use 3-hinges to denote them. The importance of 3-hinges is embodied in their maximal cortical thickness [5], axon density [6] and functional complexity [7]. These observations suggested that 3-hinges could be cortical hubs from both structural and functional perspectives. Morphology of 3-hinges were quantified in a recent work [8] by clustering them to different shape groups. This study provided an analysis approach but was only applied to health subjects and the morphology of 3-hinges was only related to their locations and global landscapes. Only developmental mechanism was inferred but not their relation to brain structure and functions.

In this study, we conduct an MRI study and aim at exploring whether 3-hinges are different between control group and ASD group in their morphology. By means of the automated data-driven pipeline in [8], we identify 3-hinges on all subjects and compute their morphological features. Then, we cluster all of them from both control and ASD groups to shape groups. Shape patterns having different proportions between groups are selected. Their morphology and spatial distribution are further studied and associated with the group difference in the respective of brain function and cognition reported in the literatures.

2 Materials and Methods

2.1 Datasets and Preprocessing

We use the NYU Langone Medical Center: Sample 1 data of Autism Brain Imaging Data Exchange (http://fcon_1000.projects.nitrc.org/indi/abide/). It includes MR scans of 33 autism subjects and 20 healthy subjects. All subjects were scanned on a 3 T Siemens Allegra. Currently, only the T1-weigthed MRI data was used. Important MRI parameters are: TR = 2530 ms, TE = 3.25 ms, Flip angle = 7 deg, FOV = 256 × 256 mm, In-plane resolution = 1.3 × 1.0 mm^2, Acquisition Time = 8 min:07 s. We use the FreeSurfer (https://surfer.nmr.mgh.harvard.edu/) to reconstruct white matter surfaces.

In general, the methods consist of four major steps: (1) identification of 3-hinges on the white matter surfaces; (2) computation of 3-hinge morphological features and the similarity between them; (3) shape clustering *via* a large-scale spectral clustering method [9]; (4) comparison between control group and ASD group in terms of the shape clusters.

2.2 3-Hinges Detection

We adopt the automatic 3-hinge detection pipeline developed in [8]. To make the paper self-contained, we provide a brief summary of the pipeline (Fig. 1).

The pipeline consists of two steps:

(1) *White matter surface gyralnet detection* (Fig. 1(b) and (d)–(f)): First, a smoothed and inflated mid-line that separates gyri from sulci, term "mid-surface" [10] is used to define gyral altitudes. A surface vertex has positive altitude value when it is above the "mid-surface", otherwise has negative value (Fig. 1(d)). Second, we apply the watershed algorithm in [11] on the gyral altitude map to separate the gyral regions and sulcal regions (Fig. 1(e)). Next, the tree marching algorithm is adopted that starts from the centers of gyral regions to neighbors to connect gyral vertices till the

borders between gyri and sulci are reached, such that a tree-shape graphs on the entire gyral regions is obtained. Finally, the redundant branches of the graphs are pruned, and the left main branches are defined as gyralnet (Fig. 1(b) and (f)).

(2) *3-hinges detection* (Fig. 1(c)): the intersection vertices of the three branches on the gyralnet are defined as 3-hinges (highlighted by red bubbles in Fig. 1(c) and (g)). For all the 3-hinges, we empirically use $r = 5$ mm as the threshold to extract the three arms from the gyralnet (the black curves in Fig. 1(c)), such that they could provide enough information to develop morphological features in the next section. Those 3-hinges whose arms are less than 5 mm are discarded.

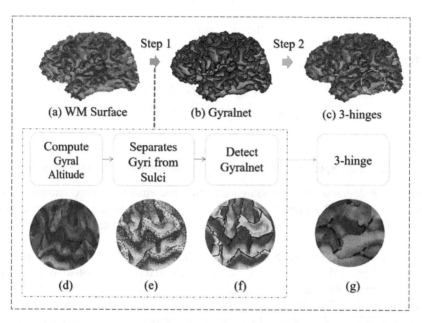

Fig. 1. 3-hinges detection pipeline. Surfaces in (a), (b), (c), (d) and (g) are color coded by gyral altitudes. Blue color indicates positive altitude and red indicates negative altitude. Red dots in (e) indicate the gyral regions while green dots indicate the sulcal regions. Black curves in (b) and (c) are the gyralnet. (g) is an enlarged view of the region highlighted by white circle in (c), and the red bubbles in them indicate the locations of 3-hinges and the black curves are the three arms of the 3-hinges extracted from gyralnet in (b). (Color figure online)

2.3   3-Hinges Morphological Feature

Before the feature development, a few preprocessing steps are conducted on 3-hinges. The three arms of the 3-hinges are smoothed by replacing the current vertices coordinates with the average of all vertices coordinates within its 1st order neighborhood. Then, 10 vertices are resampled on each arm with equal spacing. The coordinates of all arm vertices are adjusted to the same coordinate system. For this coordinate system, z-axis is represented by the surface normal on the hinge center. For x-axis, the principal component analysis (PCA) is applied to all the coordinates. The primary direction projected to the plane perpendicular to the z-axis is defined as y-axis.

After these processing steps, we extract 3 vertices (the 3rd, 6st and 9st) from each arm as representors (9 vertices in total), and the coordinates of which, a 1×27 vector, are used to develop a novel rigid transform invariant morphological feature. The feature concludes six triplets $f = \left(t_{10}, t_{20}, t_{30}, t_{10}^p, t_{20}^p, t_{30}^p\right)$, where triplet t_k includes the three edge length values of the kth vertices on three arms, and t_k^p represents the projection of three branches on the $x - y$ plane. Based this feature, the similarity between two morphological features is defined as:

$$s(i,j) = \prod_{k=1}^{6} s(i,j)_k$$

$$s(i,j)_k = 1 - \alpha_k \left\| t_{k,i} - t_{k,j} \right\|$$

(1)

where

$$\begin{cases} t_k \in \left(t_{10}, t_{20}, t_{30}, t_{10}^p, t_{20}^p, t_{30}^p\right) \\ \alpha_k = 2 \times \max_{\forall i,j} \left(\left\| t_{k,i} - t_{k,i} \right\|\right)/3. \end{cases}$$

2.4 Large-Scale Spectral Clustering on Morphological Similarity Matrix

Based on the definition of morphological feature and similarity, we construct a similarity matrix for all 3-hinges. It is worth noting that all 3-hinges from both control group and ASD group are included in order to obtain a clustering result that applies to both groups.

We apply the large-scale spectral clustering method [9]. To determine the optimal cluster number, 4 thresholds (0.005, 0.01, 0.025, 0.05) are adopted to adjust the sparsity of the similarity matrix. For each sparse similarity matrix, we use 5 predefined clustering numbers (10, 20, 30, 40, 50). For each clustering parameter option, a silhouette coefficient [12] is obtained for each sample based on the clustering result. The mean silhouette coefficient is adopted to evaluate the clustering performance for each parameter option. A larger value indicates a better performance.

2.5 Data Analysis

To identify the shape patterns that differs between control group and ASD group in numbers, we perform either 'left tail' or 'right tail' two-sampled t-test for each shape cluster to see if the number of it in control group is significantly greater or fewer than ASD group. The null hypothesis for the left tail t-test is that the mean value of ASD is larger than control and is another way around for the right tail t-test. The spatial distribution patterns of the 3-hinge locations of those identified shape patterns are studied by using Desikan-Killiany parcellation scheme [13] as the reference.

3   Results

3.1   3-Hinge Shape Clustering Results

In total, 24881 3-hinges are automatically extracted from 53 subjects (33 ASDs, 20 controls). The optimal cluster number is 20 and the optimal sparsity control parameter is 0.005. The 20 shape clusters are shown in Fig. 2.

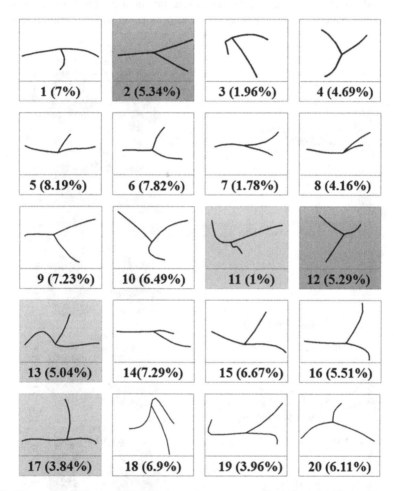

Fig. 2. Illustration of shapes of the 20 shape cluster centers. Red shade highlights those which are more on control group, while yellow shade highlights the ASD > control ones. The percentage of each cluster is listed in brackets. (Color figure online)

3.2   Distinctive Shape Patterns

On average, control group has significantly more cluster #2 and cluster #12 3-hinge shape patterns than ASD group (red shades in Fig. 2), while has less cluster #11, #13 and #17 shape patterns than ASD group (yellow shades in Fig. 2). To investigate the spatial distribution of these distinctive patterns, we adopt Desikan-Killiany parcellation as the reference. On each brain site, the 3-hinge number for each shape cluster is averaged across subjects within each group. Figure 3 shows the spatial distributions of the 5 distinctive shape patterns on all the brain sites. Superior frontal gyrus and middle frontal gyrus are identified as the two of the typical gyri where the distinctive patterns are densely located. Within the two gyri, it is interesting that the ASD < control patterns (red panel) are located relatively more on middle frontal gyrus while the ASD > control patterns (yellow panel) are located more on superior frontal gyrus.

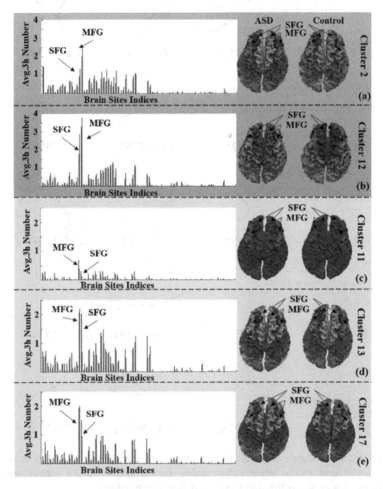

Fig. 3. The spatial distribution of the 5 distinctive shape patterns. In the left panel, brain sites (x-axis) in Desikan-Killiany parcellation scheme are used as the reference to show the numbers of the shape clusters averaged over all subjects within each group. The average numbers are also mapped to the example surfaces on the right panel. Two typical brain sites: superior frontal gyrus (SFG) and middle frontal gyrus (MFG) are highlighted. 3 h is short for 3-hinge. The color shades are of the same as the ones in Fig. 2. (Color figure online)

Based on the spatial distribution histograms in Fig. 1, we compare the 20 shape clusters within and between the two groups by using Pearson correlation coefficient as the similarity between two spatial distributions. The similarity results are shown in Fig. 4. Comparisons within ASD group and control group are in the top-left quarter and bottom-right quarter, respectively. The other two quarters are the cross-group comparison. It is seen that the distributions of the 15 3-hinge patterns that are common in both groups are similar to each other either within group (blocks 3, *avg.*: 0.85 ± 0.10 and 6, *avg.*: 0.84 ± 0.10) or across groups (block 9, *avg.*: 0.84 ± 0.1008). But the distribution of the 5 distinctive 3-hinge patterns is more different from the common ones in control group (block 5 with smaller *avg.* correlation coefficient, *avg.*: 0.78 ± 0.10) than in ASD group (block 2, *avg.*: 0.81 ± 0.10). P-value of *t*-test between blocks 2 and 3 is 0.03 while the one between blocks 5 and 6 is 4.24×10^{-4}. These results suggest that the spatial distribution of 3-hinge patterns tend to be homogenous on ASD group in contrast to the control group.

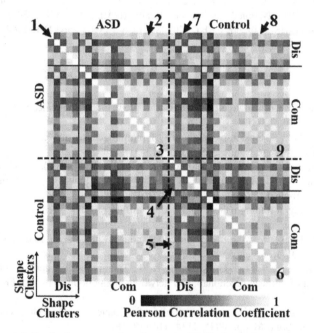

Fig. 4. The spatial distribution comparison between the 20 shape clusters on control and ASD groups. Pearson correlation coefficient is used as the similarity between the spatial distribution patterns. Dash lines separate the 20 shape clusters between ASD group and control group. Solid lines separate the 5 distinctive shape clusters (Dis) and the 15 common clusters (Com). The blocks highlighted by numbers are interpreted in the texts.

4 Conclusion

We compare the morphological patterns of 3-hinges between healthy brains and ASD brains. Five 3-hinge shape patterns distinctively between groups are identified and they are mostly found in the gyri in frontal lobes, which is in line with the previous reports that abnormal cortical folding was found in the frontal lobes [14] and with cognitive reports that malfunction in executive control network, heavily located in the frontal lobes [15]. In our previous works, 3-hinges were suggested to serve as functional hubs in the cortices. Alteration of them could suggest that critical information distributing among cortical patches or axonal pathways could be different from controls, which might provide more clues to understanding the abnormality of ASD brain function and cognition. Also, the spatial distributions of all 3-hinge pattern tend to be homogeneous on ASD brain, which could provide some new clues to investigate the formation of the abnormal cortices from the brain developmental and mechanical perspectives.

Acknowledgements. This study was funded by National Natural Science Foundation of China (31671005, 31500798), National Institutes of Health (DA033393, AG042599) and National Science Foundation (IIS-1149260, CBET-1302089, BCS-1439051 and DBI-1564736).

References

1. Fischl, B., et al.: Cortical folding patterns and predicting cytoarchitecture. Cereb. Cortex **18**(8), 1973–1980 (2008)
2. Van Essen, D.C.: A tension-based theory of morphogenesis and compact wiring in the central nervous system. Nature **385**(6614), 313–318 (1997)
3. Rakic, P.: Specification of cerebral cortical areas. Science **241**(4862), 170–176 (1988)
4. Zielinski, B.A., et al.: Longitudinal changes in cortical thickness in autism and typical development. Brain **137**(Pt 6), 1799–1812 (2014)
5. Li, K., et al.: Gyral folding pattern analysis via surface profiling. Neuroimage **52**(4), 1202–1214 (2010)
6. Ge, F., et al.: Denser growing fiber connections induce 3-hinge Gyral folding. Cereb. Cortex **28**(3), 1–12 (2017)
7. Xi, J., Lin, Z., Huan, L., Lei, G., Kendrick, K.M., Tianming, L.: A cortical folding pattern-guided model of intrinsic functional brain networks in emotion processing. Front. Neurosci. **12**, 575 (2018)
8. Zhang, T., et al.: Exploring 3-hinge gyral folding patterns among HCP Q3 868 human subjects. Hum. Brain Mapp. **39**(1), 4134–4149 (2018)
9. Liu, J., Chi, W., Danilevsky, M., Han, J.: Large-scale spectral clustering on graphs. In: International Joint Conference on Artificial Intelligence (2013)
10. Fischl, B., Sereno, M.I., Tootell, R.B., Dale, A.M.: High-resolution intersubject averaging and a coordinate system for the cortical surface. Hum. Brain Mapp. **8**(4), 272–284 (2015)
11. Bertrand, G.: On topological watersheds. J. Math. Imaging Vis. **22**(2–3), 217–230 (2005)
12. Kaufman, L., Rousseeuw, P.J.: Finding Groups in Data: An Introduction to Cluster Analysis. Wiley, Hoboken (1990)
13. Desikan, R.S., et al.: An automated labeling system for subdividing the human cerebral cortex on MRI scans into gyral based regions of interest. Neuroimage **31**(3), 968–980 (2006)

14. Holland, L., Low, J.: Do children with autism use inner speech and visuospatial resources for the service of executive control? Evidence from suppression in dual tasks. Br. J. Dev. Psychol. **28**(2), 369–391 (2011)
15. Alvarez, J.A., Emory, E., Alvarez, J.A., Emory, E.: Executive function and the frontal lobes: a meta-analytic review. Neuropsychol. Rev. **16**(1), 17–42 (2006)

Exploring Brain Hemodynamic Response Patterns via Deep Recurrent Autoencoder

Shijie Zhao[1($\boxtimes$)], Yan Cui[2], Yaowu Chen[2], Xin Zhang[1], Wei Zhang[3], Huan Liu[1], Junwei Han[1], Lei Guo[1], Li Xie[2($\boxtimes$)], and Tianming Liu[3]

[1] School of Automation, Northwestern Polytechnical University, Xi'an, China
shijiezhao@nwpu.edu.cn
[2] College of Biomedical Engineering and Instrument Science,
Zhejiang University, Hangzhou, China
xiehan@zju.edu.cn
[3] Cortical Architecture Imaging and Discovery Lab,
Department of Computer Science and Bioimaging Research Center,
The University of Georgia, Athens, GA, USA

Abstract. For decades, task-based functional MRI (tfMRI) has been widely used in exploring functional brain networks and modeling brain activities. A variety of brain activity analysis methods for tfMRI data have been developed. However, these methods are mainly shallow models and are limited in faithfully modeling the complex spatial-temporal diverse and concurrent functional brain activities. Recently, recurrent neural networks (RNNs) demonstrate great superiority in modeling temporal dependency signals and autoencoder models have been proven to be effective in automatically estimating the optimal representations of the original data. These characteristics meet the requirement of modeling hemodynamic response patterns in tfMRI data. In order to take the advantages of both models, we proposed a novel unsupervised framework of deep recurrent autoencoder (DRAE) for modeling tfMRI data in this work. The basic idea of the DRAE model is to combine the deep recurrent neural network and autoencoder to automatically characterize the meaningful functional brain networks and corresponding diverse and complex hemodynamic response patterns underlying tfMRI data simultaneously. The proposed DRAE model has been tested on the motor tfMRI dataset of HCP 900 subjects release and all seven tfMRI datasets of HCP Q1 release. Extensive experimental results demonstrated the great superiority of the proposed method.

Keywords: Task fMRI · Brain network · Hemodynamic response pattern · RNN · Autoencoder · Deep learning

---

S. Zhao and Y. Cui—Co-first authors.

D. Zhu et al. (Eds.): MBIA 2019/MFCA 2019, LNCS 11846, pp. 66–74, 2019.
https://doi.org/10.1007/978-3-030-33226-6_8

1   Introduction

Task-based functional magnetic resonance imaging (tfMRI) has been a powerful and popular noninvasive neuroimaging methodology for the study of brain activity patterns and cognitive behaviors of the human brain [1]. To model the very informative but complex tfMRI time series data, a variety of brain network reconstruction and hemodynamic response modeling techniques have been developed in the literature. These methods include model-driven methods such as the general linear model (GLM) [2], and data-driven methods like principal component analysis (PCA) [3], independent component analysis (ICA) [4] and sparse representation/dictionary learning methods [5–7]. In general, these methods reconstructed hundreds of meaningful functional brain networks and corresponding hemodynamic response patterns from tfMRI datasets and greatly advanced our understanding of the regularity of brain activities [2, 5].

However, the ability to represent and describe the tfMRI data still limited the performance of hemodynamic response patterns modeling. Therefore, developing a descriptive model that can sufficiently deal with diverse and complex tfMRI data, as well as large noises, is the key towards automatic, effective and accurate modeling of those hemodynamic response patterns in tfMRI data. Under tfMRI condition, participants need to participate in predefined sequential tasks during the whole scan session and the functional brain activity is modulated from the interactions of brain networks in different time periods, which quite coincides with the characteristics of recurrent neural network (RNN) models [8]. Therefore, it is straightforward and justified to adopt RNNs to explore and represent hemodynamic response patterns. RNNs are feed forward neural networks, which can use their internal memory units to process arbitrary sequences of inputs and model the sequential and time dependencies. They are connectionist models with the ability to selectively pass information across sequence steps. In order to characterize the tfMRI brain activities, a deep recurrent neural network (DRNN) model [9] was proposed to reconstruct the whole brain tfMRI signals from stimulus task design patterns. This framework not only identified typical brain networks by traditional methods (e.g., GLM), but also simultaneously obtain a variety of temporal brain activity patterns at multiple time scales. These results proved the great advantage of RNN model in charactering the temporal dependency signals in tfMRI data. However, the DRNN model still highly relies on the prior knowledge of task stimulus patterns which greatly limited the analysis power of the model.

In order to overcome current limitations in DRNN model, in this study, we proposed a novel unsupervised framework of deep recurrent autoencoder (DRAE) for modeling diverse and complex hemodynamic response patterns in tfMRI data. The basic idea is combing the DRNN model and autoencoder to automatically estimate the optimal task stimulus patterns of the tfMRI data and reconstruct the meaningful functional brain networks simultaneously. Autoencoder [10] is an unsupervised model that automatically learns a latent or compressed representation of the input data by minimizing the error between the input and its reconstruction. In this study, we take advantage of the autoencoder to automatically estimate the task stimulus patterns from the original tfMRI data. When the model is converged, the learned weight matrix between the FC layers and reconstructed signals represents the spatial distributions of functional brain networks underlying the tfMRI data and the output of the top RNN layer in decoding part represents the diverse and complex hemodynamic response patterns under the task condition. We adopted the motor tfMRI dataset of HCP 900 subjects release and the whole HCP Q1 release tfMRI datasets as test beds. Extensive experimental results demonstrated that the proposed DRAE model can not only automatically estimate the task stimulus patterns, but also reconstruct the meaningful functional brain networks and corresponding complex and concurrent hemodynamic response patterns with different time delays.

2 Materials and Methods

2.1 Data Acquisition and Pre-processing

The Human Connectome Project (HCP) dataset has been considered as one of the most systematic and comprehensive neuroimaging datasets. Importantly, this dataset is publicly available which makes it a good test bed for different research studies. The design paradigms are available in [11]. There are 68 subjects in HCP Q1 release dataset and over 800 subjects in HCP 900 subjects release dataset. The detailed acquisition parameters of these HCP tfMRI data are as follows: 220 mm FOV, in-plane FOV: 208×180 mm, flip angle = 52, BW = 2290 Hz/Px, $2 \times 2 \times 2$ mm spatial resolution, 90×104 matrix, 72 slices, TR = 0.72 s, TE = 33.1 ms. The preprocessing of the task fMRI data sets includes skull removal, motion correction, slice time correction, spatial smoothing, and global drift removal (high-pass filtering). All these preprocessing steps were implemented in FSL FEAT. All of these individual fMRI datasets are first registered to the MNI common space for further study.

2.2 Deep Recurrent Autoencoder

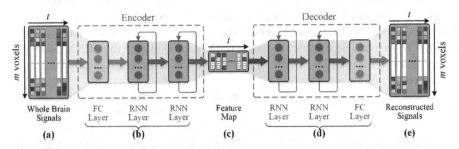

Fig. 1. Pipeline of the DRAE model. (a) Signal matrix of whole brain tfMRI signals. (b) The encoder which consists of a fully connected layer and deep RNN layers. (c) Extracted features maps. (d) The decoder which consists of deep RNN layers and a fully connected layer. (e) Matrix of reconstructed whole brain signals.

The proposed deep recurrent autoencoder (DRAE) model is summarized as Fig. 1. It consists of two components, the encoder (Fig. 1(b)) and the decoder (Fig. 1(d)). First, for each subject, the extracted and normalized whole brain tfMRI signals are aggregated into a big signal matrix (m voxels' signals with t time series, Fig. 1(a)). During the encoding stage, the signal matrix is compressed and mapped into a lower dimensional subspace representing a latent structure through a fully connected layer ([m, k], $k < m$), and then propagated through stacked RNN layers (k input units and n output units) to extract a feature map (n features with t time series, Fig. 1(c)). Next, the decoder passes the extracted feature map through another group of stacked RNN layers (n input units and k output units) to simulate diverse and complex brain activities and then maps the output of the top RNN layer into higher dimensional space (same as the original signals) by a fully connected layer ([k, m]) to reconstruct the whole brain signals (Fig. 1(e)). Specifically, the sequential output of each unit in the top RNN layer represents a temporal brain activity pattern and the corresponding weight vector in the fully connected layer which connects this unit to the reconstructed signals represents the spatial distribution of a functional brain network. The objective of the DRAE model is to minimize the reconstruction errors over all subjects of the training dataset, and the entire training progress is completely data-driven and unsupervised.

2.3   Estimation of Hemodynamic Responses

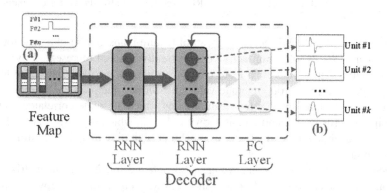

Fig. 2. A sketch map of exploring derive hemodynamic response patterns. (a) Testing feature map which keeps one feature a single impulse and set the others to zeros to stimulate the trained decoder. (b) Output of each unit in the top RNN layer representing the hemodynamic response patterns to the certain feature.

In order to further explore the hemodynamic brain response patterns, for each feature, we replaced the feature map with a testing one (Fig. 2(a)) by keeping one selected feature a single impulse and setting the others to zeros, and propagated it through the trained decoder. The decoder was stimulated by the impulse and simulates the brain activities, and the output of each unit in the top RNN layer (Fig. 2(b)) represents the hemodynamic response of the corresponding functional brain network to the certain feature.

3   Experimental Results

In this work, the training was applied on the DRAE model with 2 RNN layers of 32 LSTM units and a feature size of 16. To be specific, we extracted 244,341 voxels' signals for the motor tfMRI dataset of HCP 900 subjects release and 223,945 voxels' signals for the HCP Q1 release tfMRI dataset. During the training stage, all subjects' signals were used during the training stage, since training on grouped subjects' data will help avoid overfitting and either L1- or L2-norm regularization will increase the training loss rapidly, only MSE was taken as the loss function.

3.1   Interpretation of Feature Maps and Spatial Patterns

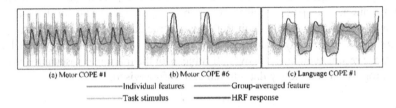

Fig. 3. Visualization of individual feature maps and group-averaged feature maps of motor task. Task design stimuli and their corresponding HRF responses are also shown for comparison.

After training of the DRAE model, a group of feature maps can be obtained for each subject. That is, the whole brain activities can be divided and represented by several feature activities. Since individual feature maps are unique, we work out group feature maps by calculating the group-average values for further interpretation. Among these group-averaged feature maps, a few feature maps which are quite correlated with the task design patterns were identified, as shown in Fig. 3, which suggests that the DRAE model has the ability to extract the whole brain activities to a lower dimensional representation.

When the model is converged, we can also obtain a trained weight matrix of the fully connected layer from the decoder. Specifically, each vector of the weight matrix represents the spatial distribution of a typical functional brain network. Figure 4 illustrates a few identified functional brain networks on the motor task of HCP tfMRI datasets using the DRAE model. As shown, the DRAE model can identify similar functional brain networks for almost all task designs and high spatial overlap rates suggest the reliability of the proposed method. Specifically, the spatial overlap rate is defined as the intersection of the identified brain networks and corresponding GLM activation results. However, the DRAE model was trained in a completely unsupervised process and the functional brain networks can be obtained without prior knowledge of the task designs. These results demonstrates the superiority of the proposed method in modeling functional brain networks.

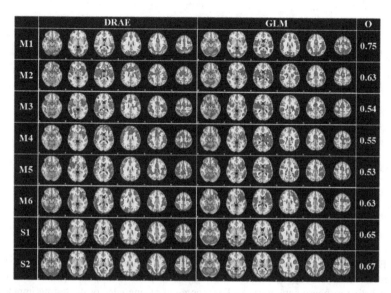

Fig. 4. Visualization of identified functional brain networks by the DRAE model. The GLM-derived group-wise activation maps are shown for comparison. M1–M6, S1 and S2 represent different task designs in motor and social tfMRI datasets, respectively. Last column O represents spatial overlap rate.

3.2 Hemodynamic Response Patterns

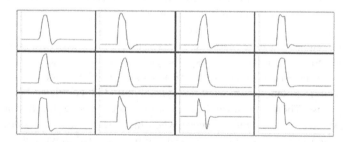

Fig. 5. A few typical and HRF-correlated hemodynamic response patterns.

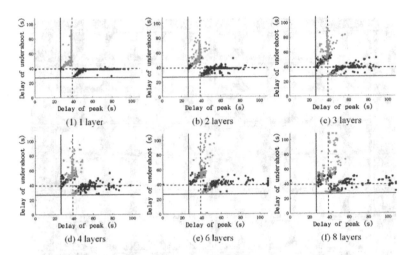

Fig. 6. Estimation of the hemodynamic response delays. X-axis represents delay of peaks, Y-axis represents delay of undershoots; red dots indicate positive response patterns, blue dots indicate negative response patterns; solid lines represent raising edge of the testing impulse and dashed lines represent falling edge of the testing impulse. Subfigures (a) to (f) show the results of 1, 2, 3, 4, 6 and 8 RNN layer(s), respectively. (Color figure online)

After model training, the feature maps represent the task stimulus patterns of the whole brain signals and these signals can be reconstructed from this feature maps. The decoder simulates the complex brain activities with its hierarchical inner cells of stacked RNN units. Diverse hemodynamic response activities are invoked by these features, thus the output of each unit in the top RNN layer just represents a temporal response pattern.

When the formatted feature maps were passed through the decoder as described in Sect. 2.3, both positive and negative response patterns were obtained. These response patterns look similar to the theoretical HRF responses but have different shapes and time delays. Figure 5 detailed shows a few typical and HRF-correlated hemodynamic response patterns. There are several minor differences among these patterns, for example, they have different raising speed when meeting the impulse; some patterns start falling down after a period of time while some don't fall down until the falling edge of the impulse; some patterns have significant undershoots while some don't have. These hemodynamic response patterns are all possible and meaningful brain activity patterns which are more specific but still interpretable, which suggests that the proposed DRAE model can obtain many more meaningful brain activities through an unsupervised method on unlabeled datasets. In order to further analyze the hemodynamic response patterns, we drew the delay estimation maps trained on the DRAE model with different depths of RNN layers (Fig. 6). Table 1 represents the average values and standard deviations of the response delays. Since positive and negative responses have similar response time delays, the negative response patterns were inverted when calculating the response delays. For the DRAE model with just one RNN layer, peak delays are almost before the falling edge (12.29 s delay) of the impulse, since the network is very simple. As RNN depth goes deeper, response peaks have larger time delays around the falling edge and larger standard deviations. These response patterns also have various undershoots delays. In general, with deep recurrent layers, the DRAE model is able to estimate diverse and complex hemodynamic response patterns.

Table 1. Statistic of the estimated hemodynamic response delays.

RNN depth	1 layer	2 layers	3 layers	4 layers	6 layers	8 layers
Average delay of peaks (s)	9.35	10.80	12.92	12.57	15.43	14.14
Standard deviation of peaks	3.76	4.46	5.64	5.40	5.47	6.26
Average delay of undershoots (s)	25.03	22.80	22.98	21.47	26.79	24.79
Standard deviation of undershoots	18.73	13.93	17.53	16.87	20.74	23.75

4 Discussion and Conclusion

In this work, we proposed a novel framework of deep recurrent autoencoder (DRAE) for modeling diverse and complex hemodynamic response patterns and functional brain networks. The proposed DRAE model combines the deep recurrent neural network (DRNN) model and autoencoder to automatically estimate the optimal task stimulus patterns of the tfMRI data, reconstruct the meaningful functional brain networks and characterize the corresponding hemodynamic response patterns underlying tfMRI data simultaneously. Diverse and complex hemodynamic response patterns can be obtained, which brings a new way to reverse engineering of the brain's response function patterns. Furthermore, with deeper stacked RNN layers, the DRAE model is able to simulate more complex hemodynamic response patterns with different time delay estimations. In general, extensive experiment results demonstrated the superiority and effectiveness of our proposed method.

Acknowledgements. This work was supported by the National Science Foundation of China (61806167, 61603399, 31627802 and U1801265), the Fundamental Research Funds for the Central Universities (3102019PJ005), Natural Science Basic Research Plan in Shaanxi Province of China (2019JQ-630) and the China Postdoctoral Science Foundation (2019T120945).

References

1. Logothetis, N.K.: What we can do and what we cannot do with fMRI. Nature **453**, 869–878 (2008)
2. Friston, K.J., Holmes, A.P., Worsley, K.J., Poline, J.P., Frith, C.D., Frackowiak, R.S.: Statistical parametric maps in functional imaging: a general linear approach. Hum. Brain Mapp. **2**, 189–210 (1994)
3. Andersen, A.H., Gash, D.M., Avison, M.J.: Principal component analysis of the dynamic response measured by fMRI: a generalized linear systems framework. Magn. Reson. Imaging **17**, 795–815 (1999)

4. Biswal, B.B., Ulmer, J.L.: Blind source separation of multiple signal sources of fMRI data sets using independent component analysis. J. Comput. Assist. Tomogr. **23**, 265–271 (1999)
5. Lv, J., et al.: Holistic atlases of functional networks and interactions reveal reciprocal organizational architecture of cortical function. IEEE Trans. Biomed. Eng. **62**, 1120–1131 (2015)
6. Zhao, S., et al.: Supervised dictionary learning for inferring concurrent brain networks. IEEE Trans. Med. Imaging **34**, 2036–2045 (2015)
7. Zhang, W., et al.: Experimental comparisons of sparse dictionary learning and independent component analysis for brain network inference from fMRI data. IEEE Trans. Biomed. Eng. **66**, 289–299 (2018)
8. Lipton, Z.C., Berkowitz, J., Elkan, C.: A critical review of recurrent neural networks for sequence learning. Computer Science (2015)
9. Cui, Y., et al.: Identifying brain networks at multiple time scales via deep recurrent neural network. IEEE J. Biomed. Health Inform. (2018)
10. Bourlard, H., Kamp, Y.: Auto-association by multilayer perceptrons and singular value decomposition. Biol. Cybern. **59**, 291–294 (1988)
11. Barch, D.M., et al.: Function in the human connectome: task-fMRI and individual differences in behavior. Neuroimage **80**, 169–189 (2013)

3D Convolutional Long-Short Term Memory Network for Spatiotemporal Modeling of fMRI Data

Wei Suo[1], Xintao Hu[1(✉)], Bowei Yan[1], Mengyang Sun[2], Lei Guo[1], Junwei Han[1], and Tianming Liu[3]

[1] School of Automation, Northwestern Polytechnical University, Xi'an, China
xhu@nwpu.edu.cn
[2] School of Computer Science, Northwestern Polytechnical University, Xi'an, China
[3] Department of Computer Science and Bioimaging Research Center, The University of Georgia, Athens, GA, USA

Abstract. Complex spatiotemporal correlation and dependency embedded in functional magnetic resonance imaging (fMRI) data introduce critical challenges in related analytical methodologies. Despite remarkable successes, most of existing approaches only model spatial or temporal dependency alone and the development of a unified spatiotemporal model is still a challenge. Meanwhile, the recent emergence of deep neural networks has provided powerful models for interpreting complex spatiotemporal data. Here, we proposed a novel convolutional long-short term memory network (3DCLN) for spatiotemporal modeling of fMRI data. The proposed model is designed to decode fMRI volumes belonging to different task events by joint training a 3D convolutional neural network (CNN) for spatial dependency modeling and a long short-term memory (LSTM) network for temporal dependency modeling. We also designed a 3D deconvolution scheme for fMRI sequence reconstruction to inspect the feature learning process in the 3DCLN. The experimental results on the motor task-fMRI data from Human Connectome Project (HCP) showed that fMRI volumes can be decoded with a relatively high accuracy (76.38%). More importantly, the proposed 3DCLN can dramatically remove noises and highlights signals of interest in the reconstructed fMRI sequence and hence improve the performance of activation detection, validating the spatiotemporal feature learning in the proposed 3DCLN model.

Keywords: Functional magnetic resonance imaging · 3D convolutional neural network · Long short-term memory network · Spatiotemporal modeling

1 Introduction

Functional magnetic resonance imaging (fMRI) is one of the widely used noninvasive imaging techniques for probing how brain functions [1]. The brain keeps undergoing massive neural processes that are highly correlated both spatially and temporally,

© Springer Nature Switzerland AG 2019
D. Zhu et al. (Eds.): MBIA 2019/MFCA 2019, LNCS 11846, pp. 75–83, 2019.
https://doi.org/10.1007/978-3-030-33226-6_9

rendering complex spatiotemporal correlation and dependency in fMRI data [2]. Thus, it is desired to develop analytical methodologies that can model such spatiotemporal complexities to extract meaningful features from fMRI data.

Recent studies have shown the promises of deep neural networks in feature learning in fMRI data. For example, Hjelm et al. applied a shallow restricted Boltzmann machine (RBM) on fMRI volumes for blind source separation (BSS) and achieved improved performance compared to independent component analysis (ICA) [3]. To reduce model complexity and increase training samples, Hu et al. proposed to interpret fMRI time series using an RBM [4]. Considering that deeper models are more powerful in feature learning compared to shallow RBMs, Li et al. proposed a BSS method based on deep belief network (DBN) consisting of multiple layers of RBM [5]. Meanwhile, long short-term memory (LSTM) network has proven to have superb capabilities in sequential and temporal data modeling [6]. Inspired by this, Wang et al. proposed a method based on LSTM to capture temporal dependency for brain states modeling [7]. However, most of existing approaches model either temporal or spatial dependency alone, and the development of a unified spatiotemporal model is still challenging.

The emergence of deep neural networks has largely improved spatiotemporal data modeling [8]. Inspired by this, we proposed a novel 3D-convolutional LSTM network (3DCLN) for spatiotemporal modeling of fMRI data. The 3DCLN takes the advantages of convolutional neural network (CNN) in modeling spatial dependency and LSTM in modeling temporal dependency. In order to inspect feature learning process in the proposed 3DCLN, we developed a 3D deconvolution scheme for fMRI sequence reconstruction. In the experiments, we used the task-fMRI dataset from Human Connectome Project (HCP) [9] for evaluation and validation. The experimental results showed that the 3DCLN can decode fMRI volumes with high accuracy. More importantly, the proposed 3DCLN can dramatically suppress noises and highlight signal of interest, showing its potential in spatiotemporal modeling of complex fMRI data.

2   Methods

2.1   Overview

The proposed 3DCLN combines a CNN and an LSTM, as shown in Fig. 1. The CNN is directly applied on 3D fMRI volumes to model spatial dependency. The feature representations of consecutive fMRI volumes in the CNN are then fed to the LSTM to model temporal dependency in an fMRI volume classification task. The CNN and LSTM are jointly trained through back propagation to capture the spatial and temporal dependency in fMRI data simultaneously.

2.2   Data Acquisition and Pre-processing

In the experiments, we used the motor task-fMRI data from HCP Q1 release (sixty-eight subjects) to validate and evaluate the proposed method. The HCP motor task consists of six events including visual cues (CUE), tapping left fingers (LF), tapping right fingers (RF), squeezing left toes (LT), squeezing right toes (RT) and moving tongue (T). The detailed parameters in fMRI data acquisition are as follows: 90 × 104 matrix, 220 mm FOV, 72 slices, TR = 0.72 s, TE = 33.1 ms, flip angle = 52°, BW = 2290 Hz/Px, 2.0 mm isotropic voxels. For fMRI images, the preprocessing included motion correction, spatial smoothing, temporal pre-whitening, slice time correction, global drift removal [10]. The time series of each voxel was normalized to have zero mean and standard deviation.

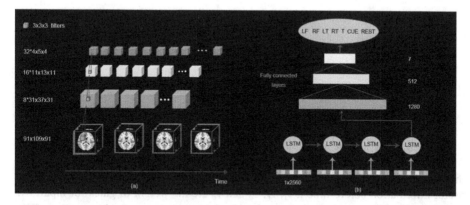

Fig. 1. The framework of the proposed 3DCLN for spatiotemporal modeling of fMRI data. (a) Spatial dependency modeling via CNN. (b) Temporal dependency modeling via LSTM. The LSTM classifies fMRI volumes using the features of consecutive fMRI volumes in the CNN.

2.3 3D-Convolutional Long Short-Term Memory Network (3DCLN)

We consider a shallow CNN and a single cell LSTM for simplified illustration. For an fMRI volume r, the s-th feature map p_s in the convolutional layer of the CNN is computed as:

$$p_s = F(q_s * r + b_s) \tag{1}$$

where $*$ denotes 3D convolution operation, q_s and b_s are the 3D-filters and bias for the s-th feature map, respectively. F is the rectified nonlinearity unit (ReLu) activation function. A convolutional layer is typically followed by a pooling layer. In this study, the pooling layer is replaced by a convolutional layer through an increased stride with step size of 3 to decrease information loss [11].

The CNN is followed by an LSTM, which have multiple gates to allow the network memory cells to store and access information over long periods of time. A typical LSTM is composed of three gates to control the proportions of information to forget and to remember [6]. The LSTM transition functions are defined as follows:

※Gates:

$$i_t = \sigma(w_i h_{t-1} + v_i x_t + b_i) \tag{2}$$

$$f_t = \sigma(w_f h_{t-1} + v_f x_t + b_f) \tag{3}$$

$$o_t = \sigma(w_o h_{t-1} + v_o x_t + b_o) \tag{4}$$

※ Input transformation:

$$m_t = \tanh(w_c h_{t-1} + v_c x_t + b_c) \tag{5}$$

※ States update:

$$c_t = f_t \odot c_{t-1} + i_t \odot m_t \tag{6}$$

$$h_t = o_t \odot \tanh(c_t) \tag{7}$$

Here, i_t, f_t, o_t are the input, forget and output gate, respectively. σ is a sigmoid function, $\odot$ is the multiplication operator, tanh is the hyperbolic tangent function. x_t is the input vector at time t, and h_t denotes the hidden state vector which stores all the useful information before time t. v_i, v_f, v_o and v_c are the weight of gates for input; w_i, w_f, w_o, w_c are the weight for hidden state h_t; b_i, b_f, b_o, b_c are the bias vectors. The output of the LSTM connects with two fully connected layers to improve the non-linearity of the output vector and then is followed by a softmax layer for fMRI volume classification.

By using the deconvolution technique, Zeiler et al. [12] have shown that the feature maps in CNN are far from being random, uninterpretable patterns. In order to inspect the feature learning process in the proposed 3DCLN model, we extended the widely used 2D deconvolution to 3D to reconstruct fMRI sequence using the learned feature maps and filters. Taking the first convolutional layer as an example, the reconstruction of input fMRI volume $\widetilde{R}$ can be achieved by summarizing the convolution between each of the feature maps p_s with the learned filters Q_s:

$$\widetilde{R} = \sum_s^S p_s * Q_s \tag{8}$$

where $*$ is the convolution operation. The filters Q are the transposed learned 3D filters, S is the number of feature maps.

2.4   Training Sample Organization and Parameter Settings

In the experiments, we treated every four consecutive fMRI volumes in a sliding window as a single training sample, as the visual cue event in the HCP motor task has the shortest duration of 4 volumes. This sliding window strategy holds the sequential structure of the input fMRI sequence and to some extent overcomes the limitation of relatively small number of fMRI volumes in the dataset. Using the fMRI data of all the sixty-eight subjects of HCP Q1 release, we obtained 680 samples for visual cues, 1904 samples for each of the five motor events (LF, RF, LT, RT and T), and 2448 samples for REST. We randomly selected 58 subjects as training set and the remaining 10 subjects as independent test set.

The structure and parameters in the proposed 3DCLN were set empirically to maximize the classification accuracy. The CNN was composed of three convolutional layers. The number of $3 \times 3 \times 3$ 3D filters in each layer was set as 8, 16 and 32, respectively (Fig. 1a). With these settings, each of the input fMRI volume was represented by a $32 * 4 \times 5 \times 4$ dimensional feature matrix. The feature matrices of four consecutive fMRI volumes were vectorized and then fed to the LSTM that consists of 4 units. The state size in the LSTM was 1280 and initial state was 0. The LSTM was followed by two fully connected layers with 1280 and 512 neurons, respectively. A softmax layer was used to classify the input fMRI volumes into 7 categories (CUE, LF, RF, LT, RT, T and REST, Fig. 1b). In order to improve the stability of model training, we used the exponential decay to adjust the learning rate per 1000 steps to 0.99 after last update with initial learning rate 0.01. To prevent overfitting, we fixed the dropout rate as 0.5 for the first fully connected layer and early stopping after 25 epochs.

3 Result

3.1 Accuracy of fMRI Volume Classification

The confusion matrix of the proposed 3DCLN in fMRI volume classification on the test set is shown in Fig. 2. The model achieved a relatively high classification accuracy (76.38%) in volume classification, indicating that the proposed 3DCLN can learn discriminative features by interpret the spatial and temporal dependency simultaneously.

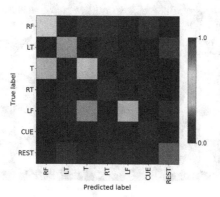

Fig. 2. The confusion matrix of the proposed 3DCLN in fMRI volume classification.

3.2   Spatial and Temporal Validation

3.2.1   Spatial Validation

In this section, we performed activation detection using the reconstructed fMRI sequence and compared the results with that by a standard general linear model (GLM) applied on the original fMRI data for spatial validation of the feature learning process in the proposed 3DCLN.

The activation map (Z > 5.7) in a standard GLM performed on the original fMRI data is shown in Fig. 3(a). Using the reconstructed fMRI sequence, we firstly performed a simple two sample *t*-test (3DCLN-TTEST) to find brain regions that have significantly higher signal magnitude against the baseline (REST) in each task event, as shown in Fig. 3(b). The activations in the 3DCLN-TTEST were highly overlapped with GLM activations in most of the events, as detailed in the second row of Table 1. For further inspection, we performed a standard GLM analysis on the reconstructed fMRI sequence (3DCLN-GLM). The activation maps are shown in Fig. 3(c). The average overlap rate

Table 1. Spatial overlap between the two methods with GLM

Methods	Events						
	RF	LF	RT	LT	T	CUE	AVG
t-test	66.2%	69.4%	60.9%	59.1%	70.2%	37.1%	60.5%
3DCLN-GLM	80.3%	71.4%	71.1%	74.8%	82.8%	32.4%	68.8%

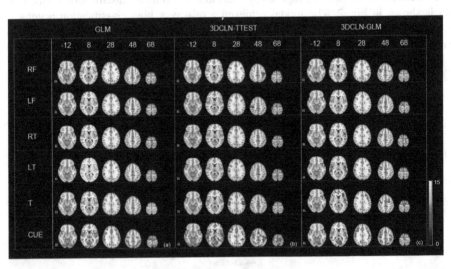

Fig. 3. Spatial validation of the feature learning process in the proposed 3DCLN model. (a) Activations in the standard GLM performed on the original fMRI data. (b) Activations in the two sample T-test applied on the reconstructed fMRI data. (c) Activations in the standard GLM applied on the reconstructed fMRI data. The average overlap rate between (a) and (b) is 60.5%. The average overlap rate between (a) and (c) is 68.8%.

between activations in the 3DCLN-GLM and that of the GLM applied on the original fMRI data was 68.8% (the second row in Table 1). Those experimental results demonstrated that the reconstructed fMRI sequence well preserved the signal contrast elicited by task performance, validating the feature learning process in the proposed 3DCLN model. It is also notable that additional activations were observed in the events of RF, RT, LT and T in 3DCLN-GLM compared to the GLM performed on original fMRI data, which will be discussed in details in next section.

3.2.2   Temporal Validation

In this section, we provided temporal validation of the feature learning process in the proposed 3DCLN by inspecting the signal patterns of the activations in the original and reconstructed fMRI sequences. The task paradigms were used as references. Taking the event of RF as an example, the white line in Fig. 4(a) shows the task paradigm. The red line is the average original fMRI signal and the blue line is the average reconstructed fMRI signal over the activations in the standard GLM applied on the original fMRI data. It is seen that the noises are remarkably suppressed in the reconstructed fMRI data (highlighted by white arrows), and the signal pattern of activations in 3DCLN-GLM is better correlated with the task paradigm (0.80 against 0.65). Similar results are observed in other events of LF, T and CUE (Fig. 4b–d). This improvement is less observed in the event of LT and RT (Fig. 4e–f, yellow arrows). Nevertheless, those experimental results showed that the feature learning process in the proposed 3DCLN can largely suppress the noises in original fMRI data and highlight the signals of interest.

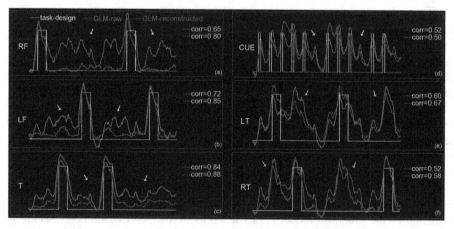

Fig. 4. Temporal validation of the feature learning process in the proposed 3DCLN model. (a) The event of RF. The white, red and blue lines show the task paradigm, averaged original fMRI signal over the activations in the standard GLM and averaged reconstructed fMRI signal over the activations in 3DCLN-GLM. (b–f) are for the events of LF, T, CUE, LT and RT respectively. (Color figure online)

As reported previously, additional activations were observed in the events of RF, RT, LT and T in 3DCLN-GLM compared to the GLM performed on original fMRI data. We further inspected the average reconstructed fMRI signal over the additional activations in 3DCLN-GLM, as shown in Fig. 5(a–d) for the events of RF, RT, LT and T, respectively. It is seen that the average reconstructed fMRI signals over the additional activations in 3DCLN-GLM for those four events are well correlated with the task paradigms, indicating that the proposed 3DCLN model may help to decrease false negative activations.

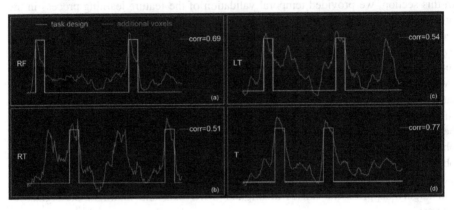

Fig. 5. The average reconstructed fMRI signals over the additional activations in 3DCLN-GLM for the events of RF, RT LT and T (a–d).

4   Conclusion

In this paper, we proposed a novel 3D-convolutional long short-term memory network (3DCLN) to model complex spatial and temporal correlation and dependency embedded in fMRI data simultaneously. The proposed 3DCLN model takes the advantage of CNN in modeling spatial dependency and LSTM in modeling temporal dependency. The experimental results on the motor task fMRI data from HCP demonstrated that fMRI volumes can be decoded with a relatively high accuracy by the proposed 3DCLN model. More importantly, the proposed model can dramatically suppress noises and highlight signals of interest in the reconstructed fMRI sequence via a deconvolution approach extended to 3D. In the future, we plan to train and evaluate and validate the 3DCLN model using the HCP 1200 subjects fMRI data release. Also, a limitation of the proposed model is that it works in a supervised fashion, making it infeasible for resting-stage fMRI data analysis. In our further studies, we plan to combine the proposed 3DCLN model with unsupervised autoencoders [13] to address this problem.

References

1. Logothetis, N.K.: What we can do and what we cannot do with fMRI. Nature **453**(7197), 869–878 (2008)
2. Friston, K.J.: Transients, metastability, and neuronal dynamics. NeuroImage **5**, 164–171 (1997)
3. Hjelm, R.D., Calhoun, V.D., Salakhutdinov, R., Allen, E.A., Adali, T., Plis, S.M.: Restricted Boltzmann machines for neuroimaging: an application in identifying intrinsic networks. NeuroImage **96**(8), 245–260 (2014)
4. Hu, X., et al.: Latent source mining in FMRI via restricted Boltzmann machine. Hum. Brain Mapp. **39**(6), 2368–2380 (2018)
5. Xia, W., Wen, X., Li, J., Li, Y.: A new dynamic Bayesian network approach for determining effective connectivity from fMRI data. Neural Comput. Appl. **24**(1), 91–97 (2014)
6. Graves, A.: Long short-term memory. Neural Comput. **9**(8), 1735–1780 (1997)
7. Wang, H., et al.: Recognizing brain states using deep sparse recurrent neural network. IEEE Trans. Med. Imag. **34**, 1058–1068 (2018)
8. Huang, S., Li, X., Zhang, Z., Wu, F., Han, J.: User-ranking video summarization with multi-stage spatio-temporal representation. IEEE Trans. Image Process. **PP**(99), 1 (2018)
9. Barch, D.M., et al.: Function in the human connectome: task-fMRI and individual differences in behavior. NeuroImage **80**(8), 169–189 (2013)
10. Glasser, M.F., Sotiropoulos, S.N., Wilson, J.A., et al.: The minimal preprocessing pipelines for the Human Connectome Project. NeuroImage **80**, 105–124 (2013)
11. Springenberg, J.T., Dosovitskiy, A., Brox, T., Riedmiller, M.: Striving for simplicity: the all convolutional net. arXiv preprint arXiv:1412.6806 (2014)
12. Zeiler, Matthew D., Fergus, R.: Visualizing and Understanding Convolutional Networks. In: Fleet, D., Pajdla, T., Schiele, B., Tuytelaars, T. (eds.) ECCV 2014. LNCS, vol. 8689, pp. 818–833. Springer, Cham (2014). https://doi.org/10.1007/978-3-319-10590-1_53
13. Huang, H., Hu, X., Zhao, Y., et al.: Modeling task fMRI data via deep convolutional autoencoder. IEEE Trans. Med. Imag. **37**(7), 1551–1561 (2017)

Biological Knowledge Guided Deep Neural Network for Brain Genotype-Phenotype Association Study

Yanfu Zhang[1], Liang Zhan[1], Paul M. Thompson[2], and Heng Huang[1(✉)]

[1] Department of Electrical and Computer Engineering, University of Pittsburgh, Pittsburgh, USA
heng.huang@pitt.edu

[2] Imaging Genetics Center, Institute for Neuroimaging and Informatics, University of Southern California, Los Angeles, USA

Abstract. Alzheimer's Disease (AD) is the main cause for age-related dementia. Many machine learning methods have been proposed to identify important genetic bases which are associated to phenotypes indicating the progress of AD. However, the biological knowledge is seldom considered in spite of the success of previous research. Built upon neuroimaging high-throughput phenotyping techniques, a biological knowledge guided deep network is proposed in this paper, to study the genotype-phenotype associations. We organized the Single Nucleotide Polymorphisms (SNPs) according to linkage disequilibrium (LD) blocks, and designed a group 1-D convolutional layer assembling both local and global convolution operations, to process the structural features. The entire neural network is a cascade of group 1-D convolutional layer, 2-D sliding convolutional layer and a multi-layer perceptron. The experimental results on the Alzheimer's Disease Neuroimaging Initiative (ADNI) data show that the proposed method outperforms related methods. A set of biologically meaningful LD groups is also identified for phenotype discovery, which is potentially helpful for disease diagnosis and drug design.

1 Introduction

Alzheimer's disease (AD) is a chronic neuro-degenerative disease. It is the 5th leading cause of death for those aged 65 or older [2] in the United States, and 5.5 million people have Alzheimer's dementia by estimation. In 2017, total payments are estimated at $259 billions for all individuals with dementia.

Based on neuroimaging and genetics techniques, computational methods [4,14] have been shown as powerful tools for understanding and assistant diagnosis on AD. As a result, many SNPs identified as risk factors for AD are listed by the AlzGene database (www.alzgene.org). Among these, early efforts attempting

This study was partially supported by U.S. NSF IIS 1836945, IIS 1836938, DBI 1836866, IIS 1845666, IIS 1852606, IIS 1838627, IIS 1837956, and NIH AG049371. NIH AG056782.

D. Zhu et al. (Eds.): MBIA 2019/MFCA 2019, LNCS 11846, pp. 84–92, 2019.
https://doi.org/10.1007/978-3-030-33226-6_10

on discovering the phenotype-genotype association mainly exploit linear regression models. Classical methods [1,10] apply individual regression at all time points, ignoring potential progressive variations of brain phenotypes. Based on linear models, sparse learning [14,21] is demonstrated to be highly effective. The Schatten p-norm is used to identify the interrelation structures existing in the low-rank subspace [16], with the idea further developed by capped trace norm [5]. Regularized modal regression model [15] is found to be robust to outliers, heavy-tailed noise, and skewed noise. Clustering analysis [6], particularly auto-learning based methods [17] to extract group structures can further help uncover the interrelations for multi-task regression.

However, the aforementioned methods are driven mainly by machine learning principles. Given the complex relation of significant SNP loci identification, an emerging interest is to integrate advanced models and biological priors simultaneously for the phenotype-genotype prediction task. In this paper, we propose a biological knowledge guided convolution neural network (CNN) benefiting from both principles of sparse learning and non-linearity, to address the genotype-phenotype prediction problem. SNPs are structural features equipped with biological priors, and in this paper, we group SNPs according to the Linkage Disequilibrium (LD) blocks, which refers to alleles that do not occur randomly with respect to each other in two or more loci. Based on LD blocks, we develop a group 1-D convolutional layer. Our design modifies naive convolutional layer by applying both group and global convolution, capable of handling structural features as well as utilizing the sparsity of SNP-LD patterns. The entire structure is composed of a cascade of the novel group 1-D convolutional layer, 2-D sliding convolutional layer, and multi-layer perceptron. The experiments verify the impression that sparse learning, group structure, and non-linearity indeed provide improvements, and the proposed method outperforms the related baselines. Also, some interesting LD blocks are identified as important biomarkers for predicting phenotypes.

The rest of this paper is organized as follow: Sect. 2 describes the biological knowledge guided neural network; Sect. 3 shows the experiment results on the Alzheimer's Disease Neuroimaging Initiative (ADNI) data; Sect. 4 concludes the paper.

2 Methodology

2.1 Problem Definition and Methodology Overview

The proposed method aims at the genotype-phenotype prediction. The SNPs of subject i are features with group structures $X_i = [g_{i,1}, g_{i,2}, \ldots, g_{i,c}]$, where $g_{i,j} \in \mathbb{R}^{c_j}$ is a feature vector of group j with size c_j, and c is the number of groups. In the proposed method, the SNPs are grouped according to the LD blocks. The phenotypes of subject i are denoted as vector $Y_i \in \mathbb{R}^m$, where m is the number of phenotypes. The task is to learn a model capturing the association between X_i and Y_i.

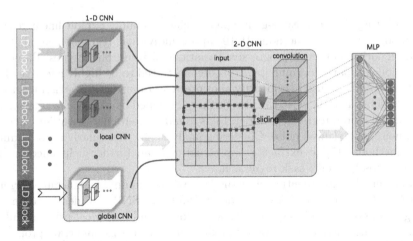

Fig. 1. The network structure of the proposed method. The inputs are grouped features (SNPs), sequentially processed by sparse group 1-D CNN and pooling, 2-D CNN, and multi-layer perceptron. The output is the prediction of phenotypes.

In this paper, we design a biological knowledge guided deep neural network based on SNP feature structures. As illustrated in Fig. 1, the network takes sparse group feature X_i as the inputs and yields the phenotype prediction $\hat{Y}_i$ as the outputs. The pipeline of the proposed method involves three steps: first, we obtain the embeddings encoding both local and global information of the structural SNP features, via the novel group 1-D convolutional layer; then, the embeddings are fed into the 2-D sliding convolutional layer for a secondary feature extraction; and at last, the prediction of phenotypes are attained using a multi-layer perceptron.

2.2 Biological Knowledge Guided CNN for Genotype-Phenotype Prediction

Naive convolution layer is not an immediate solution to the phenotype-genotype prediction problems, and the reason is two-folded. First, by definition naive convolution layer is a *global* operation, thus fails to exploit the group structure of SNPs. Second, the embeddings from the *global* operation extract the entangled relations across SNPs, blurring the association within specific LD blocks and associated phenotypes. In order to overcome these difficulty, we propose to use additional *local* convolutional operations on each LD block, besides the *global* convolutional operation encoding all SNPs. The embeddings yielded by both local and global convolution are then concatenated for the successive 2-D convolution. Formally, the group 1-D convolutional layer takes structural features X_i as input and yields concatenated embeddings h_i. A local 1-D convolution and max-pooling is operated on each group. For group j, the feature is $g_{i,j} \in \mathbb{R}^{c_j}$, and the 1-D convolution kernel is $f_j \in \mathbb{R}^{k_j \times d_h}$, here k_j is the kernel size for 1-D convolution, d_h is the number of channels. The output of a local convolution is thus,

$$h_{i,j} = P(g_{i,j} * f_j), \tag{1}$$

here $*$ is the convolution operation channel-wise, $P(\cdot)$ is 1-D max-pooling operation along each channel, and $h_{i,j}$ is the output of the local convolutions and pooling. The output $h_{i,j} \in \mathbb{R}^{d_h}$. Besides group-wise local operations, a global convolution is also applied. The global convolution is similarly defined as Eq. (2), by replacing the input with concatenated group features. The embeddings of all local convolutions and the global convolutions are then concatenated, $h_i = [h_{i,1}, h_{i,2}, \ldots, h_{i,c}, h_{i,0}]$, here $h_{i,0}$ refers to the output of the global 1-D convolution, $h_i \in \mathbb{R}^{(c+1) \times d_h}$ is the layer output defined above, and c is the number of groups. Throughout this layer, each group has a distinct convolutional kernel. The kernel size can be also tuned group-wise, as long as the channels are identical to keep the consistency of concatenation. In our data, the SNPs belongs exclusively to each LD blocks, and the size of local convolution is quite limited. Therefore we choose a shared-size local 1-D convolution for all groups, and a separate large-size 1-D convolution kernel for the global embeddings.

The embeddings from group 1-D convolutions layer can be viewed as "sentence" describing the genetic variations. Inspired by TextCNN [8], we design a variant of the standard convolutions layer. Different from images where the spatial coordinates are isotropic, in the embeddings of group SNPs, the convolution kernels are supposed to take complete block information into consideration. Thus we define the receptive field on entire neighboring block. Formally, we define the 2-D convolution kernel $f^c \in \mathbb{R}^{d_h \times d_p \times k_c}$, here the k_c is the number of channels, $d_h \times d_p$ is the kernel size, and d_h is the size of the concatenated embeddings defined above. Max-pooling $P(\cdot)$ is utilized after the convolution operations. We use h_i to denote the output of the sparse group layer and h_i^{2d} to denote the output of the 2-D sliding convolutional layer,

$$h_i^{2d} = P(h_i * f^c), \tag{2}$$

the input to the 2-D convolution layer is not padded, thus and the dimension of output of one channel after the convolution operation is $c + 2 - k_c$. $P(\cdot)$ is max-pooling operation along each channel as in group 1-D convolution layer, and the output of 2-D convolution layer $h_i^{2d} \in \mathbb{R}^{k_c}$, which is a vector ready for multi-layer perceptron. We adopt a standard MLP and mean squared error objective for regression.

The proposed 1-D group layer can also be interpreted as a method with predefined sparsity, as that the response of a local convolution can be obtained by padding zeros on group features to full size, and discarding the zero responses of padded areas after the convolution operation. Compared to classical methods such as LASSO and group LASSO, the proposed method avoids some drawbacks. In standard LASSO method, frequently only one feature is selected arbitrarily from a set of highly correlated SNPs, particularly those grouped by LD blocks, potentially misleading the identification of important SNPs. Via the proposed group convolution, the contributions of LD blocks are properly assigned to each

SNPs involved. On the other, group LASSO method applies group selections, which potentially overlooks the cross-group contributions of SNPs. This phenomenon can be alleviated by the global convolution operations.

Though the coincidence of the terminology, the proposed method is fundamentally different from previous methods exploiting the idea of processing channels of convolutional layers by groups, such as ShuffleNet [22] or ResNeXt [20]. Previous methods typically define their kernels on the entire inputs, and group the middle layer embeddings to improve computational efficiency. These networks are designed to handle large-scale problems, and the convolution kernels are still global. However in the proposed group 1-D convolutional layer, the groups are a pre-defined biological structures on SNPs, thus only proper parts of the features are visible for corresponding local convolutions operations. To sum up, the "group" in the proposed method is used under a different meaning with previous methods.

3 Experiments

3.1 Data Description

The experiments are conducted on the data obtained from the Alzheimer's Disease Neuroimaging Initiative(ADNI) database (adni.loni.usc.edu). In our experiment the genotype data [11] included all non-Hispanic Caucasian participants from the ADNI Phase 1 cohort which were genotyped using the Human 610-Quad BeadChip. Pre-processing on the SNP data include the standard quality control (QC) and imputation. The QC criteria are composed of (1) call rate check per subject and per SNP marker, (2) gender check, (3) sibling pair identification, (4) the Hardy-Weinberg equilibrium test, (5) marker removal by the minor allele frequency and (6) population stratification. The QC'ed SNPs were then imputed using the MaCH software [9] to estimate the missing genotypes. Among all, we selected only SNPs within the boundary of $\pm 20K$ base pairs of the 153 AD candidate genes, listed on the AlzGene database (www.alzgene.org) as of 4/18/2011 [3]. As a result, our analyses included 3,576 SNPs extracted from 153 genes (boundary: $\pm 20K$) using the ANNOVAR annotation (http://www.openbioinformatics.org/annovar/). The groups of SNPs are defined using the linkage disequilibrium (LD) blocks, and a total of 800 blocks are marked. 2098 SNPs are selected with sufficient group information.

Each MRI T1-weighted image was anterior commissure posterior commissure (AC-PC) aligned using MIPAV2, intensity in-homogeneity corrected using the N3 algorithm [13], skull stripped with manual editing [19], and cerebellum-removed [18]. The image is segmented using FAST [23] into gray matter (GM), white matter (WM), and cerebrospinal fluid (CSF), and registered to a common space using HAMMER [12]. GM volumes normalized by the total intracranial volume were extracted as features, from 93 ROIs defined in [7]. The data for the experiments includes all 737 subjects with sufficient data.

3.2   Experiment Settings

We compare the proposed method with several other regression methods: multivariate Linear Regression(LR), multivariate Ridge Regression(RR), Least Absolute Shrinkage and Selection Operator(LASSO), the combination of L1 norm ad L2 norm (Elastic) [14], Temporal Structure Auto-Learning Predictive Model (TSALPM) [17], Regularized Modal Regression (RMR) [15], and naive CNN. For both RR and LASSO, we set the coefficient of the regularization term through grid search ranging from 0.01 to 10. For TSALPM and RMR, we use the default parameter settings in original papers. For naive CNN, we replace the group 1-D convolutional layer with naive 1-D convolutional layer, and keep the output channels consistent with the proposed method for a fair comparison. For the proposed method, we used one sparse local CNN layer, one CNN layer and two-layer perceptron. We used a shared-size local CNN for each group, with $k_j = 10$ and $d_h = 5$. For global 1-D CNN, the kernel size is chosen as $k_j = 100$. The kernel of the first CNN layer is 400. The hidden units of the two-layer perceptron is 200, and we use a dropout rate of 0.5 during training. The coefficient of regularization term in the objective, λ, is 0.01. We use the momentum stochastic gradient descent optimization method with a learning rate of 0.001, and the momentum coefficient of 0.8. The batch size during training is 50. The scores of each ROIs are normalized to zero mean and unit variance. We reported the average root mean square error (RMSE) and mean absolute value (MAE) for each method on five runs.

Table 1. The comparison of the proposed method with baselines. For both metrics, smaller values indicate better results. The values are displayed as $\mu \pm \sigma$, here μ is the mean and σ is the standard deviation from five tests. Best performance is shown using bold font.

Method	RMSE	MAE
LR	1.5922 ± 0.0246	1.2595 ± 0.0178
RR	1.5818 ± 0.0244	1.2511 ± 0.0177
LASSO	1.2085 ± 0.0251	0.9354 ± 0.0139
Elastic	1.5123 ± 0.0262	1.1924 ± 0.0251
TSALPM	1.0942 ± 0.0216	0.8612 ± 0.0174
RMR	1.3452 ± 0.0295	1.1121 ± 0.0194
CNN	1.0113 ± 0.0180	0.7706 ± 0.0128
Proposed	$\mathbf{0.9895 \pm 0.0199}$	$\mathbf{0.7567 \pm 0.0146}$

3.3   Results and Discussions

We compare the proposed method against related baselines and the results are summarized in Table 1. On both metrics, we observe that the proposed method outperforms baselines consistently. For linear methods, sparse methods including LASSO, Elastic, and TSALPM achieve better prediction accuracy compared to non-sparse methods, LR and RR. Non-linear models, including RMR, naive CNN, and the proposed model, also improve the prediction performances against linear models in general. The group information exploited by the proposed sparse group CNN further improves the performance compared to all baselines on both metrics. The results of the proposed method shows decent improvements over naive CNN without sparse group layer. Naive CNN overlooks the group information. Meanwhile, though the dropout layer during training exerts potentially implicit sparsity in naive CNN, the linkage disequilibrium blocks in SNPs still provides additional sparse structure given our task. This demonstrates that the biological knowledge group structure is highly effective in the genotype-phenotype prediction problem.

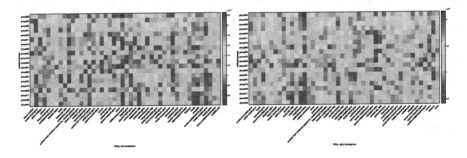

Fig. 2. Top-selected groups for phenotypes prediction.

We also include the top-selected linkage disequilibrium blocks with respect to phenotypes. The importance for LD blocks are defined as $\mathbb{I}_c = \sum_{i \in c, k, j} |g_{i,j}^k|$, here $\mathbb{I}_c$ is the importance of linkage disequilibrium block c, $i \in c$ is SNP belonging to c, and $g_{i,j}^k$ is the gradient accordingly. The results are summarized in Fig. 2. Some most notable LD blocks from our experiments are: (1) group 629, includes OLR1 1050289, OLR1 10505755, OLR1 3736234 and OLR1 3736233; (2) group 349, includes CTNNA3 1948946 and CTNNA3 13376837; (3) group 363, includes CTNNA3 10509276, CTNNA3 713250, CTNNA3 12355282. We expect the results here indicate some complex interactions within these LD blocks, which is promising for experimental assessment.

4   Conclusion

In this paper we propose a biological knowledge guided convolutional neural network to address the genotype-phenotype prediction problem. We use LD blocks to group SNPs, and develop a novel group 1-D convolutional layer to process the structural features. The prediction is attained through the sequential network of group 1-D convolutional layer, 2-D sliding convolutional layer, and a multi-layer perceptron. The experiments on ADNI data show that the proposed method outperforms related methods. Particularly, the experiments demonstrate the effectiveness of sparse structure compared to dense methods, and the advantage of local CNN layer against naive CNN methods. We also identify a set of biologically meaningful LD blocks for biomarker discovery, which is potentially helpful for disease diagnosis and drug design.

References

1. Ashford, J.W., Schmitt, F.A.: Modeling the time-course of alzheimer dementia. Curr. Psychiatry Rep. **3**(1), 20–28 (2001)
2. Association, A., et al.: 2017 alzheimer's disease facts and figures. Alzheimer's Dement. **13**(4), 325–373 (2017)
3. Bertram, L., McQueen, M.B., Mullin, K., Blacker, D., Tanzi, R.E.: Systematic meta-analyses of alzheimer disease genetic association studies: the alzgene database. Nat. Genet. **39**(1), 17 (2007)
4. Brun, C.C., et al.: Mapping the regional influence of genetics on brain structure variability–a tensor-based morphometry study. Neuroimage **48**(1), 37–49 (2009)
5. Huo, Z., Shen, D., Huang, H.: Genotype-phenotype association study via new multi-task learning model. Pac. Symp. Biocomput. World Sci. **23**, 353–364 (2017)
6. Jin, Y., et al.: Automatic clustering of white matter fibers in brain diffusion MRI with an application to genetics. Neuroimage **100**, 75–90 (2014)
7. Kabani, N.J., MacDonald, D.J., Holmes, C.J., Evans, A.C.: 3D anatomical atlas of the human brain. Neuroimage **7**(4), S717 (1998)
8. Kim, Y.: Convolutional neural networks for sentence classification. arXiv preprint (2014). arXiv:1408.5882
9. Li, Y., Willer, C.J., Ding, J., Scheet, P., Abecasis, G.R.: Mach: using sequence and genotype data to estimate haplotypes and unobserved genotypes. Genet. Epidemiol. **34**(8), 816–834 (2010)
10. Sabatti, C., et al.: Genome-wide association analysis of metabolic traits in a birth cohort from a founder population. Nat. Genet. **41**(1), 35 (2009)
11. Saykin, A.J., et al.: Alzheimer's disease neuroimaging initiative biomarkers as quantitative phenotypes: genetics core aims, progress, and plans. Alzheimer's Dement. **6**(3), 265–273 (2010)
12. Shen, D., Davatzikos, C.: Hammer: hierarchical attribute matching mechanism for elastic registration. In: Proceedings IEEE Workshop on Mathematical Methods in Biomedical Image Analysis (MMBIA 2001), pp. 29–36. IEEE (2001)
13. Sled, J.G., Zijdenbos, A.P., Evans, A.C.: A nonparametric method for automatic correction of intensity nonuniformity in MRI data. IEEE Trans. Med. imag. **17**(1), 87–97 (1998)
14. Wang, H., et al.: From phenotype to genotype: an association study of longitudinal phenotypic markers to alzheimer's disease relevant snps. Bioinformatics **28**(18), i619–i625 (2012)
15. Wang, X., Chen, H., Cai, W., Shen, D., Huang, H.: Regularized modal regression with applications in cognitive impairment prediction. In: Advances in Neural Information Processing Systems, pp. 1448–1458 (2017)
16. Wang, X., Shen, D., Huang, H.: Prediction of memory impairment with MRI data: a longitudinal study of alzheimer's disease. In: Ourselin, S., Joskowicz, L., Sabuncu, M.R., Unal, G., Wells, W. (eds.) MICCAI 2016. LNCS, vol. 9900, pp. 273–281. Springer, Cham (2016). https://doi.org/10.1007/978-3-319-46720-7_32

17. Wang, X., et al.: Longitudinal genotype-phenotype association study via temporal structure auto-learning predictive model. In: Sahinalp, S.C. (ed.) RECOMB 2017. LNCS, vol. 10229, pp. 287–302. Springer, Cham (2017). https://doi.org/10.1007/978-3-319-56970-3_18

18. Wang, Y., et al.: Knowledge-guided robust mri brain extraction for diverse large-scale neuroimaging studies on humans and non-human primates. PloS One **9**(1), e77810 (2014)

19. Wang, Y., Nie, J., Yap, P.-T., Shi, F., Guo, L., Shen, D.: Robust deformable-surface-based skull-stripping for large-scale studies. In: Fichtinger, G., Martel, A., Peters, T. (eds.) MICCAI 2011. LNCS, vol. 6893, pp. 635–642. Springer, Heidelberg (2011). https://doi.org/10.1007/978-3-642-23626-6_78

20. Xie, S., Girshick, R., Dollár, P., Tu, Z., He, K.: Aggregated residual transformations for deep neural networks. In: Proceedings of the IEEE Conference on Computer Vision and Pattern Recognition, pp. 1492–1500 (2017)

21. Yang, T., et al.: Detecting genetic risk factors for alzheimer's disease in whole genome sequence data via lasso screening. In: 2015 IEEE 12th International Symposium on Biomedical Imaging (ISBI), pp. 985–989. IEEE (2015)

22. Zhang, X., Zhou, X., Lin, M., Sun, J.: Shufflenet: an extremely efficient convolutional neural network for mobile devices. In: Proceedings of the IEEE Conference on Computer Vision and Pattern Recognition, pp. 6848–6856 (2018)

23. Zhang, Y., Brady, M., Smith, S.: Segmentation of brain mr images through a hidden markov random field model and the expectation-maximization algorithm. IEEE Trans. Med. Imag. **20**(1), 45–57 (2001)

Learning Human Cognition via fMRI Analysis Using 3D CNN and Graph Neural Network

Xiuyan Ni[1(✉)], Tian Gao[2], Tingting Wu[3], Jin Fan[3], and Chao Chen[1,4]

[1] Department of Computer Science, The Graduate Center,
City University of New York (CUNY), New York, NY, USA
xiuyanni.xn@gmail.com
[2] IBM Thomas J. Watson Research Center, Yorktown Heights, NY, USA
[3] Department of Psychology, CUNY Queens College, Flushing, NY, USA
[4] Department of Biomedical Informatics, Stony Brook University,
Stony Brook, NY, USA

Abstract. Human cognitive control involves how mental resources are allocated when the brain processes various information. The study of such complex brain functionality is essential in understanding different neurological disorders. To investigate cognition control, various cognitive tasks have been designed and functional MRI data have been collected. In this paper, we study uncertainty representation, an important problem in human cognition study, with task-evoked fMRI data. Our goals are to learn how brain region of interests (ROIs) are activated under tasks with different uncertainty levels and how they interact with each other. We propose a novel neural network architecture to achieve the two goals simultaneously. Our architecture uses a 3D convolutional neural network (CNN) to extract a high-level representation for each ROI, and uses a graph neural network module to capture the interactions between ROIs. Empirical evaluations reveal that our method significantly outperforms the existing methods, and the derived brain network is consistent with domain knowledge.

Keywords: Graph neural network · Brain network learning

1 Introduction

Cognitive control study learns how are mental resources allocated when the human brain processes various information. It involves how the brain selects and prioritizes different information processing tasks, which is crucial in understanding the mechanisms of different neurological disorders [4,20,23]. We study a particular perspective of cognitive control, the uncertainty representation. We design a task called Choice Reaction Time task to study the uncertainty representation. In our experiments, the human subjects are displayed with arrows of random directions and colors and instructed to press buttons accordingly.

© Springer Nature Switzerland AG 2019
D. Zhu et al. (Eds.): MBIA 2019/MFCA 2019, LNCS 11846, pp. 93–101, 2019.
https://doi.org/10.1007/978-3-030-33226-6_11

Depending on the number of possible directions and colors, the task may have different levels of uncertainty, measured as Shannon entropy [22].

Since our cognitive control task spans a very short time, each fMRI image is only a single 3D image (see Fig. 1 for more details), unlike resting-state fMRI or fMRI taken under tasks with long duration which can be considered 4D data with one additional dimension for time sequences. The traditional brain functional connectivity analysis methods [1,6] designed for fMRIs with time-sequential information can not be applied to our data, which leaves us low flexibility for analyzing the networks. Another method is to model the brain network using Markov Random Field (MRF). However, current methods only apply when a brain is represented by a single value [17,21,25], which can cause significant loss of information. Recently, deep neural networks have been proved to be very efficient in learning high-level representations for various types of data. For our setting, however, we are not only interested in predicting uncertainty levels, but also want to learn how different brain regions interact with each other at different uncertainty levels.

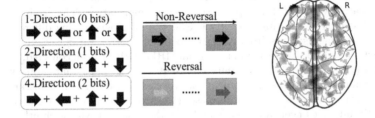

Fig. 1. Left: Experiment setting. Human subjects are shown images of arrows and click keys accordingly. The arrows may have one, two, or four possible directions, corresponding to uncertainty levels of zero, one, and two bits measured in Shannon's entropy [22]. **Middle**: More uncertainty is introduced by additional colors and corresponding actions. Green arrows require buttons with corresponding directions. Red buttons require buttons with the opposite directions. In total there are six different tasks, with various uncertainty levels. **Right**: An example of fMRI data. (Color figure online)

In this paper, we propose a new neural network architecture to solve the two tasks jointly: one as a classification task, the other as a graphical model learning task. Our architecture uses a 3D convolutional neural network (CNN). It extracts high-level feature representation for the classification of fMRIs for different uncertainties, and a graph neural network (GNN) layer for extracting the edge representations. The edge representations are further converted into a Markov Random Field (MRF) and learned through a loss derived from the likelihood of the MRF. Our architecture learns both ROI representations for tasks of different uncertainty levels and a graphical model to encode how different ROIs interacts. We test our method on a task-evoked fMRI dataset, and found that our model outperforms the existing state-of-the-art classifiers. In the meantime, our model generates a brain network for uncertainty representation.

Related Work. The fMRI data are widely used for analyzing neurological disorders and locating task-related key regions [8,15]. Recently, neural network models have been broadly applied to fMRI data based study [2,5,30], and also for learning brain networks [2,26,30]. Nie et al. [16] use 3D CNN for predicting the overall survival time for brain tumor patients. Belilovsky et al. [2] use convolutional neural networks for learning brain networks. Their model takes pre-computed covariance matrices as inputs and outputs the same dimensional matrices. The outputs can be viewed as adjacency matrices of the brain network. Nonetheless, their method requires each region to be represented by one single value, which might lose a lot of information. Instead of using pre-calculated covariance matrix, we take all the information from brain regions as inputs for our architecture and extract high-level features for each region. In our architecture, valuable information is leveraged by the neural networks and can be used for multitask learning. Zhang et al. [30] apply Graph Convolutional Network to brain image analysis for the prediction of Parkinson's disease. However, their graph convolutional network is not used for learning brain networks.

2 Method

2.1 Network Architecture

We propose a novel neural network architecture to classify fMRI images, and learn a brain network at the same time (Fig. 2). For our input, each fMRI image is a 3D volumetric image with uncertainty level ranging between 1 and 6. Our architecture uses a 3D convolutional layer for extracting high-level feature embeddings for brain ROIs, and a GNN layer with MRF for structure learning of human brain networks. We use traditional cross entropy loss for the classifying uncertainty levels and meanwhile a maximum-likelihood-loss for MRF learning. For each fMRI image, we extract R ROIs. The size of each ROI is $7 \times 7 \times 7$. The size of the input for the model is $R \times 1 \times 7 \times 7 \times 7$, which can be viewed as R single-channel 3D images. Let the number of inputs be N, and the number of ROIs be R. For each image $k \in \{1, \ldots, N\}$, we denote each ROI r as $x_r^k, r \in \{1, \ldots, R\}$. Each image is labeled with an uncertainty level $y^k \in \{1, \ldots, 6\}$.

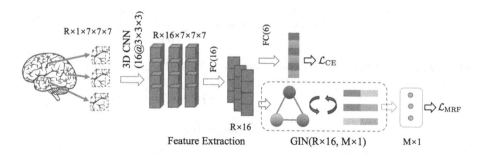

Fig. 2. The architecture of our model.

Our model starts with feature extraction for each ROI. This is done with a 3D CNN layer of 16 channels with kernel size $3 \times 3 \times 3$ (CNN($16@3 \times 3 \times 3$)) followed by a fully connected layer ($FC(16)$). The output feature is a vector of length 16 for each ROI. We perform two tasks on the output features:

- For the uncertainty classification task, we map the concatenation of the output of all R ROIs to a 1D vector of length 6 with a fully connected layer ($FC(6)$). The 1D vector is then fed to a softmax layer to calculate the label probability. The loss from this task is the cross entropy loss $\mathcal{L}_{\mathrm{CE}}$.
- For brain network structure learning, we feed the R output features to the graph neural network layer and then use MRF to estimate the connection between each ROI. More details will be discussed in Sect. 2.2. The loss from this task is $\mathcal{L}_{\mathrm{MRF}}$.

Our overall loss to minimize is $\mathcal{L} = \mathcal{L}_{\mathrm{CE}} + \mathcal{L}_{\mathrm{MRF}}$.

2.2   Graph Neural Network Layer for Brain Network Learning

Graph neural network (GNN) has been proposed for learning the efficient representation for many graph-structured data [10]. GNN usually employs a message-passing schema, which means each node aggregates the information of its neighbors and transforms into new representation using the information. The generated new representation of the nodes captures the structured information of the inherited graph [13,27].

In this work, we build a brain network learning layer based on an existing graph neural network called Graph Isomorphism Network (GIN) [29]. The input of the layer is a set of 16-dimensional vectors, each of which represents one ROI in the human brain. The output is edge potentials for each possible edge between the ROIs. GIN is used for helping with the message passing between nodes and edges in the graph. We use multi-layer perceptrons (MLPs) as our message-passing function in our model. We assume the initial graph is a fully connected graph with all possible edges. Thus, we have $M = R \times (R - 1)/2$ edges. We use the initial graph as input for GNN layer. Let $\mathcal{N}(v)$ be the neighbours of node v, $h_{t,v}$ be the representation of node v at t^{th} iteration, and ϵ_t be an arbitrarily small number, the GIN updates the node representation as

$$h_{t,v} = MLP_t\Big((1 + \epsilon_t) \cdot h_{t-1,v} + \sum_{u \in \mathcal{N}(v)} h_{t-1,u}\Big) \qquad (1)$$

where $h_{0,v}$ is the high-level representation of vth ROI after feature extraction. We denote the final output of GIN layer as $h_v = h_{T,v}$.

After the GIN layer, we construct the edge representation as

$$\phi_{i,j} = [h_i; h_j]\mathbf{W}_{\mathrm{edge}} + \mathbf{b}_{\mathrm{edge}},$$

where $\mathbf{W}_{\mathrm{edge}} \in \mathbb{R}^{16 \times 32}$ and $\mathbf{b}_{\mathrm{edge}} \in \mathbb{R}^{16}$ are the weights for the linear layer, and $[\cdot; \cdot]$ is the concatenation operation.

For image k, the energy function $E(x_1^k, \ldots, x_R^k)$ can be calculated as the sum of potentials for each edge $f_{i,j}$. Thus, the MRF probability of data x^k can be calculated as:

$$P(x^k) = \frac{1}{Z} \exp(-E(x^k)) = \frac{1}{Z} \exp\left(-\sum_{(i,j)\in\mathcal{E}} f_{i,j}(h_i^k, h_j^k)\right)$$

$$= \frac{1}{Z} \exp\left(-\sum_{(i,j)\in\mathcal{E}} w_{i,j} \cdot \langle \phi_{i,j}^k, \theta_{i,j}\rangle\right),$$

where $\theta_{i,j} \in \mathbb{R}^{16}$ is used to map the edge representation to a real value potential, $w_{i,j} \in \mathbb{R}$ is used to re-weight each edge, and Z is the partition function.

In theory, Z should be calculated over all distribution space, which is impractical. To alleviate this problem, Z can be approximated using all samples of the data, which is still very expensive to evaluate. In this paper, we approximate Z with all examples in the same training batch. $Z \approx \sum_{k=1}^{B} \exp\left(-E(x^k)\right)$, in which B is the batch size. Our MRF learning module uses the negative log-likelihood as the loss, for data k, the MRF learning loss is:

$$\mathcal{L}_{\mathrm{MRF}} = -\log \prod_{k=1}^{N} P(x^k) = \sum_{k=1}^{N} \left[E(x^k) + \log Z\right]. \tag{2}$$

3 Experiments and Discussions

We apply our method to task-evoked fMRI images. Our dataset is collected when the subjects are instructed to perform Choice Reaction Time (CRT) tasks [28]. At each CRT task, the subjects are presented with an arrow and instructed to press the corresponding buttons. The details can be found in Fig. 1. There are 6 uncertainty conditions manipulated by the directions and colors of the arrows, corresponding to 6 labels for the classification task. Our data contains 16 subjects. Each subject is asked to perform around 1000 trials. Each CRT task trial only lasts for two seconds, thus only one 3D image is collected for each trial. We collect 17226 fMRI 3D images in total from the 16 subjects. The images are preprocessed using SPM8. Each gradient-echo planar imaging (EPI) image volume was realigned to the first volume, registered with structural MRI, and normalized to the Montréal Neurological Institute (MNI) ICBM152 space. Then all the images are resampled to a voxel size of $2 \times 2 \times 2\,\mathrm{mm}$, and spatially smoothed. The dimension of the processed images is $79 \times 95 \times 68$.

Neuroscience studies state that cognitive control network (CCN) and default mode network (DMN) [12,18,24,28] are two major networks in the human brain that are related to uncertainty tasks. In this work, we focus on $R = 19$ regions of interests (ROIs) from the two brain networks. Control network (CCN) [7] is composed of anterior cingulate cortex (ACC), anterior insula (AI), and frontal eye field (FEF), etc. Default mode network (DMN) [9] consists of domain-specific networks such as visual, auditory, etc. Each ROI is with dimension $7 \times 7 \times 7$.

Table 1. The average classification accuracy (%) for 16 subjects.

	RF	LG	SVM	3D-CNN	Our model
Accuracy	33.54	61.34	56.68	71.03	**75.59**

Our method is compared with Random Forest Classifier (RF), Linear Regression Classifier (LG), and SVM with Linear kernel (SVM) [3]. To prove the effectiveness of our graph neural network layer, we also conduct an ablation experiment which uses a simple 3D CNN model. The 3D CNN model is similar to our model, but did not use the GNN layer, and only trained on cross-entropy loss. For each subject, we test all methods. For all methods, we reserve the same 80% of subject's data as the training set, 10% as the validation set and 10% as the testing set. The 3D-CNN model and our model are trained using stochastic gradient descent optimizer (SGD) with learning rate = 0.001, $\epsilon = 0$ for 1000 epochs. The classification results are summarized in Table 1. We can find from Table 1 that 3D CNN model outperforms the traditional classifiers, and our GNN layer further improves the classification performance.

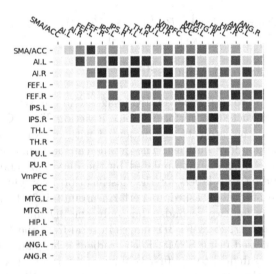

Fig. 3. The brain network learned among the 19 ROIs. SMA/ACC: supplementary motor area extending to anterior cingulate cortex. AI: anterior insular cortex. FEF: frontal eye find. IPS: area around and along the intraparietal sulcus. TH: thalamus. vmPFC: ventral medial prefrontal cortex. PCC: posterior cingulate cortex. MTG: middle temporal gyrus. ANG: angular gyrus. L: ROI located in left hemisphere of the brain. R: ROI located in the right hemisphere. The red box indicates positive connection and the blue box indicates the negative connection. Darker color means stronger connection.

For brain network learning, we visualize the results in Fig. 3. In Neuroscience studies, the CCN is known as a network responsible for cognitive processes [9,11]. The DMN is considered as the network handling human's self-related activities such as emotion and autobiographical memory [19]. The two networks work together for processing uncertainty tasks [9,14]. From Fig. 3, we can find quantitative proof for the above statements. That is, we observe both intra-network and inter-network edges. We further visualize the network in CCN and DMN in brain templates respectively as in Fig. 4. The positive and negative edges are colored in warm and cool colors respectively. We can find from Fig. 4 clearly that the more connections can be found from CCN than DMN. The stronger intra-network connection in CCN means that CCN is more crucial in uncertainty processing, which is consistent with neuroscience knowledge about uncertainty representation [11,28]. Overall, the GNN not only helps with the classification task but also generates meaningful brain network for uncertainty processing.

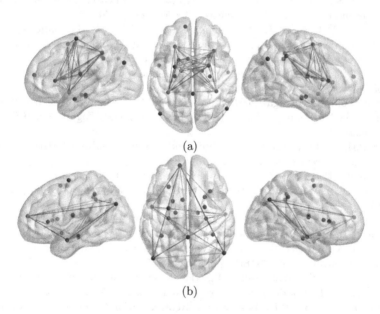

Fig. 4. The network in CCN (a) and DMN (b) in three views of brain templates. The nodes in red are the ROIs in CCN and blue nodes are the ROIs in DMN. The positive edges are in warm color, while the negative edges are in cool colors. (Color figure online)

4   Conclusions

In this paper, we propose a novel neural network framework to classify the CRT task-evoked fMRI data, and learn the brain network. Our framework integrates a 3D CNN for extracting high-level features for brain ROIs, a traditional softmax block trained on cross-entropy loss for classifying the fMRI images at different uncertainty levels, and a graph neural network layer trained on MRF loss for learning the structures of the brain network. Our method outperforms the traditional classifiers and the plain 3D CNN model. Besides, our model also learns the structure of the brain network, which is, how the brain ROIs interact with each other during the uncertainty tasks. Our model provides a quantitative assessment for cognitive control study and has the potential to be applied to any other labeled data with underlying graph structures.

Acknowledgement. This work was partially supported by NSF IIS-1855759 and CCF-1855760.

References

1. Bassett, D.S., Yang, M., Wymbs, N.F., Grafton, S.T.: Learning-induced autonomy of sensorimotor systems. Nat. Neurosci. **18**(5), 744 (2015)
2. Belilovsky, E., Kastner, K., Varoquaux, G., Blaschko, M.B.: Learning to discover sparse graphical models. In: Proceedings of the 34th International Conference on Machine Learning, vol. 70, pp. 440–448. JMLR. org (2017)
3. Bishop, C.M.: Pattern Recognition and Machine Learning. Springer, New York (2006)
4. Castellanos, F.X., Sonuga-Barke, E.J., Milham, M.P., Tannock, R.: Characterizing cognition in ADHD: beyond executive dysfunction. Trends Cognit. Sci. **10**(3), 117–123 (2006)
5. Chen, P.H., et al.: A convolutional autoencoder for multi-subject FMRI data aggregation. arXiv preprint (2016). arXiv:1608.04846
6. Cole, M.W., Bassett, D.S., Power, J.D., Braver, T.S., Petersen, S.E.: Intrinsic and task-evoked network architectures of the human brain. Neuron **83**(1), 238–251 (2014)
7. Cole, M.W., Schneider, W.: The cognitive control network: integrated cortical regions with dissociable functions. Neuroimage **37**(1), 343–360 (2007)
8. Diamond, A., Barnett, W.S., Thomas, J., Munro, S.: Preschool program improves cognitive control. Science **318**(5855), 1387 (2007)
9. Elton, A., Gao, W.: Task-positive functional connectivity of the default mode network transcends task domain. J. Cognit. Neurosci. **27**(12), 2369–2381 (2015)
10. Hamilton, W.L., Ying, R., Leskovec, J.: Representation learning on graphs: methods and applications. IEEE Data Eng. Bull. **40**(3), 52–74 (2017)
11. Hellyer, P.J., Shanahan, M., Scott, G., Wise, R.J., Sharp, D.J., Leech, R.: The control of global brain dynamics: opposing actions of frontoparietal control and default mode networks on attention. J. Neurosci. **34**(2), 451–461 (2014)
12. Kelly, A.C., Uddin, L.Q., Biswal, B.B., Castellanos, F.X., Milham, M.P.: Competition between functional brain networks mediates behavioral variability. Neuroimage **39**(1), 527–537 (2008)
13. Kipf, T.N., Welling, M.: Semi-supervised classification with graph convolutional networks. arXiv preprint (2016). arXiv:1609.02907
14. Leech, R., Kamourieh, S., Beckmann, C.F., Sharp, D.J.: Fractionating the default mode network: distinct contributions of the ventral and dorsal posterior cingulate cortex to cognitive control. J. Neurosci. **31**(9), 3217–3224 (2011)

15. Ni, X., Yan, Z., Wu, T., Fan, J., Chen, C.: A region-of-interest-reweight 3D convolutional neural network for the analytics of brain information processing. In: Medical Image Computing and Computer Assisted Intervention - MICCAI, pp. 302–310 (2018)
16. Nie, D., Zhang, H., Adeli, E., Liu, L., Shen, D.: 3D deep learning for multi-modal imaging-guided survival time prediction of brain tumor patients. In: Ourselin, S., Joskowicz, L., Sabuncu, M.R., Unal, G., Wells, W. (eds.) MICCAI 2016. LNCS, vol. 9901, pp. 212–220. Springer, Cham (2016). https://doi.org/10.1007/978-3-319-46723-8_25
17. Nielsen, A.N., Greene, D.J., Gratton, C., Dosenbach, N.U., Petersen, S.E., Schlaggar, B.L.: Evaluating the prediction of brain maturity from functional connectivity after motion artifact denoising. Cereb. Cortex **29**(6), 2455–2469 (2018)
18. Power, J.D., Schlaggar, B.L., Lessov-Schlaggar, C.N., Petersen, S.E.: Evidence for hubs in human functional brain networks. Neuron **79**(4), 798–813 (2013)
19. Raichle, M.E., MacLeod, A.M., Snyder, A.Z., Powers, W.J., Gusnard, D.A., Shulman, G.L.: A default mode of brain function. Proc. National Acad. Sci. **98**(2), 676–682 (2001)
20. Ridderinkhof, K.R., Ullsperger, M., Crone, E.A., Nieuwenhuis, S.: The role of the medial frontal cortex in cognitive control. Science **306**(5695), 443–447 (2004)
21. Schmidt, M., Murphy, K., Fung, G., Rosales, R.: Structure learning in random fields for heart motion abnormality detection. In: 2008 IEEE Conference on Computer Vision and Pattern Recognition, pp. 1–8. IEEE (2008)
22. Shannon, C.E., Weaver, W.: The Mathematical Theory of Communication. University of Illinois Press, Champaign (1949)
23. Solomon, M., Ozonoff, S.J., Ursu, S., Ravizza, S., Cummings, N., Ly, S., Carter, C.S.: The neural substrates of cognitive control deficits in autism spectrum disorders. Neuropsychologia **47**(12), 2515–2526 (2009)
24. Spreng, R.N., Sepulcre, J., Turner, G.R., Stevens, W.D., Schacter, D.L.: Intrinsic architecture underlying the relations among the default, dorsal attention, and frontoparietal control networks of the human brain. J. Cognit. Neurosci. **25**(1), 74–86 (2013)
25. Tan, M., Shi, Q., van den Hengel, A., Shen, C., Gao, J., Hu, F., Zhang, Z.: Learning graph structure for multi-label image classification via clique generation. In: Proceedings of the IEEE Conference on Computer Vision and Pattern Recognition, pp. 4100–4109 (2015)
26. Van Den Heuvel, M.P., Mandl, R.C., Kahn, R.S., Hulshoff Pol, H.E.: Functionally linked resting-state networks reflect the underlying structural connectivity architecture of the human brain. Hum. Brain Mapp. **30**(10), 3127–3141 (2009)
27. Veličković, P., Cucurull, G., Casanova, A., Romero, A., Lio, P., Bengio, Y.: Graph attention networks. In: International Conference on Learning Representations (2018)
28. Wu, T., et al.: Hick-hyman law is mediated by the cognitive control network in the brain. Cereb. Cortex **28**(7), 1–16 (2017)
29. Xu, K., Hu, W., Leskovec, J., Jegelka, S.: How powerful are graph neural networks? In: International Conference on Learning Representations (2019)
30. Zhang, X., He, L., Chen, K., Luo, Y., Zhou, J., Wang, F.: Multi-view graph convolutional network and its applications on neuroimage analysis for parkinson's disease. arXiv preprint (2018). arXiv:1805.08801

CU-Net: Cascaded U-Net with Loss Weighted Sampling for Brain Tumor Segmentation

Hongying Liu[1], Xiongjie Shen[1], Fanhua Shang[1(✉)], Feihang Ge[2],
and Fei Wang[3]

[1] Key Lab of Intelligent Perception and Image Understanding of Ministry
of Education, School of Artificial Intelligence, Xidian University, Xi'an, China
{hyliu,fhshang}@xidian.edu.cn, shenxiongjie123@gmail.com
[2] School of Information Science and Technology,
Aichi Prefectural University, Nagakute, Japan
fhge2018@163.com
[3] Weill Cornell Medical School, Cornell University, New York, NY, USA
feiwang.cornell@gmail.com

Abstract. This paper proposes a novel cascaded U-Net for brain tumor segmentation. Inspired by the distinct hierarchical structure of brain tumor, we design a cascaded deep network framework, in which the whole tumor is segmented firstly and then the tumor internal substructures are further segmented. Considering that the increase of the network depth brought by cascade structures leads to a loss of accurate localization information in deeper layers, we construct between-net connections to link features at the same resolution and transmit the detailed information from shallow layers to the deeper layers. Then we present a loss weighted sampling (LWS) scheme to eliminate the issue of imbalanced data. Experimental results on the BraTS 2017 dataset show that our framework outperforms the state-of-the-art segmentation algorithms, especially in terms of segmentation sensitivity.

Keywords: Brain tumor segmentation · Cascaded U-Net · Feature fusion · Loss weighted sampling

1 Introduction

Glioma is the most common primary central nervous system tumor with high morbidity and mortality. For glioma diagnosis, four standard Magnetic Resonance Imaging (MRI) modalities are generally used: T1-weighted MRI (T1), T2-weighted MRI (T2), T1-weighted MRI with gadolinium contrast enhancement (T1ce) and Fluid Attenuated Inversion Recovery (FLAIR). Usually, it is a challenging and time-consuming task for doctors to combine these four modalities to complete a fine segmentation of brain tumors.

© Springer Nature Switzerland AG 2019
D. Zhu et al. (Eds.): MBIA 2019/MFCA 2019, LNCS 11846, pp. 102–111, 2019.
https://doi.org/10.1007/978-3-030-33226-6_12

Since deep learning has attracted considerable attentions from researchers, convolutional neural network (CNN) has been widely applied to the brain tumor segmentation. Havaei et al. [2] proposed a CNN architecture with two pathways to extract features in different scales. Such an multi-scale idea was validated to be effective in improving the segmentation results in many works [2,3,5]. In [12], a triple cascaded framework was put forward according to the hierarchy of brain tumor, though novel in framework, the patch-wise and sequential training process leads to a somewhat inefficient processing. Shen et al. [9] built a tree-structured, multi-task fully convolutional network (FCN) to implicitly encode the hierarchical relationship of tumor substructures. The end-to-end network structure was much efficient than the patch-based methods. To improve the segmentation accuracy of tumor boundaries, Shen et al. [10] proposed a boundary-aware fully convolutional network (BFCN) and constructed two branches to learn two tasks separately, one for tumor tissue classification and the other for tumor boundary classification. However, the flaw inherent in the traditional FCN still exists, that is, rough multi-fold up-sampling operation makes the results less refined. To avoid the loss of location information caused by down-sampling operations in traditional CNNs, Lopez et al. [7] designed a dilated residual network (DRN) and abandoned pooling operations. This may be an effective solution to prevent the network from losing the details, but is too time-consuming and memory-consuming.

Ronneberger et al. [8] proposed a U-shape convolutional network (called U-Net) and introduced skip-connections to fuse multi-level features, so as to help the net decode more precisely. Many experimental results show that U-Net performs well in various medical image segmentation tasks. Dong et al. [1] applied U-Net to brain tumor segmentation and took the soft dice loss as loss function to solve the issue of imbalanced data in brain MRI data. Though soft dice loss may have better performance than cross entropy loss in some extremely class-imbalanced situation, it has less stable gradient, which may make the training process unstable even not convergent.

Inspired by the hierarchical structure within the brain tumor, we propose a novel cascaded U-shape convolutional network for the multistage segmentation of brain tumors. To mitigate the vanishing gradient problem caused by the increasing depth of neural networks, each basic block in our cascaded U-shape convolutional network is designed as a residual block as in [4]. Moreover, the decoding-layer supervision information is also considered during the training process, and this is expected to further alleviate the problem of vanishing gradients. To reduce the information loss in the deeper layers, we design between-net connections to facilitate the efficient transmission of high resolution information from the shallow layers to the corresponding deeper layers, which leads to obtain more refined segmentation results. Additionally, to address the class-imbalanced problem, we define a new cross entropy loss function by introducing a loss weighted sampling scheme.

The main contributions of this paper can be summarized as follows.

- We propose a novel cascaded U-Net framework for brain tumor segmentation.
- Some between-net connections are designed to facilitate the efficient transmission of high resolution information from shallow layers to deeper layers. And the residual block is introduced to fit in with the excessive depth.
- Moreover, we also present a loss weighted sampling scheme to address the severe class-imbalance problem.
- Finally, our experimental results show that our method performs much better than state-of-the-art methods in terms of dice score and sensitivity.

2   The Proposed Cascaded U-Net Method

2.1   Our Cascaded U-Net Architecture

Our network is a novel end-to-end architecture mainly composed of two cascaded U-Nets with each for different task, as shown in Fig. 1. Such a cascaded framework is inspired by the underlying hierarchical structure within the brain tumor that the tumor comprises a tumor core, and the tumor core contains an enhancing tumor.

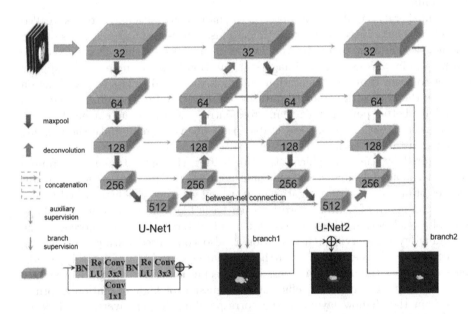

Fig. 1. Our cascaded U-Net architecture (CU-Net or CUN) for brain tumor segmentation. The digital number on each block denotes the number of output channels. Before every supervision, including 8 auxiliary supervisions and 2 branch supervisions, there is a 1 × 1 convolution to squeeze the channels of output into the same quantity as target. Besides, in each auxiliary supervision, a deconvolution is used to up-sample the feature maps to the same resolution as input. All the arrows denote the operations. (Color figure online)

Given the input brain MRI images, we extract a non-brain mask firstly and prevent the network from learning the masked areas by loss weight sampling. Then the first-stage U-Net separates the whole tumor from background, and sends the extracted features into the second-stage U-Net, which further segments tumor substructures. Such a cascade structure is designed to take advantage of the underlying physiological structure within the brain tumor. The cascade structure will multiply the network depth, which on the one hand will enhance the ability of a network to extract semantic features, but on the other hand exacerbate the vanishing gradient problem. In our architecture, we design the following three strategies to avoid the above problem and fulfill the coarse-to-fine segmentation of brain tumor.

Firstly, inspired by the residual network, each basic unit in our network is constructed by a residual block stacked by two 3×3 convolution blocks. Secondly, the auxiliary supervisions are considered in our cascaded U-Net. Specifically, each decoding layer in the network expands a branch composed by a deconvolution and a 1×1 convolution to up-sample the feature maps to the same resolution as input and squeeze the output channels. Then the training labels are added for the supervised learning (see the thinner orange arrows in Fig. 1). This allows the introduction of additional gradients during training and further alleviates the vanishing gradient problem. In some extent, it can be also regarded as an additional regulation for the network to avoid overfitting. Finally, the between-net connections are designed. The features from the decoding layers of the first U-Net are transmitted to the corresponding encoding layers in the second U-Net by concatenation operation. These between-net connections enable the high-resolution information in some shallow layers to be preserved and sent to the deeper layers for a fine segmentation of tumor substructures.

2.2 Training with Loss Weighted Sampling

Our proposed network is an end-to-end architecture, in which the two cascaded U-Nets are trained jointly, ensuring the efficiency of the data processing procedure. To address the extremely imbalance of the positive and negative samples in the brain tumor dataset, we present a loss weighted sampling scheme and combine it with the cross entropy loss function. Specifically, the sampled loss function is formulated as follows:

$$
\mathcal{L} = \frac{\sum\limits_{n=1}^{b} \sum\limits_{i=1}^{l} \sum\limits_{j=1}^{w} \left[\left(- \sum\limits_{m=1}^{c} (L \cdot \log Y) \right) \cdot W \right]}{\sum\limits_{n=1}^{b} \sum\limits_{i=1}^{l} \sum\limits_{j=1}^{w} W}
\tag{1}
$$

where $Y \in \mathbb{R}^{b \times c \times l \times w}$ denotes the predicted probability for the one-hot label $L \in \mathbb{R}^{b \times c \times l \times w}$ after softmax functions. b is the number of batches, c is the number of channels, l and w are the length and width of the image, respectively. Sample matrix $W \in \mathbb{R}^{b \times l \times w}$ is computed according to specific tasks, and $W_{n,i,j} \in \{0, 1\}$ denotes the loss weight of the pixels at the spatial location (n, i, j).

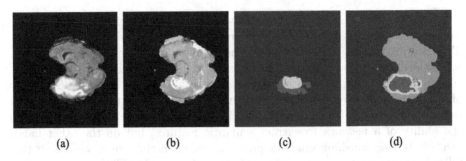

(a)   (b)   (c)   (d)

Fig. 2. A brain tumor training sample is divided into four regions according to the input data and ground truth: (a) FLAIR. (b) T1ce. (c) Ground truth (Purple: Non-tumor; Blue: Edema; Yellow: enhancing tumor; Green: necrosis.) (d) Four regions of a training sample. S_1: Black background; S_2: Normal brain region; S_3: Tumor region obtained from (c); S_4: Tumor contour region obtained by a contour detection algorithm. (Color figure online)

The brain MRI image is divided into four regions: S_1, S_2, S_3 and S_4, which represent the black background, normal brain region, tumor region, and tumor contour region, respectively (see Fig. 2(d)). Then the sample matrix W can be computed as follows:

$$W = \sum_{i=1}^{3} Sample\left(S_i, p_i\right) + \alpha Sample\left(S_4, p_4\right) \tag{2}$$

where $Sample(S_i, p_i)$ denotes a binary matrix obtained by random sampling in S_i with probability p_i. The hyper-parameter α is greater than or equal to 1, which is introduced for adjusting the loss weight of contour regions and is expected to enhance the ability of our network to recognize the tumor contour. Note that α becomes α_1 and α_2 for the U-Net1 and U-Net2 in the proposed cascaded U-Net, respectively.

For most of the MRI images, the black background S_1, also referred as non-brain mask in this paper, contains a large number of pixels but provides little useful information for the segmentation task. According to this prior knowledge, we let p_1 be 0 and extract a non-brain mask in advance and merge it with the prediction maps when testing.

To compute the branch loss function $\mathcal{L}_1$ and auxiliary loss function $\mathcal{L}_{a_i}$ $(i = 1, 2, \ldots, 4)$ in U-Net1, we let $p_3 = 1, p_4 = 1$. Then p_2 is calculated as follows:

$$p_2 \cdot N_{S_2} = \beta \cdot p_3 \cdot N_{S_3} \tag{3}$$

where N_{S_i} denotes the pixel number in region S_i, and β, usually more than 1, is for adjusting the proportion of positive and negative samples in a training batch, thus eliminating the class imbalance problem [6]. Because $Sample(S_i, p_i)$ is a random sampling operation, as long as $\beta \cdot p_2 \cdot epoch \geq 1$ is guaranteed, where *epoch* is the times of the network to traverse the whole training set, all pixels in the dataset are expected to participate in the calculation of loss for at least one time so that no information from the brain tumor will be lost.

For the branch loss function $\mathcal{L}_2$ and auxiliary loss function $\mathcal{L}_{a_i}$ $(i = 5, 6, \ldots, 8)$ in U-Net2, we let: $p_1 = 0, p_2 = 0, p_3 = 1, p_4 = 1, \alpha_2 = 1$, which means that U-Net2 only learns the segmentation of tumor substructures. Thus, the loss function of our network is

$$\mathcal{L}_{Total} = \mathcal{L}_1 + \mathcal{L}_2 + \omega \sum_{i=1}^{8} \mathcal{L}_{ai} + \lambda\psi \tag{4}$$

where $\mathcal{L}_{ai}$ is the auxiliary loss function $(i = 1, 2, \ldots, 8)$, ω is the weighted coefficient, and ψ is the regularization term with the hyper-parameter λ for tradeoff with the other terms.

For the testing process, we extract the non-brain mask in advance and fuse it with the outputs of branch1 and branch2 to get the final segmentation result.

3   Experimental Results

In this section, we apply the proposed cascaded U-Net for brain tumor segmentation tasks. We also compare our cascaded U-Net with the state-of-the-art methods: U-Net [8], BFCN [10] and DRN [7].

3.1   Datasets and Pre-processing

We evaluate our method on the training data of BraTS challenge 2017. It consists of 210 cases of high-grade glioma and 75 cases of low-grade glioma. In each case, four modal brain MRI scans: T1, T2, T1ce and FLAIR, are provided, respectively. The resolution of MRI scans is $240 \times 240 \times 155$. Pixel-level labels provided by the radiologists are: 1 for necrotic (NCR) and the non-enhancing tumor (NET), 2 for edema (ED), 4 for enhancing tumor (ET), and 0 for everything else. In our experiments, 210 high-grade cases are divided into three subsets at a ratio of 3:1:1, i.e., 126 training data, 42 validation data and 42 testing data are attained. Low-grade cases are not used. Besides, about 30% scans that don't contain any tumor structure are discarded in the training process. All the input images are processed by N4-ITK bias field correction and intensity normalization. In addition, data augmentation including random rotation and random flip is used in all the algorithms.

3.2   Implementation Details

All the algorithms were implemented on a computer with NVIDIA GeForce GTX1060Ti (6 GB) GPU and Intel Core i5-7300HQ CPU @ 2.5 GHz (8GB), together with the open-source deep learning framework pytorch. The contour weight α_1 is set to 2, and β is set to 1.5. The extracted tumor contour is about 10 pixels wide. In the training phase, we use stochastic gradient descent (SGD) with momentum to optimize the loss function as in [11]. The momentum parameter is 0.9, and the initial learning rate is 10^{-3} and decreased by a factor of 10 every ten epochs until a minimum threshold of 10^{-7}. The weight decay λ is set to 5×10^{-5}. The models are trained for about 50 iterations until there is an obvious uptrend in the validation loss. The weighted coefficient ω is set to 0.1 initially and decreased by a factor of 10 every ten epochs until a minimum threshold of 10^{-3}.

For segmentation results, we evaluate the following three parts: (1) Whole Tumor (WT); (2) Tumor Core (TC); and (3) Enhancing Tumor (ET). For each part, dice score (called Dice), sensitivity (called Sens) and specificity (called Spec) are defined as follows:

$$\text{Dice}(P, T) = \frac{2|P_1 \wedge T_1|}{|P_1| + |T_1|}, \qquad \text{Sens}(P, T) = \frac{|P_1 \wedge T_1|}{|T_1|},$$
$$\text{Spec} = \frac{|P_0 \wedge T_0|}{|T_0|}, \tag{5}$$

where P, T denote the segmentation results and labels, and P_0, P_1, T_0, T_1 denote negatives in P, positives in P, negatives in T and positives in T, respectively.

3.3 Results and Analysis

To verify the effectiveness of our proposed network and loss weighted sampling scheme, we compare our CUN method with several state-of-the-art deep learning algorithms including U-Net [8], BFCN [10] and DRN [7].

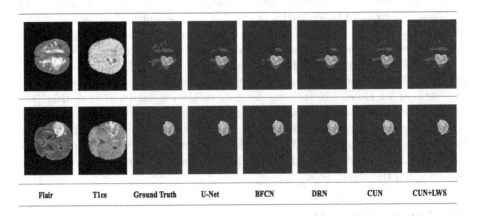

| Flair | T1ce | Ground Truth | U-Net | BFCN | DRN | CUN | CUN+LWS |

Fig. 3. Segmentation results of different methods on the local testing data. From left to right: Flair, T1ce, Ground Truth and results of U-Net, BFCN, DRN, CUN, CUN+LWS, respectively. In ground truth and segmentation results, purple, blue, yellow, green represent Non-tumor, Edema, Enhancing Tumor, and Necrosis, respectively. (Color figure online)

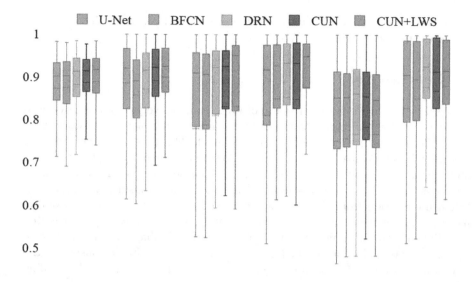

Fig. 4. Distributions of dice score and sensitivity of the five methods for whole tumor (WT), tumor core (TC) and enhancing tumor (ET). The solid lines and dotted lines in the boxes represent the median value and the average value, respectively.

The visual results are shown in Fig. 3. It can be seen that our proposed CUN+LWS has the best segmentation sensitivity among the five methods, and is better at segmenting the tiny sub-structures within a brain tumor. The distributions of the obtained dice scores and sensitivities are presented in Fig. 4. The quantitative results of the five models on the testing set are listed in Table 1. As we can see, our CUN method outperforms the three state-of-the-art methods by approximately 1.5% in dice score and 2% in sensitivity. Besides, when LWS

Table 1. Dice score, sensitivity and specificity of the five methods for Whole Tumor, Tumor Core and Enhancing Tumor on the testing set.

Method	Whole Tumor			Tumor Core			Enhance Tumor		
	Dice	Sens	Spec	Dice	Sens	Spec	Dice	Sens	Spec
U-Net [8]	0.872	0.885	0.996	0.779	0.811	**0.999**	0.751	0.829	**0.999**
BFCN [10]	0.874	0.857	**0.997**	0.788	0.850	0.998	0.757	0.851	0.998
DRN [7]	0.881	0.871	0.996	0.810	0.854	0.998	0.768	0.878	0.998
CUN	0.886	0.892	**0.997**	0.830	0.849	**0.999**	**0.784**	0.869	0.998
CUN+LWS	**0.888**	**0.903**	0.996	**0.831**	**0.877**	0.998	0.768	**0.881**	0.998

is adopted, there is an additional average growth of 1.5% in sensitivity, which indicates the effectiveness of LWS.

4 Conclusions

Inspired by the hierarchical structure of brain tumors, we proposed a novel cascaded U-Net for the segmentation of brain tumor. To make the network work more effectively, three strategies were designed. The residual blocks and the auxiliary supervision can help gradient flow more smoothly during training, and alleviate the vanishing gradient problem caused by the increasing depth of neural networks. The between-net connections can transmit the high resolution information from the shallow layer to the deeper layer and help obtain more refined segmentation results. Furthermore, we presented a loss weighted sampling scheme to adjust the number of samples in different classes to solve the severe class imbalance problem. Our experimental results demonstrated the advantages of our network and the effectiveness of the loss weighted sampling scheme.

Acknowledgments. This work was supported by the State Key Program of National Natural Science of China (No. 61836009), the Project supported the Foundation for Innovative Research Groups of the National Natural Science Foundation of China (No. 61621005), the Major Research Plan of the National Natural Science Foundation of China (Nos. 91438201 and 91438103), the Fund for Foreign Scholars in University Research and Teaching Programs (the 111 Project) (No. B07048), the National Natural Science Foundation of China (Nos. 61976164, 61876220, 61876221, U1701267, U1730109, 61473215, 61871310, 61472306, and 61502369), the Program for Cheung Kong Scholars and Innovative Research Team in University (No. IRT_15R53), the Science Foundation of Xidian University (Nos. 10251180018 and 10251180019), the Fundamental Research Funds for the Central Universities under Grant (No. 20101195989), the National Science Basic Research Plan in Shaanxi Province of China (No. 2019JQ-657), and the Key Special Project of China High Resolution Earth Observation System-Young Scholar Innovation Fund.

References

1. Dong, H., Yang, G., Liu, F., Mo, Y., Guo, Y.: Automatic brain tumor detection and segmentation using u-net based fully convolutional networks. In: Annual Conference on Medical Image Understanding and Analysis, pp. 506–517 (2017)
2. Havaei, M., et al.: Brain tumor segmentation with deep neural networks. Med. Image Anal. **35**, 18–31 (2017)
3. Havaei, M., Dutil, F., Pal, C., Larochelle, H., Jodoin, P.M.: A convolutional neural network approach to brain tumor segmentation. In: International Workshop on Brainlesion: Glioma, Multiple Sclerosis, Stroke and Traumatic Brain Injuries, pp. 195–208 (2015)
4. He, K., Zhang, X., Ren, S., Sun, J.: Deep residual learning for image recognition. In: IEEE Conference on Computer Vision and Pattern Recognition (CVPR), pp. 770–778 (2016)

5. Kayalibay, B., Jensen, G., van der Smagt, P.: CNN-based segmentation of medical imaging data. arXiv preprint (2017). arXiv:1701.03056
6. Liu, H., Shang, F., Yang, S., Gong, M., Zhu, T., Jiao, L.: Sparse manifold regularized neural networks for polarimetric sar terrain classification. IEEE Trans. Neural Netw. Learn. Syst. (2019)
7. Lopez, M.M., Ventura, J.: Dilated convolutions for brain tumor segmentation in MRI scans. In: International MICCAI Brainlesion Workshop, pp. 253–262 (2017)
8. Ronneberger, O., Fischer, P., Brox, T.: U-net: convolutional networks for biomedical image segmentation. In: International Conference on Medical Image Computing and Computer-Assisted Intervention, pp. 234–241 (2015)
9. Shen, H., Wang, R., Zhang, J., McKenna, S.: Multi-task fully convolutional network for brain tumour segmentation. In: Annual Conference on Medical Image Understanding and Analysis, pp. 239–248 (2017)
10. Shen, H., Wang, R., Zhang, J., McKenna, S.J.: Boundary-aware fully convolutional network for brain tumor segmentation. In: Descoteaux, M., Maier-Hein, L., Franz, A., Jannin, P., Collins, D.L., Duchesne, S. (eds.) MICCAI 2017. LNCS, vol. 10434, pp. 433–441. Springer, Cham (2017). https://doi.org/10.1007/978-3-319-66185-8_49
11. Wang, D., et al.: signADAM: learning confidences for deep neural networks (2019). arXiv: 1907.09008
12. Wang, G., Li, W., Ourselin, S., Vercauteren, T.: Automatic brain tumor segmentation using cascaded anisotropic convolutional neural networks. In: International MICCAI Brainlesion Workshop, pp. 178–190 (2017)

BrainPainter: A Software for the Visualisation of Brain Structures, Biomarkers and Associated Pathological Processes

Răzvan V. Marinescu[1,2(✉)], Arman Eshaghi[2,3], Daniel C. Alexander[2], and Polina Golland[1]

[1] Computer Science and Artificial Intelligence Laboratory, MIT, Cambridge, USA
`razvan@csail.mit.edu`
[2] Centre for Medical Image Computing, University College London, London, UK
[3] Queen Square MS Centre, UCL Institute of Neurology, London, UK

Abstract. We present BrainPainter, a software that automatically generates images of highlighted brain structures given a list of numbers corresponding to the output colours of each region. Compared to existing visualisation software (i.e. Freesurfer, SPM, 3D Slicer), BrainPainter has three key advantages: (1) it does not require the input data to be in a specialised format, allowing BrainPainter to be used in combination with any neuroimaging analysis tools, (2) it can visualise both cortical and subcortical structures and (3) it can be used to generate movies showing dynamic processes, e.g. propagation of pathology on the brain. We highlight three use cases where BrainPainter was used in existing neuroimaging studies: (1) visualisation of the degree of atrophy through interpolation along a user-defined gradient of colours, (2) visualisation of the progression of pathology in Alzheimer's disease as well as (3) visualisation of pathology in subcortical regions in Huntington's disease. Moreover, through the design of BrainPainter we demonstrate the possibility of using a powerful 3D computer graphics engine such as Blender to generate brain visualisations for the neuroscience community. Blender's capabilities, e.g. particle simulations, motion graphics, UV unwrapping, raster graphics editing, raytracing and illumination effects, open a wealth of possibilities for brain visualisation not available in current neuroimaging software. BrainPainter (Source code: https://github.com/mrazvan22/brain-coloring) is customisable, easy to use, and can run straight from the web browser: http://brainpainter.csail.mit.edu. It can be used to visualise biomarker data from any brain imaging modality, or simply to highlight a particular brain structure for e.g. anatomy courses.

1 Introduction

Efficient visualisation of brain structure, function and pathology is crucial for understanding the mechanisms underlying neurodegenerative diseases and eases

---

D. C. Alexander and P. Golland—Joint senior authors with equal contribution.

© Springer Nature Switzerland AG 2019
D. Zhu et al. (Eds.): MBIA 2019/MFCA 2019, LNCS 11846, pp. 112–120, 2019.
https://doi.org/10.1007/978-3-030-33226-6_13

the interpretation of results in neuroimaging studies. This is especially important in populations studies, where two or more populations are compared for group differences in biomarkers derived from e.g. Magnetic Resonance Imaging, Positron Emission Tomography (PET) or Computer Tomography (CT). The results are best visualised as brain images, where regions-of-interest (ROIs) are highlighted based on the magnitude of the difference between the two groups. These visualisation are generally done by the same software that performs the registration, segmentation and statistical analysis. However, for traumatic brain injury or less common neurodegenerative diseases such as Parkinson's disease and Multiple Sclerosis, visualisations of statistical results is sometimes not performed due to the inability to register images to a common template or lack of robust registration software. Therefore, many studies such as [1,2] only report differences between patients and controls in tables or as box plots. There is therefore a lack of visualisation tools that can highlight neuroimaging findings for these complex diseases.

When registration to a common population template is possible, e.g. in Alzheimer's disease (AD), excellent 3D visualisation software exists which allows interactive visualisation of population differences – e.g. 3D Slicer [3], Freesurfer [4] or SPM [5]. However, they have several inherent limitations. First, such software – e.g. Freesurfer – generally require inputs in their proprietary data format, which is usually difficult and time-consuming to create without using their pipeline. While creating these proprietary data formats is necessary when users need to display voxelwise visualisations, often users only need to highlight entire ROIs – in this simpler case the user could only provide a list of RGB colors for each ROI in a csv file, removing the need to create input data in a specialised format. Another limitation of existing visualisation software is their difficulty in highlighting complex patterns of pathology in a single slice of a 3D volumetric image. To overcome this, some authors show multiple slices (sometimes up to 8 slices [6]), although this takes too much space on the academic paper being published. While Freesurfer solves this problem using a cortical surface-based representation that captures most of the complexity of pathology patterns in a single image, this surface representation is not supported for subcortical structures such as the hippocampus. Third, current visualisation software cannot be easily used to generate e.g. a movie showing a dynamic process, e.g. propagation of pathology within the human brain, as most of them have been intended for interactive visualisation and have no application programming interface (API) that allows automatic generation of hundreds of images using pre-defined settings.

We present BrainPainter, a software for easy visualisation of structures, pathology and biomarkers in the brain. As opposed to previous visualisation software, the input data is very simple: a generic .csv file containing numbers for each ROI, each number mapping to a different colour to be assigned to that ROI – such a simple input allows BrainPainter to be used in conjunction with any other neuroimaging analysis software. Secondly, BrainPainter can visualise both cortical and subcortical structures using a surface representation, removing the need to show multiple slices of the same 3D scan. Third, the images are

INPUT

Biomarkers (.csv file)	Hippocampus	Inferior temporal	Superior parietal ...	
Brain 1	0.6	2.3	1.3	..
Brain 2	1.2	0.0	3.0	..
...		...		

User-defined color gradient

0	1	2	3

OUTPUT

Brain 1

Brain 2

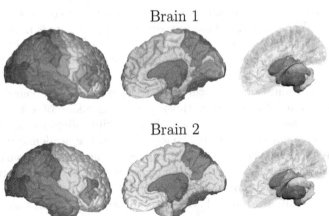

Fig. 1. Given a .csv file with region-of-interest (ROI) biomarkers and a user-defined color gradient, BrainPainter can automatically generate brain images with the cortical surface (left and middle) as well as with subcortical structures (right). The input .csv file can contain multiple rows, one for each set of output images. The color gradient is a list of RGB colours given by the user. Final colours are interpolated using the numbers from the input .csv file based on the color gradient – e.g. if the hippocampus has an associated value of 1.2, it's final color in the output image will be an interpolation of colors 1 and 2 from the gradient. (Color figure online)

generated automatically from pre-defined view-points, and can be easily used to create a movie showing e.g. the propagation of pathology, without the need to write any extra software code or interface with an API.

2 Design

BrainPainter has a very simple yet effective workflow. Given an input csv file with biomarkers for each region, it produces high-quality visualisations of cortical and subcortical structures. For this, it uses Blender as a rendering engine, and loads 3D meshes from a template brain (one 3D mesh for each ROI), which are then coloured according to the input numbers. Instead of providing a list of RGB colours for each ROI, we choose a simpler interface of providing one number for each ROI which maps to an RGB color using a user-defined color gradient. For example, the gradient can range from white → yellow → orange → red, as in the example from Fig. 1. In this case, the input numbers for each ROI need to be in the range [0,3], where a value of 1.3 would interpolate between colour 1 (yellow) and color 2 (orange).

BrianPainter uses open-source software Blender as the rendering engine. We chose Blender for three reasons. First, it is open-source, allowing us to distribute it already integrated with BrainPainter, thus requiring no further installation. Secondly, Blender is a powerful 3D graphics software, which allowed us to create realistic lightning conditions and handle transparency required for the glass-brain. Third, it also supports creating movies of complex temporal processes such as pathology spread along the brain. The software also supports a variety of object formats for the brain template, including the popular .obj mesh format. As BrainPainter is written in Python, it allows interfacing with any Blender function.

The software is able to colour and visualise regions belonging to a pre-defined atlas. Currently, we support three widely-used atlases: (i) the Desikan-Killiany (DK) atlas [7], (ii) the Destrieux atlas [8] and (iii) the Tourville atlas [9]. However, a custom atlas can also be used by mapping those regions to any of the three atlases currently supported, through the modification a simple mapping in the main configuration file.[1]

3 Customisation

BrainPainter can be easily customised in several ways, as shown in Fig. 2. First of all, the colours assigned to each region can be changed by modifying both the control points of the color gradient and the input numbers selecting colors along the gradient. The background colour and image resolution can also be changed.

The 3D structures being visualised can also be customised. We currently support three atlases (Desikan-Killiany, Destrieux and Tourville) as well as two types of brain surfaces: inflated, which is a brain surface that is smoothed out and

---

[1] https://github.com/mrazvan22/brain-coloring/blob/master/config.py.

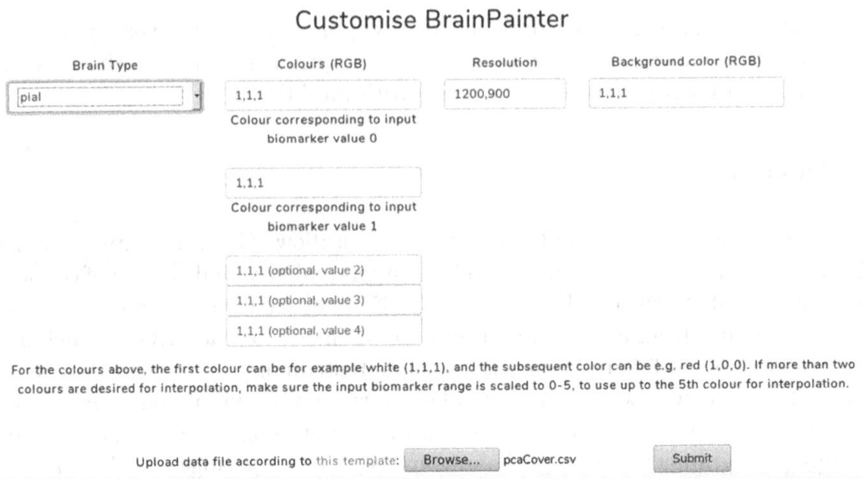

Customise BrainPainter

Brain Type	Colours (RGB)	Resolution	Background color (RGB)
pial	1,1,1	1200,900	1,1,1
	Colour corresponding to input biomarker value 0		
	1,1,1		
	Colour corresponding to input biomarker value 1		
	1,1,1 (optional, value 2)		
	1,1,1 (optional, value 3)		
	1,1,1 (optional, value 4)		

For the colours above, the first colour can be for example white (1,1,1), and the subsequent color can be e.g. red (1,0,0). If more than two colours are desired for interpolation, make sure the input biomarker range is scaled to 0-5, to use up to the 5th colour for interpolation.

Upload data file according to this template: Browse...   pcaCover.csv   Submit

Fig. 2. BrainPainter website interface at http://brainpainter.csail.mit.edu, showing how it can be easily customised. Here, the user selects the brain type, colours and resolution, and finally uploads the input .csv file with ROI biomarkers. The server then generates the output images, which can be downloaded by the user. More customisation features will be added in future versions.

where no gyri appear, and also pial, the standard brain surface with gyri. The software allows one to remove some 3D structures – for example, Fig. 5 shows the subcortical structures with the cerebellum removed from the visualisation – contrast this with Fig. 4.

BrainPainter also support two types of surfaces, cortical and subcortical structures. For the cortical surface, we only show the left hemisphere (although the right hemisphere can also be added), and provide two default viewing angles (front and back). For the subcortical structures, we show them for both hemispheres and also show the right hemisphere as a glass brain, for reference.

More complex settings such as the viewing angle and luminosity can also be customised, but currently require minor modifications to the source code. In the future, we plan to enable these customisations from the main configuration file.

4   First Use Case: Visualising the Degree of Pathology

In the first use case, we want to visualise the degree of pathology in Alzheimer's disease. During the progression of Alzheimer's disease, some regions of the brain such as the hippocampus and temporal lobes will be more affected compared to other regions of the brain such as the occipital lobe. Visualisation of pathology in AD is important in order to understand its underlying mechanisms and generate new hypotheses.

The notion of pathology here is abstract, and can refer to atrophy as measured by volume loss or cortical thinning, white matter degradation as measured

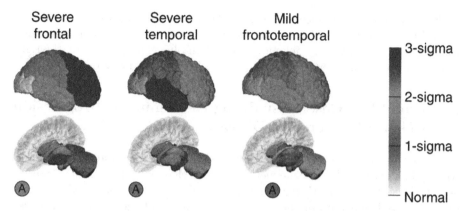

Fig. 3. Demonstration of BrainPainter for showing degree of pathology for three subtypes of Alzheimer's disease. The vertical bar on the right shows the degree of atrophy as standard deviations from the control population. Image courtesy of [10]. (Color figure online)

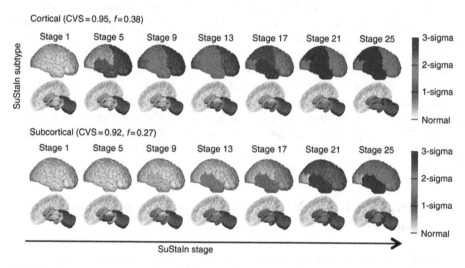

Fig. 4. Demonstration of BrainPainter for showing the temporal progression of atrophy in two subtypes of Alzheimer's disease, as a sequence of snapshots at different disease stages. Image reproduced and adapted from [10]. (Color figure online)

by diffusion tensor imaging (DTI) changes in fractional anisotropy (FA), or the level of abnormal conformations of proteins such as amyloid-beta or tau as measured by Positron Emission Tomography. However, BrainPainter is agnostic to the meaning of these biomarkers and can be used with any imaging modality, including markers derived from several modalities together.

Figure 3 shows an application of BrainPainter by [10] to highlight the degree of atrophy in Alzheimer's disease. Regions with no atrophy are coloured in white, while regions with severe atrophy are coloured in blue. The gradient on the right shows, for every color, the number of standard deviations away from controls.

5   Second Use Case: Visualising the Temporal Progression of Neurodegenerative Diseases

In the second use case, we would like to visualise the temporal progression of Alzheimer's disease (AD). Alzheimer's disease is characterised by a slow, continuous progression – while it's mechanisms are still not fully understood, it is currently believed that initial abnormalities in the amyloid and tau proteins cause a cascade of events that eventually lead to axonal degradation, neural death and cognitive decline [11]. Therefore, being able to visualise the progression of these events, including their timing and speed, is crucial for understanding the mechanisms of Alzheimer's disease.

Figure 4, reproduced and adapted from [10], demonstrates the ability of BrainPainter to visualise the evolution of atrophy in two subtypes of Alzheimer's disease – *cortical* and *subcortical* – characterised by prominent atrophy in the cortical and subcortical regions respectively. This study done by [10] used data from the Alzheimer's disease Neuroimaging Initiative to disentangle the heterogeneity of AD into subtypes with different progression. Here, visualisations provided by BrainPainter were able to characterise not only the degree of atrophy in each region (white/red to blue colors), but also the timing of atrophy events. For example, even in the *cortical* subtype, the hippocampus becomes affected by stage 13, while similarly, in the *subcortical* subtype the temporal lobe becomes affected by stage 13.

6   Third Use Case: Visualising Pathology in Subcortical Structures

The ability to visualise subcortical structures is crucial for neurodegenerative diseases that cause damage to these regions. Apart from Alzheimer's disease, Huntington's disease (HD) is also known for targetting subcortical regions [12,13]. The neurodegeneration in HD is believed to begin in the striatum and pallidum, and later followed by other subcortical and cortical regions [12].

Figure 5, reproduced and adapted with permission from [13], shows visualisations generated by BrainPainter of atrophy progression in subcortical areas, for Huntington's disease. The images show early involvement of the putamen, caudate and pallidum in the progression of Huntington's disease, and demonstrate the potential of BrainPainter in visualising pathology dynamics in subcortical regions using parsimonious glass-brain images.

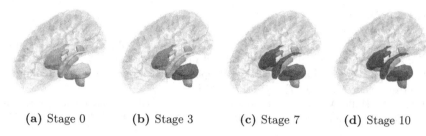

(a) Stage 0   (b) Stage 3   (c) Stage 7   (d) Stage 10

Fig. 5. Progression of pathology in Huntington's disease, shown in subcortical regions, using images generated with BrainPainter. Images adapted from [13].

7   Conclusion

We presented BrainPainter, an open-source software that can be used to visualise structures, biomarkers and pathologies in the human brain. The visualisations generated by BrainPainter can be used to significantly enhance the interpretation of neuroimaging research and can be easily embedded by researchers into scientific articles. While not demonstrated here, BrainPainter can also easily generate movies showing dynamic processes, e.g. propagation of brain pathology.

Our software has several limitations that can be addressed in future versions. First, it can currently only highlight entire regions-of-interest from an atlas. However, this was a design choice, as it removes the need for users to create specialised input files with voxelwise measurements, thus increasing usability. Nevertheless, in future versions we might add the ability to highlight fine-grained patterns of pathology. Yet another limitation of BrainPainter is that it cannot visualise more complex structures such as white-matter tracts, although we plan to add such functionality in future releases.

The use of the powerful Blender engine opens numerous avenues not possible with current neuroimaging software: motion graphics can be used to generate realistic movies showing e.g. the evolution of biomarkers, particle simulations can be used to visualise toxic proteins accumulating in certain regions, soft-body simulations can be used to model brain deformations due to head trauma, while camera-based rendering allows the creation of educational videos.

Acknowledgements. RVM was supported by the NIH grants NIBIB NAC P41EB015902 and NINDS R01NS086905, as well as the EPSRC Centre For Doctoral Training in Medical Imaging with grant EP/L016478/1. AE received a McDonald Fellowship from the Multiple Sclerosis International Federation (MSIF, www.msif.org), and the ECTRIMS – MAGNIMS Fellowship. DCA was supported by EuroPOND, which is an EU Horizon 2020 project, and by EPSRC grants J020990, M006093 and M020533. PG was supported by NIH grants NIBIB NAC P41EB015902 and NINDS R01NS086905.

We are also particularly grateful to Anderson Winkler for creating the 3D brain templates for all three atlases, which are used in this work (https://brainder.org/research/brain-for-blender/).

References

1. Coughlin, J.M., et al.: Neuroinflammation and brain atrophy in former NFL players: an in vivo multimodal imaging pilot study. Neurobiol. Dis. **74**, 58–65 (2015)
2. Schoonheim, M.M., et al.: Subcortical atrophy and cognition: sex effects in multiple sclerosis. Neurology **79**(17), 1754–1761 (2012)
3. Pieper, S., Halle, M., Kikinis, R.: 3D slicer. In: 2nd IEEE International Symposium on Biomedical Imaging: Nano to Macro (IEEE Cat No. 04EX821), pp. 632–635. IEEE (2004)
4. Fischl, B.: FreeSurfer. Neuroimage **62**(2), 774–781 (2012)
5. Penny, W.D., Friston, K.J., Ashburner, J.T., Kiebel, S.J., Nichols, T.E.: Statistical Parametric Mapping: The Analysis of Functional Brain Images. Elsevier, Amsterdam (2011)
6. Migliaccio, R., et al.: Mapping the progression of atrophy in early-and late-onset Alzheimer's disease. J. Alzheimer's Dis. **46**(2), 351–364 (2015)
7. Desikan, R.S., et al.: An automated labeling system for subdividing the human cerebral cortex on MRI scans into gyral based regions of interest. Neuroimage **31**(3), 968–980 (2006)
8. Destrieux, C., Fischl, B., Dale, A., Halgren, E.: Automatic parcellation of human cortical gyri and sulci using standard anatomical nomenclature. Neuroimage **53**(1), 1–15 (2010)
9. Klein, A., Tourville, J.: 101 labeled brain images and a consistent human cortical labeling protocol. Front. Neurosci. **6**, 171 (2012)
10. Young, A.L., et al.: Uncovering the heterogeneity and temporal complexity of neurodegenerative diseases with Subtype and Stage Inference. Nature communications **9**(1), 4273 (2018)
11. Mudher, A., Lovestone, S.: Alzheimer's disease-do tauists and baptists finally shake hands? Trends Neurosci. **25**(1), 22–26 (2002)
12. Douaud, G., et al.: In vivo evidence for the selective subcortical degeneration in Huntington's disease. Neuroimage **46**(4), 958–966 (2009)
13. Wijeratne, P.A., et al.: An image-based model of brain volume biomarker changes in Huntington's disease. Ann. Clin. Transl. Neurol. **5**(5), 570–582 (2018)

Structural Similarity Based Anatomical and Functional Brain Imaging Fusion

Nishant Kumar[1]([✉]), Nico Hoffmann[2], Martin Oelschlägel[3], Edmund Koch[3], Matthias Kirsch[4], and Stefan Gumhold[1]

[1] Computer Graphics and Visualisation, Technische Universität Dresden, 01062 Dresden, Germany
nishant.kumar@tu-dresden.de
[2] Institute of Radiation Physics, Helmholtz-Zentrum Dresden-Rossendorf, 01328 Dresden, Germany
[3] Clinical Sensoring and Monitoring, Technische Universität Dresden, 01307 Dresden, Germany
[4] Department of Neurosurgery, University Hospital Carl Gustav Carus, 01307 Dresden, Germany

Abstract. Multimodal medical image fusion helps in combining contrasting features from two or more input imaging modalities to represent fused information in a single image. One of the pivotal clinical applications of medical image fusion is the merging of anatomical and functional modalities for fast diagnosis of malign tissues. In this paper, we present a novel end-to-end unsupervised learning based Convolutional neural network (CNN) for fusing the high and low frequency components of MRI-PET grayscale image pairs publicly available at ADNI by exploiting Structural Similarity Index (SSIM) as the loss function during training. We then apply color coding for the visualization of the fused image by quantifying the contribution of each input image in terms of the partial derivatives of the fused image. We find that our fusion and visualization approach results in better visual perception of the fused image, while also comparing favorably to previous methods when applying various quantitative assessment metrics.

Keywords: Medical image fusion · MRI-PET · Convolutional neural networks (CNN) · Structural similarity index (SSIM)

1 Introduction

A rapid advancement in sensor technology has improved medical prognosis, surgical navigation and treatment. For example, anatomical modalities such as Magnetic resonance imaging (MRI) and Computed Tomography (CT) reveals the structural information of the brain like the location of tumor as well as white and gray matter while modalities such as Positron emission tomography (PET) provides functional information like glucose metabolism. The hybrid blend of

© Springer Nature Switzerland AG 2019
D. Zhu et al. (Eds.): MBIA 2019/MFCA 2019, LNCS 11846, pp. 121–129, 2019.
https://doi.org/10.1007/978-3-030-33226-6_14

PET-CT acquisition hardware provides fast and accurate attenuation correction and helps in combining anatomical and functional information. However it exposes patients to high level of X-Ray and ionizing radiation. The integrated MRI-PET scanners results in high tissue contrast with significantly low radiation dose. But the development of a robust hybrid MRI-PET hardware is challenging due to compatibility issue of PET detectors in a high magnetic field environment of MRI. The post-hoc fusion of MRI-PET image pairs overcomes the challenges of fully integrated MRI-PET scanners and helps medical personnel to better diagnose brain abnormalities such as glioma and Alzheimer's disease [1,2].

Most of the past image fusion methods proposed a three step approach to the fusion problem. First, the source images were transformed into a particular domain using approaches such as multi-scale decomposition [3–7], sparse representation [8,9], mixture of multi-scale decomposition and sparse representation [10] and Intensity-Hue-Saturation [11] among others. Then, the transformed coefficients are combined using a predefined coefficient grouping based fusion strategy such as max selection and weighted-averaging. Finally, the fused image is reconstructed by taking the inverse of the transformation strategy. However, the intricacy of these methods leads to the computational inefficiency making them unrealistic for the real time setup [12]. CNN based medical image fusion [13] has been actively studied in the past. However, these methods train the network on natural images due to the unavailability of large preregistered medical image pairs. The acquisition method of natural images differ from PET images since PET accumulates nuclear tracers depending on positron range, photon collinearity or the width of the detector element that results in a smooth low resolution acquisition without clear interfaces between certain tissues. The high resolution MRI such as T1-MPRAGE on the other hand are acquired in spatial frequency domain by varying the sequence of RF pulses. Hence, the aspects of human visual system that are tuned to process natural images are not equally useful for MRI-PET images due to which the selection of a proper objective assessment metric is challenging [14]. Secondly, there are no ground truth in a fusion problem due to which proper selection of the loss layer becomes critical.

Therefore, we propose a fast grayscale anatomical and functional medical image fusion approach in an end-to-end unsupervised learning network trained on publicly available medical image pairs. Additionally, the fusion result is visualized based on the contribution of the input images to the fused output image. The computational efficiency of our combined fusion and visualisation framework has the potential of real time clinical application in future.

2   Methods

2.1   Fusion Framework

The fusion architecture in Fig. 1 takes two grayscale input images I_1 and I_2 and generates a grayscale fused image I_F. The network consist of three different strategies named feature extraction, fusion and reconstruction to preserve most of the details from the input modalities. We train the parameters of the feature extraction and reconstruction layers by maximising the structural similarity and minimising the euclidean distance between fused image and the input images.

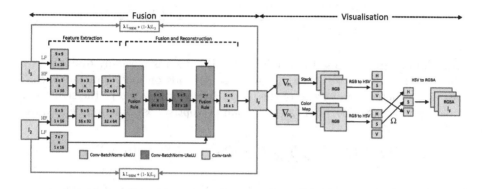

Fig. 1. The proposed fusion and visualisation framework.

Feature Extraction: In the first feature extraction layer, we perform two different convolution operations on each of the input images to decompose it into high and low frequency feature maps. Since blurry PET images has higher low frequency components than sharp MRI images, we define a kernel filter of size 9×9 for the anatomical input I_1 to capture low frequency (LF) features in a larger window while we select a smaller kernel size of 7×7 to capture the LF features of the functional input I_2 efficiently. For the high frequency (HF) layer, we define a kernel size of 3×3 for anatomical input I_1 to capture the sharp local features such as edges and corners better in smaller neighborhoods while we choose a kernel size of 5×5 for functional input I_2 due to less number of edges. We add two more hidden HF layers with increasing number of channels to preserve the deep high frequency features at the boundary regions.

Fusion and Reconstruction: HF features contain detailed information about texture and edges that has direct impact on the edge distortion of the fused image. Therefore, proper selection of the fusion strategy of HF features is crucial for robust fusion results. Max pooling strategy extracts edges from the features maps whereas average pooling is efficient in preserving textures. We utilise the advantage of each of the methods and propose max-average pooling as 1st fusion rule for the HF features. We implemented weighted averaging strategy as the 2nd fusion rule for LF features containing global information of inputs. Our reconstruction strategy contains three hidden layers and we define *tanh* activation function at the last layer due to its steeper gradients than a sigmoid function making backpropagation effective. Let $H_1(\phi)$ and $H_2(\phi)$ be the high frequency features of I_1 and I_2 at channel ϕ in the third hidden HF layer, $L_1(\tau)$ and $L_2(\tau)$ the low frequency features of I_1 and I_2 at channel τ in the first hidden LF layer and $R_i(\tau)$ the feature map generated from the second reconstruction layer, then the outputs of first fusion layer $H_o(\phi)$ and the second fusion layer $R_o(\tau)$ are:

$$H_o(\phi) = \frac{max\left(H_1(\phi), H_2(\phi)\right)}{H_1(\phi) + H_2(\phi)}, \quad R_o(\tau) = \frac{L_1(\tau) + L_2(\tau) + R_i(\tau)}{3} \qquad (1)$$

Loss Function: The fused image in medical domain is normally evaluated by a human observer whose sensitivity to noise depends on local luminance, contrast and structural properties of the image. Therefore, we adopt the structural similarity index ($SSIM$ [15]) as the human perceptive loss function defined as:

$$SSIM(I, J) = \frac{1}{N} \sum_{k=1}^{N} [l(i_k, j_k)]^\alpha \cdot [c(i_k, j_k)]^\beta \cdot [s(i_k, j_k)]^\gamma \qquad (2)$$

where I and J are the two input images and N is the number of local windows in the image. In our paper, $\alpha = \beta = \gamma = 1$ gives equal importance to luminance $l(i_k, j_k)$, structural $s(i_k, j_k)$ and contrast $c(i_k, j_k)$ comparisons of the image contents i_k and j_k at k^{th} local window with C_l, C_c, C_s as constants given as:

$$l(i_k, j_k) = \frac{2\mu_{i_k}\mu_{j_k} + C_l}{\mu_{i_k}^2 \mu_{j_k}^2 + C_l}, \quad c(i_k, j_k) = \frac{2\sigma_{i_k}\sigma_{j_k} + C_c}{\sigma_{i_k}^2 \sigma_{j_k}^2 + C_c}, \quad s(i_k, j_k) = \frac{\sigma_{i_k j_k} + C_s}{\sigma_{i_k} + \sigma_{j_k} + C_s} \qquad (3)$$

where μ_{i_k}, μ_{j_k} are the mean and σ_{i_k}, σ_{j_k} are the standard deviations of image contents i_k and j_k computed using a Gaussian filter with standard deviation σ_g and $\sigma_{i_k j_k}$ being the correlation coefficient. By empirically setting only SSIM as the loss function, we observed a shift in brightness of the fused image since the smaller σ_g preserves edges and contrast better than the luminance in the flat areas of the image. Therefore, in addition to SSIM we employ pixel level loss ℓ_2 which preserves luminance better. With I_1 and I_2 as the two source images and F as the final fused image, we express our steerable total loss function as:

$$L_{total} = \lambda * L_{SSIM} + (1 - \lambda) * L_{\ell_2} \qquad (4)$$

where $L_{SSIM} = (1 - SSIM(I_1, F)) + (1 - SSIM(I_2, F))$ and $L_{\ell_2} = (||F - I_1||_2 + ||F - I_2||_2)$ while λ controls the weightage of each of the sub-losses.

2.2   Visualization Framework

We visualised the functional and anatomical information in the fused grayscale image by first calculating the partial derivative of each pixel of the fused image with respect to each of the input images. Assuming n and m as the dimensions of the anatomical input I_1 and functional input I_2 while k and l are the dimensions of the fused image I_F, so the gradients $\nabla_{FI_1}(n, m)$ and $\nabla_{FI_2}(n, m)$ will be:

$$\nabla_{FI_1}(n, m) = \sum_{i=0}^{k} \sum_{j=0}^{l} \frac{\partial F[i, j]}{\partial I_1[n, m]}, \quad \nabla_{FI_2}(n, m) = \sum_{i=0}^{k} \sum_{j=0}^{l} \frac{\partial F[i, j]}{\partial I_2[n, m]} \qquad (5)$$

We then color coded the functional gradient image ∇_{FI_2} and performed Hue Saturation Value (HSV) transformation on both the images. The Hue and Saturation channels of ∇_{FI_2} and the Value channel from ∇_{FI_1} were stacked and inverse transformed to get the fused colored image. The factor Ω is multiplied with the saturation channel of ∇_{FI_2} to prevent the occlusion of anatomical information.

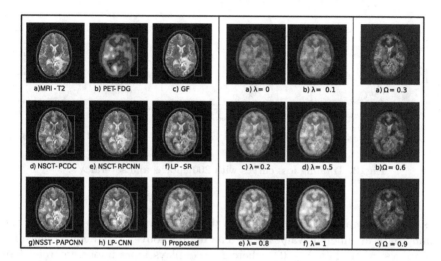

Fig. 2. The three sets of images shows visual results of compared methods, proposed fusion results based on λ and the visualisation results based on Ω. (Color figure online)

3   Experiments and Results

3.1   Training

Data Acquisition: We obtained 500 MRI-PET image pairs publicly available at the Alzheimer's Disease Neuroimaging Initiative (ADNI) [16] with subject's age between 55–90 years among both genders. All images were analyzed as axial slices with a voxel size of $1.0 \times 1.0 \times 1.0 \, \text{mm}^3$. The MRI images were skull stripped T1 weighted N3m MPRAGE sequences while PET-FDG images were co-registered, averaged, standardized voxel sized with uniform resolution of the same subject. We aligned the MRI-PET image pairs using the Affine transformation tool of 3D Slicer registration library.

Initialisation of Hyperparameters: The kernel filters of our fusion network are initialised as truncated normal distributions with standard deviation of 0.01 while the bias is zero. The stride in each layer is 1 with no padding during convolution since every down-sampling layer will erase detailed information in the input images which is crucial for medical image fusion. We employ batch normalization and Leaky ReLU activation with slope 0.2 to avoid the issue of vanishing gradient. The network is trained for 200 epochs with the batch size of 1 and varied $\lambda \in [0,1]$ on a single GeForce GTX 1080 Ti GPU. The Adam optimizer is used as the optimization function during backpropagation step with learning rate of 0.002. Our approach has been implemented in Python 2.7 and Tensorflow 1.10.1 on a Linux Ubuntu 17.10 x86_64 system with 12 Intel Core i7-8700K CPU @ 3.70 GHz and 64-GB RAM.

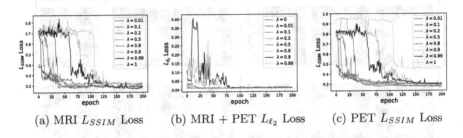

(a) MRI L_{SSIM} Loss   (b) MRI + PET L_{ℓ_2} Loss   (c) PET L_{SSIM} Loss

Fig. 3. Training loss curves with 200 epochs and several $\lambda's$.

Loss Curve Analysis: Figure 3 shows the loss curves L_{SSIM} and L_{ℓ_2} for the training data at different values of λ. The figures convey rapid convergence for all λ values other than $\lambda \geq 0.9$ where L_{SSIM} plays more important role than L_{ℓ_2} in the total loss function L_{total}. It is to be noted that L_{SSIM} has higher sensitivity to smaller errors such as luminance variations in flat texture-less regions while L_{ℓ_2} is more sensitive to larger errors irrespective of the underlying regions within the image. This property leads to delayed convergence of L_{SSIM} for visually perceptive results at edges as well as flat regions of the fused image.

3.2   Testing

We performed cross-validation on our trained model with a disjoint test dataset that contain 100 MRI-PET image pairs of 100 unique subjects from ADNI and Harvard Whole Brain Atlas [17] databases. 90 MR-T1 and PET-FDG image pairs obtained from ADNI were mutually exclusive from training image pairs. In order to test our method on datasets distinct from ADNI, the remaining 10 pre-registered image pairs were a combination of MR-T1 and PET-FDG or MR-T2 and PET-FDG images obtained from Harvard Whole Brain Atlas [17] with subjects suffering from either Glioma or Alzeihmer's disease.

3.3   Evaluation Settings

The visualisation results of the test images were evaluated with 10 values of $\lambda, \Omega \in [0,1]$ on four objective assessment metrics namely nonlinear correlation information entropy (Q_{IE}) [18], xydeas metric (Q_G) [19], feature mutual information (Q_{FMI}) [20], structural similarity metric (Q_{SSIM}) [15] and human perceptive visual information fidelity (Q_{VIFF}) [21] with higher values means better performances. The evaluation resulted in highest scores with $\lambda = 0.8$ and $\Omega = 0.6$ for three of the mentioned metrics. We then used six different medical image fusion methods from recent past namely guided filtering (GF) [7], nonsubsampled contourlet transform (NSCT-PCDC) [3] and (NSCT-RPCNN) [22], combination of multi-scale transform and sparse representation (LP-SR) [10], nonsubsampled shearlet transform (NSST-PAPCNN) [6] and convolutional neural networks (LP-CNN) [13] for quantitative comparisons in a MATLAB R2018a environment. Our code is publicly available at: https://github.com/nish03/FunFuseAn/.

Table 1. Assessment of fusion methods based on objective metrics and runtime.

Metrics	GF	NSCT-PCDC	LP-SR	NSCT-RPCNN	NSST-PAPCNN	LP-CNN	Proposed
Q_{IE}	0.8169	0.8080	0.8092	0.8132	0.8102	0.8076	0.8104
Q_G	0.7555	0.5457	0.6501	0.6702	0.6685	0.5665	0.5707
Q_{FMI}	0.9224	0.8754	0.8969	0.8941	0.8997	0.8958	0.8885
Q_{SSIM}	0.8260	0.7992	0.7837	0.8492	0.8318	0.7176	0.8610
Q_{VIFF}	0.2776	0.3415	0.5990	0.5430	0.6001	0.5326	0.6005
Time (s)	13.43	221.07	75.69	775.31	521.36	481.73	0.37

3.4   Comparison to the State of the Art

Visual Results: The first set of Fig. 2 conveys negligible contribution of PET features in the fused image by GF while NSCT-PCDC, NSST-PAPCNN, LP-SR and NSCT-RPCNN has uneven distribution of structural edges and contrast leading to splotchy visual artifacts. The results from LP-CNN are better than other methods but like other methods it fails to preserve the edges from functional modality i.e. PET. Our method conserve structural information better in both of the image pairs and is robust in preserving the edges (see PET features in red box). The second set of Fig. 2 reveals that the luminance of the proposed fusion results increases with greater λ values leading to brightness artifacts at corner cases of $\lambda = 0$ and $\lambda = 1$. The third set of Fig. 2 shows proposed visualisation results at $\lambda = 0.8$ controlled by parameter Ω where a shift in occlusion of the anatomical information with different values of Ω could be observed.

Objective Assessment: Table 1 summarizes the average scores of 100 test image pairs computed for different fusion methods along with our proposed method at $\lambda = 0.8$ and $\Omega = 0.6$. A method with a higher score performs better than a method with a lower score which is applicable for all the mentioned metrics. The results convey that our method performs better with the quality metric Q_{SSIM} and Q_{VIFF}. This is assertive from the fact that the neural network optimizes the loss function and subsequently improves the structural information in the fused image. Overall, the competitive scores reflects the robustness of our method for human perceptive fusion results.

Computational Efficiency: We evaluated the total runtime of each of the methods for 100 test images in the MATLAB R2018a environment. Table 1 conveys that our fusion and visualisation method achieved best timings since the network parameters are optimized during the training phase and with a fixed batch size it requires just one forward propagation through the fusion network to generate the fused images. Therefore, our fusion network could also be utilized in a real time neurosurgical intervention setup where a continuous feed of live images in a form of time series will generate fused output video stream with very low time delay.

4   Conclusion and Discussion

We presented a novel image fusion and visualisation framework which is highly suitable for diagnosing malignant brain conditions. The end-to-end learning based fusion model utilised the structural similarity loss to construct artifact free fusion images and the gradient based visualisation delineated the anatomical features of MRI from the functional features of PET in the fused image. The extensive evaluation of our approach conveyed significant improvements in human perceptive results compared to past methods. In future, our method could further be extended to include other combination of anatomical and functional imaging modalities by changing the fusion architecture especially the feature extraction layers. Additionally, we plan to immersively visualise the proposed results in an augmented reality based real time preoperative setup, thereby enabling medical experts to make robust clinical decisions.

Acknowledgements. This work was supported by the European Social Fund (project no. 100312752) and the Saxonian Ministry of Science and Art.

References

1. James, A.P., Dasarathy, B.V.: Medical image fusion: a survey of the state of the art. Inf. Fusion **19**, 4–19 (2014)
2. Nensa, F., Beiderwellen, K., Heusch, P., Wetter, A.: Clinical applications of PET/MRI: current status and future perspectives. Diagn. Interv. Radiol. **20**(5), 438–447 (2014)
3. Bhatnagar, G., Wu, Q.M.J., Liu, Z.: Directive contrast based multimodal medical image fusion in NSCT domain. IEEE Trans. Multimedia **15**(5), 1014–1024 (2013)
4. Du, J., Li, W., Xiao, B., Nawaz, Q.: Union Laplacian pyramid with multiple features for medical image fusion. Neurocomputing **194**, 326–339 (2016)
5. Du, J., Li, W., Xiao, B.: Anatomical-functional image fusion by information of interest in local Laplacian filtering domain. IEEE Trans. Image Process. **26**(12), 5855–5866 (2017)
6. Yin, M., Liu, X., Liu, Y., Chen, X.: Medical image fusion with parameter-adaptive pulse coupled neural network in nonsubsampled shearlet transform domain. IEEE Trans. Instrum. Meas. **68**(1), 49–64 (2019)
7. Li, S., Kang, X., Hu, J.: Image fusion with guided filtering. IEEE Trans. Image Process. **22**(7), 2864–2875 (2013)

8. Li, H., He, X., Tao, D., Tang, Y., Wang, R.: Joint medical image fusion, denoising and enhancement via discriminative low-rank sparse dictionaries learning. Pattern Recogn. **79**, 130–146 (2018)

9. Yang, B., Li, S.: Pixel-level image fusion with simultaneous orthogonal matching pursuit. Inf. Fusion **13**(1), 10–19 (2012)

10. Liu, Y., Liu, S., Wang, Z.: A general framework for image fusion based on multi-scale transform and sparse representation. Inf. Fusion **24**, 147–164 (2015)

11. Daneshvar, S., Ghassemian, H.: MRI and PET image fusion by combining IHS and retina-inspired models. Inf. Fusion **11**(2), 114–123 (2010)

12. Hoffmann, N., Weidner, F., Urban, P., et al.: Framework for 2D–3D image fusion of infrared thermography with preoperative MRI. Biomed. Eng./Biomedizinische Technik **62**(6), 599–607 (2017)

13. Liu, Y., Chen, X., Cheng, J., Peng, H.: A medical image fusion method based on convolutional neural networks. In: 20th International Conference on Information Fusion (Fusion), Xi'an, pp. 1–7 (2017). https://doi.org/10.23919/ICIF.2017.8009769

14. Liu, Y., Chen, X., Wang, Z., Wang, Z.J., Ward, R.K., Wang, X.: Deep learning for pixel-level image fusion: recent advances and future prospects. Inf. Fusion **42**, 158–173 (2018)

15. Wang, Z., Bovik, A.C., Sheikh, H.R., Simoncelli, E.P.: Image quality assessment: from error visibility to structural similarity. IEEE Trans. Image Process. **13**(4), 600–612 (2004)

16. Clifford, R.J., et al.: The Alzheimer's Disease neuroimaging initiative (ADNI). J. Magn. Reson. Imaging **27**(4), 685–691 (2008)

17. Johnson, K., Becker, J.: http://www.med.harvard.edu/AANLIB/home.html

18. Wang, Q., Shen, Y.: Performances evaluation of image fusion techniques based on nonlinear correlation measurement. In: 21st IEEE Instrumentation and Measurement Technology Conference (IEEE Cat. No. 04CH37510), vol. 1, pp. 472–475 (2004)

19. Xydeas, C., Petrovic, V.: Objective image fusion performance measure. Electron. Lett. **36**, 308–309 (2000)

20. Haghighat, M.B.A., Aghagolzadeh, A., Seyedarabi, H.: A non-reference image fusion metric based on mutual information of image features. Comput. Electr. Eng. **37**(5), 744–756 (2011)

21. Han, Y., Cai, Y., Cao, Y., Xu, X.: A new image fusion performance metric based on visual information fidelity. Inf. Fusion **14**(2), 127–135 (2013)

22. Das, S., Kundu, M.K.: NSCT-based multimodal medical image fusion using pulse-coupled neural network and modified spatial frequency. Med. Biol. Engi. Comput. **50**(10), 1105–1114 (2012)

Multimodal Brain Tumor Segmentation Using Encoder-Decoder with Hierarchical Separable Convolution

Zhongdao Jia, Zhimin Yuan, and Jialin Peng[✉]

College of Computer Science and Technology,
Huaqiao University, Xiamen 361021, China
2004pjl@163.com

Abstract. To address automatic segmentation of brain tumor from multi-modal MRI volumes, a light-weight encoder-decoder network is presented. Exploring effective way to trade off the range of spatial contexts and computational efficiency is crucial to address challenges of 3D segmentation. To this end, we introduce *hierarchical* separable convolution (HSC), an integration of *view-* and *group-wise* separable convolution, which can simultaneously encode multi-scale context in 3D and reduce memory overhead without sacrificing accuracy. Specifically, typical 3D convolution is replaced with complementary 2D convolutions at multiple scales and thus multiple fields-of-view, which results in a light-weight but stronger model. Moreover, thanks to the decomposed convolutions, we ensemble 3D segmentations with different focal views to further improve segmentation accuracy. Experiments on the BRATS 2017 benchmark showed that our method achieved state-of-the-art performance in Dice, i.e., 0.901, 0.809 and 0.762 for the whole tumor, tumor core and enhancing tumor core, respectively.

Keywords: Brain tumor segmentation · Hierarchical separable convolution · Contextual information

1 Introduction

Glioma, one of the most common types of brain tumors, are typically imaged using multiple MRI sequences, i.e., T1-weighted (T1), contrast-enhanced T1-weighted (T1ce), T2-weighted (T2), and Fluid-Attenuated Inversion Recovery (FLAIR) image. However, manual delineation of brain tumors and their substructures is time-consuming and also subjective due to the ambiguity of precise annotation. Therefore, an automatic brain tumor segmentation method can not only improve the diagnostic efficiency of brain tumors, but also has advantage to provide more reproducible results.

Supported by National Natural Science Foundation of China (11771160) and Fujian Science and Technology Project (2019H0016).

D. Zhu et al. (Eds.): MBIA 2019/MFCA 2019, LNCS 11846, pp. 130–138, 2019.
https://doi.org/10.1007/978-3-030-33226-6_15

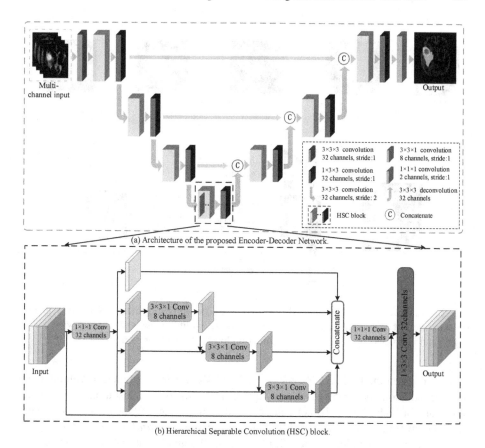

(a) Architecture of the proposed Encoder-Decoder Network.

(b) Hierarchical Separable Convolution (HSC) block.

Fig. 1. Overall architecture of the proposed encoder-decoder with a novel HSC module. (a) indicates the structure of proposed encoder-decoder, and (b) indicates the detailed structure of the HSC module. Images from multiple sequences are concatenated, forming a 4-channel input to the model.

Convolutional Neural Networks (CNNs) have been widely used in multi-modal brain tumor segmentation [2–6, 12]. Especially, the notable U-Net [1] with encoder-decoder structure and 2D convolution has inspired many CNN models for brain tumorsegmentation. For example, Marcinkiewicz *et al.* [11] proposed a modified U-Net models with three encoders, which take three different modalities of images as inputs, respectively, and are fused before inputting to the decoder. However, the 2D U-Net and their variants [1, 11] are only able to process 3D medical images slice by slice, ignoring inter-slice information. To cope with this issue, researches [4, 8] have tried to fuse segmentations on multiple 2D views of a 3D volume.

Contextual cues are crucial for the success of accurate segmentation. To capture 3D spatial context information, volumetric CNN including 3D variants of U-Net, such as V-Net [9], were also investigated. For instance, Casamitjana *et al.* [10] used two cascades V-Net [9] network to sequentially locate brain tumor and segment its sub-regions.

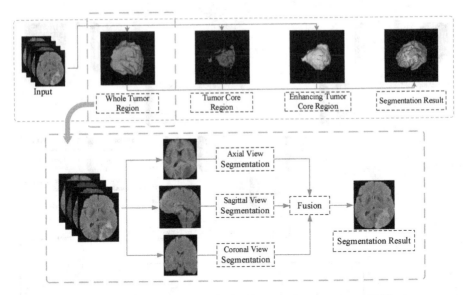

Fig. 2. Framework of the proposed method. We use three separate CNNs to segment substructures of the brain tumor in the axial view, sagittal view and coronal view. The segmentation process of whole tumor region is highlighted for illustration.

However, given the limited GPU memory, 3D CNNs for large amount of volume data are computationally prohibitive due to the huge memory consumption. To take advantage of both 3D and 2D convolution, Qiu et al. [15] and Wang et al. [3] replaced the 3D convolution (such as $3 \times 3 \times 3$) with *depth-wise separable convolution*, i.e., a 2D ($3 \times 3 \times 1$) convolution and a 1D ($1 \times 1 \times 3$) convolution, which can obviously reduce computational cost and memory demand. However, the 3D spatial information captured by the 1D convolution is limited.

In this paper, we introduce a light-weight encoder-decoder network to address challenges in brain tumor segmentation. To encode multi-scale 3D spatial contexts with low computation cost, *hierarchical separable convolution* (HSC) is introduced. Specifically, (a) to improve the perception of spatial contextual cues, we introduce *view-wise separable convolution* (VSC), that is decomposing a standard 3D convolution into two complementary types of 2D convolutions, which can obviously reduce computation complexity; (b) inspired by Res2Net [2] and spatial pyramid pooling [16], we encode cues from multiple fields-of-view by introducing *group-wise separable convolution* (GSC), that is applying parallel convolutions of 2D on subgroups of feature channels with hierarchical connections. In this way, our 3D segmentation model can have focal view on a 3D volume, which is desirable for both isotropic and anisotropic medical volumes. Thus, we further ensemble 3D segmentations focusing on different 2D views, which have widely used for 2D method to improve the segmentation accuracy.

2   Method

The proposed network consists of an encoder and a decoder with a novel HSC block, which is shown in Fig. 1. The backbone of our network is a lightweight variant of U-Net with reduced number of convolution channels (only 32 channels) and down-sampling stages (3 down-sampling stages). Volume images from multiple modalities are concatenated, forming a 4-channel input to the model. For the multi-label brain tumor segmentation task, we decompose it into three binary segmentation subtasks to mitigate interference between brain tissues, which is shown in Fig. 2. Ensemble of 3D segmentations using different decompositions of 3D convolution is further employed.

2.1   Hierarchical Separable Convolution (HSC) Block

Compared with 2D convolution, 3D convolutional kernel allows the neural network to extract 3D context information, but brings more memory burden. Although CNNs with 2D slices or 2.5D slices as input can reduce the memory consumption, they are limited to capture the 3D spatial context information. In order to tackle these issues, we propose *an integration of view-wise and group-wise separable convolutions* to incorporate *multi-scale 3D contextual information* with *focal view*.

View-wise Separable Convolution (VSC). For the sake of using 3D context information more effectively while reducing the number of parameters, we spatially decompose a 3D convolution kernel of $3 \times 3 \times 3$ into two complementary 2D convolutions, i.e., a $3 \times 3 \times 1$ convolution and a $1 \times 3 \times 3$ convolution, which work on different 2D views of a 3D volume. As the kernel decomposition is asymmetrical in spatial view, the network with VSC is flexible to have focus on specific views. Specifically, the first 2D convolution is used to capture inner-slice features on one view and the second 2D convolution is to fuse spatial consistency and contexts on another view. For our network, we use VSC that consists of four consecutive layers of three $3 \times 3 \times 1$ convolutions and one $1 \times 3 \times 3$ convolutions, which further lays different emphasis on different spatial views.

Group-wise Separable Convolution (GSC). The capture of multi-scale information is critical to the representation strength of the neural network model and the final segmentation accuracy. Inspired by Res2Net [2] and depth-wise separable convolution, we apply *group-wise separable 2D convolutions* ($3 \times 3 \times 1$) on subgroups of feature channels with hierarchical connections, as shown in Fig. 1(b). After $1 \times 1 \times 1$ convolution, HSC block groups the feature channels into s subgroups. Then, $3 \times 3 \times 1$ convolution is hierarchically performed on $s - 1$ of the s groups with fusion connections; shortcut connections on the remaining subgroup of feature is to reformulate HSC as learning residual function. After concatenating of all the output feature maps, a $1 \times 3 \times 3$ convolution is performed to encode cues on an alternative view. By integration of group-wise separable convolutions, hierarchical connections and view-wise separable convolutions, (1) semantic features from multiple fields-of-view can be extracted, and multi-scale information can be exploited; (2) the ability of perception of 3D spatial contextual cues with focal views can be improved than that of 2D methods;

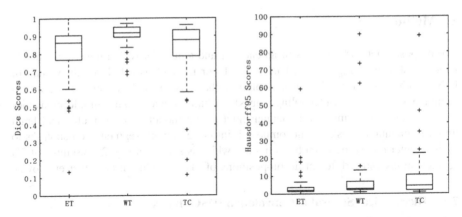

Fig. 3. Dispersion of Dice Scores and Hausdorff95 Scores for segmentation results on the BRATS 2017 validation dataset. ET, WT, TC denote enhancing tumor core, whole tumor and tumor core, respectively.

(3) the model is asymmetrical in view and thus facilitates to use ensemble methods to obtain better and robust predictive performance.

2.2   Ensemble of 3D Segmentations with Focal Views

Since the model is asymmetrical in view, we propose to ensemble several 3D segmentations with different 2D focal views to obtain better predictive performance. Specifically, we permute axes of a 3D volume and independently perform 3 times of 3D segmentation with inherent focus on axial view, sagittal view and coronal view, respectively. During the test stage, the softmax outputs from the three views are averaged as the final segmentation result.

3   Experiments and Results

3.1   Dataset and Implementation Details

The proposed model was evaluated on the data from the 2017 MICCAI BRATS Challenge[1]. The BRATS 2017 training dataset consists of 285 cases and the validation set contains 46 cases. The three measure regions are enhancing tumor core (ET), whole tumor (WT), and tumor core (TC). The results of segmentation are reported from online evaluation. All the data were skull-stripped and re-sampled to 1 mm^3 resolution. Thereafter, each sequence of the training dataset was normalized by the mean value and standard deviation to cope with the inconsistency of image gray values.

---

[1] http://www.med.upenn.edu/sbia/brats2017.html.

The proposed network was implemented in Python 2.7, using the 1.4.0 version Tensorflow framework[2] and NiftyNet platform[3]. All the experiments were completed on a standard workstation equipped with 120 GB of memory, an INTEL XEON E5-2630V3 working at 2.4 GHz, and a Nvidia Tesla K40 GPU with 12 GB of video memory. The

Table 1. Result of ablation study in terms of Dice score on the BRATS 2017 validation dataset. ET, WT, TC denote enhancing tumor core, whole tumor and tumor core, respectively. The number of parameters is in millions.

Methods	ET	WT	TC	Params
V-Net	0.631	0.869	0.719	59.74M
2D U-Net	0.530	0.793	0.620	31.03M
Our Model (Backbone)	0.620	0.828	0.609	0.46M
Our Model without GSC	0.730	0.884	0.786	1.38M
Our Model without Ensemble	0.674	0.855	0.633	0.26M
Our Model using ($3 \times 3 \times 1$ and $1 \times 1 \times 3$)	0.749	0.891	0.788	0.66M
Our Model using ($3 \times 3 \times 1$ and $1 \times 3 \times 3$)	**0.762**	**0.901**	**0.809**	0.78M

Adaptive Moment Estimation [17] was used with an initial learning rate 0.001 to optimize the network, with a weight decay of $1e-07$. The maximum number of iterations was 30k and the Dice coefficient was used as the cost function to deal with the problem of label imbalance.

3.2   Results and Ablation Study

Following BRATS 2017 Challenge, the Dice scores and Hausdorff95 Scores were used to assess the accuracy of segmentation results. On the BRATS 2017 validation dataset, our method achieved average Dice scores of 0.762, 0.901, 0.809 for enhancing tumor core, whole tumor, and tumor core, respectively. Boxplots with the distributional characteristics of our segmentation scores are shown in Fig. 3.

To evaluate the effectiveness of our model, (1) we compared the performance of the proposed method with two widely used models, i.e., 2D U-Net that performs segmentation with slice-by-slice strategy, and V-Net that performs 3D segmentation using 3D convolutions; (2) we tested the proposed model using different building blocks and their combinations. Note that in default, our model uses the combination of HSC (VSC +GSC) and the Ensemble strategy. The backbone of our model is the one using only VSC but without GSC and Ensemble.

As shown in Table 1, in comparison with 2D U-Net, V-Net achieved higher Dice scores in all segmentation tasks, which confirmed the effectiveness of using 3D spatial contextual cues. Although the backbone of our method is inferior to V-Net, our full

---

[2] http://www.tensorflow.org.

[3] http://niftynet.io.

model gained significant improvement over 2D U-Net and V-Net. More specifically, the backbone of our method with ensemble strategy (i.e., Our Model without GSC) can obviously performed better than V-Net, which was further improved by using GSC. To validate the effectiveness of VSC, we compared it with depth-wise separable convolution, that is replacing the 2D convolution of $1 \times 3 \times 3$ with 1D convolution of $1 \times 1 \times 3$, which showed degenerated performance (see the second to last row of Table 1). This indicates that the 3D spatial contextual information captured by 1D $1 \times 1 \times 3$ convolution is limited, and the use of 2D convolution of $1 \times 3 \times 3$ can take advantage of contextual information in larger range to improve the segmentation result.

Table 2. Comparisons (in Dice score) with recent methods on the BRATS 2017 validation dataset. ET, WT, TC denote enhancing tumor core, whole tumor and tumor core, respectively.

Methods	ET	WT	TC
Li [4]	0.750	0.880	0.710
Isensee [7]	0.732	0.896	0.797
Casamitjana [10]	0.714	0.877	0.637
Pereira [12]	0.719	0.884	0.771
Kamnitsas [13]	0.738	**0.901**	0.797
Islam [14]	0.701	0.879	0.781
Our method	**0.762**	**0.901**	**0.809**

Meanwhile, we compared the parameters of our model and variants with baseline models, i.e., V-Net and 2D U-Net. Since 2D U-Net and V-Net both have a large number of feature channels with symmetric structure, and V-Net uses a large number of 3D convolution kernels, this causes 2D U-Net and V-Net to have significantly more parameters than our model. As shown in the last column of Table 1, despite using considerably fewer parameters than 2D U-Net (0.78M vs. 31.03M) and V-Net (0.78M vs. 59.74M), our model performed better in the result of segmentation for enhancing tumor core, whole tumor and tumor core, respectively.

3.3   Comparison with Other Methods

We compared the performance of our method with other recent methods on the BRATS 2017 validation dataset, which is summarized in Table 2. To be specific, we compared our method with (1) the method of Li et al. [4], which fused 2D segmentations from three views of 3D volumes; (2) the method of Isensee et al. [7], which used a 3D version of U-Net and integrated different levels of segmentation layers in the localization path and the final output; (3) the method of Casamitjana et al. [10], which used a cascade of two V-Net networks, where the first network is to locate the brain tumor area and the second network is to finely segment the tumor tissue; (4) the method of Pereira et al. [12], which cascaded two CNN networks with the function similar to [10], and used recombination and recalibration Seg-SE block in the second network; (5) the method of Kamnitsas et al. [13], which integrated multiple 3D CNN models with different architectures and averaged the segmentation predictions from each model to obtain the final result; (6) the method of Islam *et al.* [14], which used a class-balanced PixelNet by randomly sampling a small number of pixels instead of the whole image. As shown in Table 2, we obtained superior segmentation accuracy for all the three segmentation tasks.

4 Conclusion

In this paper, we proposed an efficient Convolution Neural Networks model for the challenging multi-modal brain tumor segmentation. Specifically, we proposed a hierarchical separable convolution block consist of both view-wise and group-wise separable convolutions to capture multi-scale 3D context information while reducing memory consumption. Besides, thanks to the separated convolutions, we can ensemble three 3D segmentations network with focal views to improve the segmentation accuracy and the robustness of the model. The experimental results showed that we achieved state-of-the-art result on the BRATS 2017 validation dataset without complicated post-processing techniques. In future work, we will investigate how to incorporate spatial regularization [18] and adaptively feeding hard or easy image sample [19] to enhance the label prediction.

References

1. Ronneberger, O., Fischer, P., Brox, T.: U-Net: convolutional networks for biomedical image segmentation. In: Navab, N., Hornegger, J., Wells, W.M., Frangi, A.F. (eds.) MICCAI 2015. LNCS, vol. 9351, pp. 234–241. Springer, Cham (2015). https://doi.org/10.1007/978-3-319-24574-4_28
2. Gao, S., Cheng, M., Zhao, K., et al.: Res2Net: a new multi-scale backbone architecture. In: 32th CVPR, Long Beach, CA (2019)
3. Wang, G., Li, W., Ourselin, S., Vercauteren, T.: Automatic brain tumor segmentation using cascaded anisotropic convolutional neural networks. In: Crimi, A., Bakas, S., Kuijf, H., Menze, B., Reyes, M. (eds.) BrainLes 2017. LNCS, vol. 10670, pp. 178–190. Springer, Cham (2018). https://doi.org/10.1007/978-3-319-75238-9_16
4. Li, Y., Shen, L.: Deep learning based multimodal brain tumor diagnosis. In: Crimi, A., Bakas, S., Kuijf, H., Menze, B., Reyes, M. (eds.) BrainLes 2017. LNCS, vol. 10670, pp. 149–158. Springer, Cham (2018). https://doi.org/10.1007/978-3-319-75238-9_13
5. Havaei, M., Davy, A., Warde-Farley, D., et al.: Brain tumor segmentation with deep neural networks. Med. Image Anal. **35**, 18–31 (2017)
6. Kamnitsas, K., Ledig, C., Newcombe, V.F., et al.: Efficient multi-scale 3D CNN with fully connected CRF for accurate brain lesion segmentation. Med. Image Anal. **36**, 61–78 (2017)
7. Isensee, F., Kickingereder, P., Wick, W., Bendszus, M., Maier-Hein, K.H.: Brain tumor segmentation and radiomics survival prediction: contribution to the BRATS 2017 challenge. In: Crimi, A., Bakas, S., Kuijf, H., Menze, B., Reyes, M. (eds.) BrainLes 2017. LNCS, vol. 10670, pp. 287–297. Springer, Cham (2018). https://doi.org/10.1007/978-3-319-75238-9_25
8. Zhao, X., Wu, Y., Song, G., et al.: A deep learning model integrating FCNNs and CRFs for brain tumor segmentation. Med. Image Anal. **43**, 98–111 (2018)

9. Milletari, F., Navab, N., Ahmadi, S.A.: V-Net: fully convolutional neural networks for volumetric medical image segmentation. In: 4th International Conference on 3D Vision, Stanford, CA, pp. 565–571. IEEE (2016)

10. Casamitjana, A., Català, M., Sánchez, I., Combalia, M., Vilaplana, V.: Cascaded V-Net using ROI masks for brain tumor segmentation. In: Crimi, A., Bakas, S., Kuijf, H., Menze, B., Reyes, M. (eds.) BrainLes 2017. LNCS, vol. 10670, pp. 381–391. Springer, Cham (2018). https://doi.org/10.1007/978-3-319-75238-9_33

11. Marcinkiewicz, M., Nalepa, J., Lorenzo, P.R., Dudzik, W., Mrukwa, G.: Segmenting brain tumors from MRI using cascaded multi-modal U-Nets. In: Crimi, A., Bakas, S., Kuijf, H., Keyvan, F., Reyes, M., van Walsum, T. (eds.) BrainLes 2018. LNCS, vol. 11384, pp. 13–24. Springer, Cham (2019). https://doi.org/10.1007/978-3-030-11726-9_2

12. Pereira, S., Alves, V., Silva, C.A.: Adaptive feature recombination and recalibration for semantic segmentation: application to brain tumor segmentation in MRI. In: Frangi, A.F., Schnabel, J.A., Davatzikos, C., Alberola-López, C., Fichtinger, G. (eds.) MICCAI 2018. LNCS, vol. 11072, pp. 706–714. Springer, Cham (2018). https://doi.org/10.1007/978-3-030-00931-1_81

13. Kamnitsas, K., et al.: Ensembles of multiple models and architectures for robust brain tumour segmentation. In: Crimi, A., Bakas, S., Kuijf, H., Menze, B., Reyes, M. (eds.) BrainLes 2017. LNCS, vol. 10670, pp. 450–462. Springer, Cham (2018). https://doi.org/10.1007/978-3-319-75238-9_38

14. Islam, M., Ren, H.: Class balanced PixelNet for neurological image segmentation. In: 6th ICBCB, Chengdu, China, pp. 83–87. ACM (2018)

15. Qiu, Z., Yao, T., Mei, T.: Learning spatio-temporal representation with pseudo-3D residual networks. In: 16th ICCV, Venice, Italy, pp. 5533–5541. IEEE (2017)

16. He, K., Zhang, X., Ren, S., et al.: Spatial pyramid pooling in deep convolutional networks for visual recognition. IEEE Trans. Pattern Anal. Mach. Intell. **37**(9), 1904–1916 (2015)

17. Kingma, D. P., Ba, J.: Adam: a method for stochastic optimization. arXiv preprint arXiv: 1412.6980 (2014)

18. Hu, P., Wu, F., Peng, J., et al.: Automatic 3D liver segmentation based on deep learning and globally optimized surface evolution. Phys. Med. Biol. **61**(24), 8676 (2016)

19. Zhou, H. Y., Gao, B. B., Wu, J.: Adaptive feeding: Achieving fast and accurate detections by adaptively combining object detectors. In: 16th ICCV, Venice, Italy, pp. 3505–3513. IEEE (2017)

Prioritizing Amyloid Imaging Biomarkers in Alzheimer's Disease via Learning to Rank

Bo Peng[1], Zhiyun Ren[1], Xiaohui Yao[2], Kefei Liu[2], Andrew J. Saykin[3], Li Shen[2(✉)], Xia Ning[1(✉)], and for the ADNI

[1] The Ohio State University, Columbus, OH 43210, USA
peng.707@buckeyemail.osu.edu, {ren.685,ning.104}@osu.edu
[2] University of Pennsylvania, Philadelphia, PA 19104, USA
{xiaohui.yao,kefei.liu,li.shen}@pennmedicine.upenn.edu
[3] Indiana University School of Medicine, Indianapolis, IN 46202, USA
asaykin@iupui.edu

Abstract. We propose an innovative machine learning paradigm enabling precision medicine for AD biomarker discovery. The paradigm tailors the imaging biomarker discovery process to individual characteristics of a given patient. We implement this paradigm using a newly developed learning-to-rank method `PLTR`. The `PLTR` model seamlessly integrates two objectives for joint optimization: pushing up relevant biomarkers and ranking among relevant biomarkers. The empirical study of `PLTR` conducted on the ADNI data yields promising results to identify and prioritize individual-specific amyloid imaging biomarkers based on the individual's structural MRI data. The resulting top ranked imaging biomarker has the potential to aid personalized diagnosis and disease subtyping.

Keywords: Amyloid PET · Structural MRI · Imaging biomarker prioritization · Learning to rank · Alzheimer's disease

1 Introduction

Alzheimer's disease (AD) is a national priority, with 5.5 million Americans affected at an annual cost of $259 billion in 2017 and no available cure [1]. Brain characteristics related to AD progression may be captured by multimodal magnetic resonance imaging (MRI) and positron emission tomography (PET) scans. Thus, there is a large body of neuroimaging studies in AD, aiming to develop

Data used in preparation of this article were obtained from the Alzheimer's Disease Neuroimaging Initiative (ADNI) database (ad-ni.loni.usc.edu). As such, the investigators within the ADNI contributed to the design and implementation of ADNI and/or provided data but did not participate in analysis or writing of this report. A complete listing of ADNI investigators can be found at: https://adni.loni.usc.edu/wp-content/uploads/how_to_apply/ADNI_Acknowledgement_List.pdf.

© Springer Nature Switzerland AG 2019
D. Zhu et al. (Eds.): MBIA 2019/MFCA 2019, LNCS 11846, pp. 139–148, 2019.
https://doi.org/10.1007/978-3-030-33226-6_16

image-based predictive machine learning models for early detection of AD as well as identification of relevant imaging biomarkers (e.g., [8]). These models are typically designed to accomplish learning tasks such as regression, classification and/or survival analysis. As a result, the identified imaging biomarkers are at the population level and not specific to an individual subject.

In this work, we propose a novel learning paradigm that embraces the concept of precision medicine and tailors the imaging biomarker discovery process to the individual characteristics of a given patient. Specifically, we perform an innovative application of a newly developed learning-to-rank method, denoted as PLTR [5], to the structural MRI and amyloid PET data of the Alzheimer's Disease Neuroimaging Initiative (ADNI) cohort [9]. Using structural MRI as the individual characteristics, our goal is to not only identify individual-specific amyloid imaging biomarkers but also prioritize them according to AD-specific abnormality. Compared with traditional biomarker studies at the population level, the uniqueness of our study is twofold: (1) the identified biomarkers are tailored to each individual patient; and (2) the identified biomarkers are prioritized based on the individual's characteristics, which has the potential to enable personalized diagnosis and disease subtyping.

2 Materials and Data Processing

To demonstrate the effectiveness of the learning-to-rank method for personalized prioritization of the amyloid imaging biomarkers, we applied it to the ADNI cohort [9]. The ADNI was launched in 2003 as a public-private partnership, led by Principal Investigator Michael W. Weiner, MD. The primary goal of ADNI has been to test whether serial MRI, PET, other biological markers, and clinical and neuropsychological assessment can be combined to measure the progression of mild cognitive impairment (MCI, a prodromal stage of AD) and early AD. For up-to-date information, see www.adni-info.org.

Data used in the preparation of this article were obtained from the 2017 ADNI TADPOLE grand challenge (tadpole.grand-challenge.org/), and was downloaded from the ADNI website (adni.loni.usc.edu). The TADPOLE data used in this study consists of structural MRI and AV45-PET (amyloid) imaging data as well as diagnostic information. Both MRI and amyloid imaging data have been pre-processed with standard ADNI pipelines as described previously in [7].

In this study, we included all the regional MRI measures with field name containing "UCSFFSX" in the TADPOLE D1 and D2 data sets. Specifically, these are FreeSurfer regional volume and cortical thickness measures processed by the ADNI UCSF team. We also included all the regional amyloid measures with field name containing "UCBERKELEYAV45" in the TADPOLE D1 and D2 data sets. These are cortical and subcortical amyloid deposition measures processed by the ADNI UC Berkeley team.

Originally, there are totally 12,741 participant visit records with 103 amyloid features, 125 FreeSurfer features and diagnostic information corresponding to each visit. To convert this longitudinal data set into a cross-sectional one as well as handle the missing data issue, we use the following procedure to generate a clean set of cross-sectional data: (1) remove visit records that have more than 50% of null values across 103 amyloid features, with 10,623 records removed; (2) extract the earliest AV45-PET visit for each participant, with 1,091 records kept; (3) remove visit records that have more than 50% of null values across 125 FreeSurfer features, with 58 records removed; (4) remove features that have more than 50% of null values across records, with 16 FreeSurfer features removed; (5) remove 3 participants with no diagnostic information. Finally, 1,030 participants with 103 amyloid and 109 FreeSurfer measures are studied, including 351 health control (HC), 501 MCI and 178 AD participants. We treat both MCI and AD subjects as patients, and so have a total of 679 cases and 351 controls.

3   Methods

We use the joint push and learning-to-rank method as developed in He *et al.* [5], denoted as PLTR, for personalized patient feature prioritization. Our goal is to prioritize amyloid features for each patient that are most relevant to his/her disease diagnosis using patients' existing information. The underlying hypothesis is that patients with similar FreeSurfer feature profiles would have similar ranking structures among their amyloid features. In the context of AD feature prioritization, PLTR learns and uses latent vectors of patients and amyloid features to score each amyloid feature for each patient, and ranks the features based on their scores; patients with similar FreeSurfer feature profiles will have similar latent vectors. During the learning process, PLTR explicitly pushes the most relevant amyloid features on top of the less relevant ones for each patient, and therefrom optimizes the latent patient and amyloid feature vectors so they will reproduce the pushed ranking structures.

3.1   Overview of PLTR

In PLTR, the ranking of features in terms of their relatedness to MCI/AD in a patient is determined by their latent scores on the patient. For a feature f_i and a patient $\mathcal{P}_p$, f_i's latent score on $\mathcal{P}_p$, denoted as $s_p(f_i)$, is calculated as the dot product of f_i's latent vector $\mathbf{v}_i \in \mathbb{R}^{l \times 1}$ and $\mathcal{P}_p$'s latent vector $\mathbf{u}_p \in \mathbb{R}^{l \times 1}$, where l is the latent dimension, as follows,

$$s_p(f_i) = \mathbf{u}_p^{\mathsf{T}} \mathbf{v}_i, \tag{1}$$

where the latent vectors $\mathbf{u}_p$ and $\mathbf{v}_i$ will be learned. All the features are then sorted based on their scores on $\mathcal{P}_p$, with the most relevant features having the highest scores and ranked higher than irrelevant features.

Overall, PLTR seeks the patient latent vectors and feature latent vectors that will be used in feature scoring function s (Eq. (1)) such that for each patient, the relevant features will be ranked on top and in right orders using the latent vectors. In PLTR, such latent vectors are learned by solving the following optimization problem:

$$\min_{U,V} \mathcal{L}_s = (1-\alpha)P_s^{\uparrow} + \alpha O_s^+ + \frac{\beta}{2}R_{uv} + \frac{\gamma}{2}R_{\text{csim}}, \tag{2}$$

where $\mathcal{L}_s$ is the overall loss function; $P_s^{\uparrow}$ measures the number of irrelevant features that are ranked on top of relevant features; O_s^+ measures the ranking among relevant features. R_{uv} is a regularizer on U and V to prevent overfitting, defined as

$$R_{uv} = \frac{1}{m}\|U\|_F^2 + \frac{1}{n}\|V\|_F^2, \tag{3}$$

where m and n are the number of patients and the number of features, respectively; $\|X\|_F$ is the Frobenius norm of matrix X. R_{csim} is a regularizer on patients to constrain patient latent vectors, defined as

$$R_{\text{csim}} = \frac{1}{m^2}\sum_{p=1}^{m}\sum_{q=1}^{m} w_{pq}\|\mathbf{u}_p - \mathbf{u}_q\|_2^2, \tag{4}$$

where w_{pq} is the similarity between $\mathcal{P}_p$ and $\mathcal{P}_q$ that is calculated using FreeSurfer features of the patients. Details of these terms can be found in He et al. [5].

3.2 Patient Similarities from FreeSurfer Features

We consider 109 FreeSurfer features and represent each patient as a FreeSurfer feature vector, denoted as $\mathbf{r}_p = [r_{p1}, r_{p2}, \cdots, r_{pn_r}]$, where r_{pi} ($i = 1, \cdots, n_r$) is a FreeSurfer feature for patient p. Thus, for all the patients, we construct a FreeSurfer feature matrix $R_{\text{AD}} = [\mathbf{r}_1^+; \mathbf{r}_2^+; \cdots; \mathbf{r}_{m^+}^+] \in \mathbb{R}^{m^+ \times n_r}$ and for all the health control subjects (HCs), a FreeSurfer feature matrix $R_{\text{HC}} = [\mathbf{r}_1^-; \mathbf{r}_2^-; \cdots; \mathbf{r}_{m^-}^-] \in \mathbb{R}^{m^- \times n_r}$, where m^+ and m^- are the numbers of AD/MCI patients and HCs, respectively, and n_r is the number of FreeSurfer features. We scale R_{AD} values into the unit interval by dividing each column of R_{AD} (i.e., each FreeSurfer feature) using its maximum value. The normalized R_{AD} matrix is denoted as $\bar{R}_{\text{AD}}$, and the similarities between patients are calculated over $\bar{R}_{\text{AD}}$ using the radial basis function (RBF) kernel:

$$w_{pq} = \exp(-\frac{\|\bar{R}_{\text{AD}}(p,:) - \bar{R}_{\text{AD}}(q,:)\|^2}{2\sigma^2}), \tag{5}$$

where w_{pq} is the patient similarity used in Eq. (4). This patient similarity measurement is denoted as simU.

3.3 Patient Amyloid Features in Ground Truth

Similarly, each patient is also represented by an amyloid feature vector, denoted as $\mathbf{c}_p = [c_{p1}, c_{p2}, \cdots, c_{pn_c}]$, where c_{pi} ($i = 1, \cdots, n_c$) is an amyloid feature for patient p. Thus, we construct an amyloid feature matrix $C_{\text{AD}} = [\mathbf{c}_1^+; \mathbf{c}_2^+; \cdots, \mathbf{c}_{m^+}^+]$ for AD/MCI patients, and an amyloid feature matrix

$C_{\mathrm{HC}} = [\mathbf{c}_1^-; \mathbf{c}_2^-; \cdots, \mathbf{c}_{m-}^-]$ for HC subjects. We normalize C_{AD} by dividing each column of C_{AD} (i.e., each amyloid feature) by the mean value of the corresponding column in C_{HC}. Thus, the normalization results in C_{AD} measure the extent to which an amyloid feature in patients deviates from that in HCs. The normalized matrix, denoted as $\bar{C}_{\mathrm{AD}}$, is used as the ground truth of amyloid feature ranking. That is, the optimization problem (2) tries to learn the latent vectors that reconstruct the ordering structures in $\bar{C}_{\mathrm{AD}}$, and prioritize amyloid features that are most relevant to patients. The reason why we use FreeSurfer features to quantitatively measure patients and prioritize amyloid features correspondingly is that MRI imaging is non-invasive and relatively low-cost as compared to PET imaging.

4 Experiments

4.1 Experimental Protocol

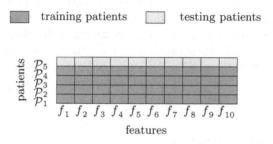

Fig. 1. Data split

We split patients into training set and testing set, such that a certain patient and all his/her features will be either in the training set or in the testing set. We train the PLTR model using training patients and test its performance on the testing patients. This corresponds to the use scenario in which we want to identify the most potentially useful AD biomarkers for new patients, based on the existing information of the patients, when such biomarkers have not been tested on the new patients. Figure 1 demonstrates the data split process.

We define average hit at k, denoted as AH@k, to evaluate the ranking performance. AH@k is defined as follows:

$$\mathrm{AH}@k(\tau, \tilde{\tau}) = \sum_{i=1}^{k} \mathbb{I}(\tilde{\tau}_i \in \tau), \tag{6}$$

where τ is the ground-truth ranking list, $\tilde{\tau}$ is the predicted ranking list, and $\tilde{\tau}_i$ is the i-th ranked item in $\tilde{\tau}$. That is, AH@k calculates the number of items among top k in the predicted lists that are also in the ground truth (i.e., hits). Higher AH@k values indicate better prioritization performance.

We define a second evaluation metric weighted average hit at k, denoted as WAH@k as follows:

$$\text{WAH@}k(\tau, \tilde{\tau}) = \sum_{j=1}^{k} \sum_{i=1}^{j} \mathbb{I}(\tilde{\tau}_i \in \tau)/j, \tag{7}$$

that is, WAH@k is a weighted version of AH@k that calculates the average hit up to top k. Higher WAH@k indicate more hits and those hits are ranked on top in the ranking list. By default, the ground-truth τ has k items (i.e., the top-k items among all the sorted items) in Eqs. (6) and (7).

4.2   Baseline Methods

We compare PLTR with another two methods: the Bayesian Multi-Task Multi-Kernel Learning (BMTMKL) method [2] and the Kernelized Rank Learning (KRL) method [4]. BMTMKL uses kernels over FreeSurfer features to predict amyloid feature values. KRL uses kernel regression with a ranking loss to predict amyloid feature values. These two methods represent two strong baseline methods for the biomarker feature prioritization problem. We use the patient similarity matrix 5 as the kernels for BMTMKL and KRL. We conducted parameter grid search to identify the best parameters for each model, and present the best performance of the models.

5   Experimental Results

5.1   Overall Performance

We first hold out 35 and 163 patients as testing patients, respectively. These testing patients are determined such that they have more than 10 similar patients in the training set, and the corresponding patient similarities are higher than 0.75 and 0.65, respectively. Patient latent vectors and feature latent vectors are learned on the training patients. The feature scores for the testing patients are calculated as the weighted sum of the predicted feature scores from their top-10 most similar training patients, where the weights are the corresponding patient similarities. The patient similarities are calculated using simU (Eq. (5), $\sigma = 1$). The patient amyloid features are normalized as described in Sect. 3.3. Please note that we only use patients (i.e., MCI and AD subjects) for model training and testing, and only use controls (i.e., HC subjects) to set the standard for patient data normalization, as feature prioritization for healthy controls has limited clinical interests.

Table 1 presents the best performance of PLTR in terms of AH@5 for each latent dimension. When 35 patients are hold out for testing, the best AH@5 is 1.886 when latent dimension $d = 20$, and the corresponding WAH@5 is 1.632.

Table 1. Overall performance of PLTR (simU, $\sigma = 1$)

n	Method	Parameters					AH@5	WAH@5	AH@10	WAH@10
		α	β	γ	d	λ				
35	PLTR	0.3	0.5	1.0	10	–	1.857	1.545	**3.371**	2.249
		0.3	0.5	1.0	20	–	**1.886**	**1.632**	3.286	1.987
		0.3	0.5	1.0	50	–	1.857	1.560	3.314	2.007
	BMTMKL	–	–	–	–	–	0.971	0.916	2.171	**2.573**
	KRL	–	–	–	–	3.0	0.429	0.426	1.086	1.245
163	PLTR	0.5	1.0	1.0	10	–	1.343	0.930	3.080	**2.497**
		0.5	1.0	1.0	20	–	**1.429**	**1.067**	3.074	2.402
		0.5	1.0	1.0	50	–	**1.429**	1.012	**3.110**	2.437
	BMTMKL	–	–	–	–	–	0.282	0.288	0.957	0.929
	KRL	–	–	–	–	0.1	0.356	0.389	1.025	1.054

The column "n" corresponds to the number of hold-out testing patients. Best performance under each evaluation metric is in **bold**.

This performance is significantly better than those of the baseline methods. Note that we use predicted feature scores to prioritize features for the testing patients. Table 1 also shows that PLTR significantly outperforms the baseline methods in terms of AH@10. PLTR is slightly worse than BMTMKL on WAH@10 (2.249 vs 2.573). This indicates that among top 10 drugs in the ranking list, PLTR is able to rank more relevant features on top than BMTMKL, although the positions of those hits are not as high as BMTMKL. When 163 patients are hold out for testing, the best performance of PLTR (i.e., AH@5 1.429 when $d = 20$) is still better than those of the baseline methods. This indicates that PLTR is able to capture the signals that lead to accurate feature rankings among training data, potentially correct the noise in the data and use the signals to prioritize features for new patients.

Table 1 also shows that the best performance for the 35 testing patients is better than that for the 163 testing patients (e.g., AH@5 $= 1.886$ for 35 testing patients vs AH@5 $= 1.429$ for 163 testing patients). This indicates that when there are more similar patients for model training, PLTR is able to achieve better performance. However, when there are more testing patients and thus the similarities between training and testing patients are smaller, PLTR achieves more significant improvement compared to the baseline methods (e.g., $1.429/0.356 = 4.01$ for 163 testing patients vs $1.886/0.971 = 1.94$ for 35 patients). This indicates that when patient similarities are smaller, PLTR is able to achieve much better improvement over the baseline methods.

Feature Prioritization on Population Level. We also investigate which features are frequently prioritized for all the testing patients. We sort all the top-5 ranked features from all the testing patients, weighted by their aggregated ranking positions among the patients, so that features that are frequently ranked high among many patients will be sorted on top. Table 2 lists the top 10 frequently prioritized features by PLTR among the 163 testing patients. Among these 10 features, 8 of them are among the top 10 identified from the ground truth. Similarly, for the 35 testing patients, 7 of the top 10 most frequently prioritized features are among the top 10 identified from the ground truth. This indicates the capability of PLTR to find common AD biomarkers on a population level.

Table 2. Top-10 frequent features by PLTR (simU, $\sigma = 1$)

Rank	Features	p-value	GT
1	ctx-lh-frontal pole	8.67e−20	Y
2	ctx-rh-frontal pole	5.68e−20	Y
3	right-lateral ventricle	4.34e−04	Y
4	ctx-rh-medial orbitofrontal	4.79e−23	Y
5	left-lateral ventricle	1.09e−04	Y
6	ctx-lh-rostral middle frontal	5.12e−21	Y
7	right-choroid plexus	4.41e−05	N
8	ctx-rh-rostral middle frontal	3.68e−20	N
9	ctx-lh-precuneus	3.19e−19	Y
10	non-wm-hypointensities	8.75e−01	Y

The p-value measures whether the feature means are statistically different between controls and patients. Column "GT" indicates if the feature is in ground truth (Y) or not (N). These features are frequently prioritized by PLTR when 163 patients are hold out for testing.

Most of the above top ranked amyloid features are related to AD or its biomarkers. For example, frontal lobe, the region where frontal pole, rostral middle frontal gyrus and medial orbitofrontal cortex are located, shows significantly higher amyloid deposition in AD/MCI patients than in controls [3]. Furthermore, Huang et al. [6] report that both frontal lobe and precuneus show significantly higher amyloid deposition in both MCI and AD compared to HC. Additionally, they report the negative correlation between Mini-Mental State Examination (MMSE) score with amyloid deposition in frontal lobe and precuneus, which further validates increased amyloid deposition in these regions of MCI and AD patients.

5.2 Study on Patient-Patient Similarities

Table 3 presents the best performance when a different patient similarity is applied. In this case, the patient similarities are calculated using an RBF kernel ($\sigma = 5$) on the FreeSurfer features of the patients, after the FreeSurfer features are divided by the corresponding feature mean from normal patients. This feature normalization measures how much the FreeSurfer features in patients deviate from those in HCs. This similarity measurement is denoted as simN.

Table 3. Overall performance of PLTR (simN, $\sigma = 5$)

n	Method	Parameters					AH@5	WAH@5	AH@10	WAH@10
		α	β	γ	d	λ				
62	PLTR	0.5	1.0	1.0	10	–	1.371	1.161	**3.129**	**2.295**
		0.5	1.0	1.0	20	–	1.387	**1.186**	3.081	2.162
		0.5	1.0	1.0	50	–	**1.403**	1.165	3.113	2.117
	BMTMKL	–	–	–	–	–	0.790	0.670	1.871	1.982
	KRL	–	–	–	–	0.5	0.306	0.299	0.968	1.046

The column "n" corresponds to the number of hold-out testing patients.
Best performance under each evaluation metric is in **bold**.

62 patients are hold out for testing, who have at least 10 training patients each with patient similarities higher than 0.65. The feature ranking is done in the same way as in Sect. 5.1. Table 3 shows that the PLTR substantially outperforms BMTMKL and KRL. Tables 1 and 3 together demonstrate that regardless of similar functions used to measure patient similarities in FreeSurfer features, PLTR is robust in outperforming baseline given that the testing patients have sufficient similar training patients.

6   Conclusions and Discussions

We have proposed an innovative machine learning paradigm enabling precision medicine for AD imaging biomarker prioritization. The paradigm tailors the imaging biomarker discovery process to individual characteristics of a given patient, and has been implemented based on a newly developed learning-to-rank method PLTR. To the best of our knowledge, this learning-to-rank method has never been applied to the AD imaging biomarker studies. It is a paradigm shifting strategy to facilitate precision medicine research in brain imaging study of AD. The PLTR model seamlessly integrates two objectives for joint optimization: pushing up relevant biomarkers and ranking among relevant biomarkers. The empirical study of PLTR has been performed on the ADNI data and yielded promising results to identify and prioritize individual-specific amyloid imaging biomarkers based on the individual's structural MRI data.

Acknowledgements. This work was supported in part by NIH R01 EB022574, R01 LM011360, U19 AG024904, R01 AG019771, and P30 AG010133; NSF IIS 1837964 and 1855501. The complete ADNI Acknowledgement is available at http://adni.loni.usc.edu/wp-content/uploads/how_to_apply/ADNI_Acknowledgement_List.pdf.

References

1. Alzheimer's Association: 2017 Alzheimer's disease facts and figures (2017)
2. Costello, J.C., et al.: A community effort to assess and improve drug sensitivity prediction algorithms. Nat. Biotechnol. **32**(12), 1202 (2014)

3. Forsberg, A., et al.: Pet imaging of amyloid deposition in patients with mild cognitive impairment. Neurobiol. Aging **29**(10), 1456–1465 (2008)
4. He, X., Folkman, L., Borgwardt, K.: Kernelized rank learning for personalized drug recommendation. Bioinformatics **34**(16), 2808–2816 (2018)
5. He, Y., Liu, J., Ning, X.: Drug selection via joint push and learning to rank. IEEE/ACM Trans. Comput. Biol. Bioinform., 1 (2018)
6. Huang, K.L., et al.: Regional amyloid deposition in amnestic mild cognitive impairment and alzheimer's disease evaluated by [18f]av-45 positron emission tomography in chinese population. PLoS ONE **8**(3), 1–8 (2013)
7. Marinescu, R.V., Oxtoby, N.P., et al.: TADPOLE Challenge: Prediction of Longitudinal Evolution in Alzheimer's Disease. arXiv e-prints arXiv:1805.03909, May 2018
8. Ten Kate, M.: Amyloid-independent atrophy patterns predict time to progression to dementia in mild cognitive impairment. Alzheimer's Res. Ther. **9**(1), 73 (2017)
9. Weiner, M.W., Veitch, D.P., et al.: The Alzheimer's disease neuroimaging initiative 3: continued innovation for clinical trial improvement. Alzheimers Dement. **13**(5), 561–571 (2017)

MFCA

Diffeomorphic Metric Learning and Template Optimization for Registration-Based Predictive Models

Ayagoz Mussabayeva[1], Maxim Pisov[1,3], Anvar Kurmukov[1,4],
Alexey Kroshnin[1,4], Yulia Denisova[1], Li Shen[5], Shan Cong[6], Lei Wang[7],
and Boris Gutman[1,2(✉)]

[1] The Institute for Information Transmission Problems, Moscow, Russia
bgutman1@iit.edu
[2] Department of Biomedical Engineering, Illinois Institute of Technology,
Chicago, IL, USA
[3] Moscow Institute of Physics and Technology State University, Moscow, Russia
[4] Higher School of Economics, Moscow, Russia
[5] Department of Biostatistics, Epidemiology and Informatics,
University of Pennsylvania, Philadelphia, PA, USA
[6] Indiana University, Indianapolis, IN, USA
[7] Department of Psychiatry and Behavioral Sciences,
Northwestern University Feinberg School of Medicine, Chicago, IL, USA

Abstract. We present a method for metric optimization and template
construction in the Large Deformation Diffeomorphic Metric Mapping
(LDDMM) framework. The construction treats the Riemannian metric on the space of diffeomorphisms as a data-embedding kernel in the
context of predictive modeling, here Kernel Logistic Regression (KLR).
The task is then to optimize kernel parameters, including the LDDMM
metric parameters as well as the registration template, resulting in a
parameterized argminimum optimization. In practice, this leads to a
group-wise registration problem with the goal of improving predictive
performance, for example by focusing the metric and template on discriminating patient and control populations. We validate our algorithm
using two discriminative problems on a synthetic data set as well as 3D
subcortical shapes from the SchizConnect cohort. Though secondary to
the template and kernel optimization, accuracy of schizophrenia classification is improved by LDDMM-KLR compared to linear and RBF-KLR.

Keywords: Image registration · Machine learning · Subcortical
shape · Metric learning · LDDMM

1 Introduction

The problem of image registration arises in a number of medical imaging contexts. The process of registering images underlies concurrent use of spatially

© Springer Nature Switzerland AG 2019
D. Zhu et al. (Eds.): MBIA 2019/MFCA 2019, LNCS 11846, pp. 151–161, 2019.
https://doi.org/10.1007/978-3-030-33226-6_17

distributed information from multiple data sets, possibly collected at different times or using different imaging modalities.

The practical goal of registration is spatial alignment. In addition, a subset of registration algorithms has the benefit of establishing a formal distance between images as a byproduct of spatial normalization. Of particular interest among this class of methods is the Large Deformation Diffeomorphic Metric Mapping (LDDMM) [1]. The distance between images defined by LDDMM derives from a Riemannian metric on velocity fields. The distance is then a metric on diffeomorphisms, or the deformations themselves. The Riemannian structure implies the possibility of using the metric as a kernel in a machine learning (ML) context. Such a distance can be derived in a straightforward manner, as in [2] or as the initial momentum "slope". The latter approach is taken here. Yet, to date, little effort in this direction has been undertaken, in part due to the computational complexity of the task. Further, the fact that the LDDMM distance is defined on diffeomorphisms means that in practice the metric in a group of images will be heavily dependent on the choice of the template image. The parameters of the metric itself also significantly influence the registration results [3]. In light of this, applying the LDDMM Riemannian metric as a kernel in a predictive model requires optimization of both the metric parameters and the template. This is the problem we address here. Kernel optimization is an established ML problem. Several canonical kernel forms exist [4], many of which have been studied in the context of metric learning [5,6]. In line with this research, we extend previous work on diffeomorphic metric learning in [2].

A related, though conceptually different notion of learning the LDDMM metric focuses instead on spatially varying the kernel parameters [7] This method allows to find more flexible metric representation, while still satisfying the metric properties. However, the key difference lies in the cost function. In [7] and related work, the metric is optimized with respect to standard registration costs, with additional novel regularization on the LDDMM parameter distribution. Though far more flexible than LDDMM with global parameters, the framework is still conceptually similar to standard LDDMM in that it targets traditional pair-wise registration problems. The metric is not learned in a predictive modeling (group-wise) sense, and its inner product properties are not exploited in the sense of a machine learning "kernel trick".

Similarly to what we do here, the authors in [2] developed an automatic method to find LDDMM metric parameters for optimal classification accuracy. However, there are two important distinctions: (1) rather than using the LDDMM Riemannian product, a distance-derived image similarity measure was used instead. The previous method would be more accurately described as a similarity learning approach. (2) Because only pairwise image distances were used, no template optimization was performed. In fact, the improved template construction, along with optimal registration parameters, potentially has greater practical value to the imaging researcher than the classification tool itself. By optimizing the template for a specific biological question, we enable a more meaningful interpretation of traditional localized registration-based measures, e.g. Jacobian determinant or momentum operator maps, in neuroimaging studies. The focus is thus not on classification accuracy, though it is indeed improved over simpler models, but on template and parameter optimization. In this respect, this work closely parallels the template construction and metric parameter optimization in [8].

The remainder of the paper is organized as follows. Section 2 briefly describes LDDMM. Section 3 builds the model and optimization specifics of LDDMM kernel and template learning in the context of kernel logistic regression. Section 4 describes the synthetic and real brain MRI-based experiments, and 5 concludes the paper.

2   Image Registration in the LDDMM Framework

Large Deformation Diffeomorphic Metric Mapping (LDDMM) was first introduced and implemented in [1]. Since then, LDDMM has been extended into a several methods. The main idea remains the same: to compute a matching diffeomorphism $\phi: [0,1] \times \Omega \to \Omega$, where Ω is the image domain and $[0,1]$ is the time interval. The diffeomorphism ϕ can be seen from different points of view. In its original definition, ϕ belonged to a large class of functions. For the purposes of explicit computation, diffeomorphism ϕ can be considered as the flow generated by the evolution equation:

$$\frac{\partial \phi(t,x)}{\partial t} = v(t, \phi(t,x)),$$
$$\phi(0,x) = x, \tag{1}$$

where $v \in V$ is an element in the space of smooth vector fields.

Let $I, J \in \Omega$ be the source and target images, respectively. The optimization problem for registering I, J is generally formulated as a cost function comprised of a similarity measure between warped source and target images and a regularization term:

$$E(v) = \frac{1}{\sigma^2} d(I \circ \phi, J) + R(v) \tag{2}$$

where σ^2 is the normalization coefficient.

Here, we define similarity as the sum of squared differences (SSD) $d(I \circ \phi, J) = \|I \circ \phi - J\|_{L_2}^2$, where $I \circ \phi$ is the warped image.

The diffeomorphism space is a Lie Group with respect to (1) and it suggests a right-invariance property, allowing to recall the adjoint representation and the scalar product on the tangent space. Smoothness of the warp can be enforced by defining an appropriate regularization term. As long as the tangent space V has a well-defined inner product, regularization is defined by $\|\cdot\|_V$ through a Riemannian metric L. The operator L should be naturally defined by the geometric structure of the domain and implies smoothness. As it was in [1] L is defined as an adjoint differential operator (3). Finally, regularization is defined as the inner product integrated along the path of the diffeomorphism ϕ^v and shown in Eq. (3). Note that here the superscript of ϕ defines the dependence on v; we omit this below:

$$R(v) = \int_0^1 \|v_t\|_V^2 \, dt = \int_0^1 <Lv_t, v_t> dt \tag{3}$$

$$L = (\alpha\Delta + \gamma E)^2,$$

where Δ is the laplacian operator and E is identity operator.

The regularization term can also be thought of as a distance between images, i.e. the minimal length of diffeomorphic path required to transform the appearance of I to be as similar as possible to J. Path length is defined as an integration of the velocity norm based on the corresponding Riemannian metric along the path. Importantly, the velocity field is defined on vector space with all the implicit properties.

The choice of the operator L is a trade-off between simplicity and expressivity. We choose operator L as in the original paper [1]. It consists of two scalar parameters, providing minimal flexibility for metric tuning. Parameters of the operator (α, γ) correspond to convexity and normalization terms, respectively. These parameters significantly affect the quality of the registration, as shown in [3].

2.1   Kernel Construction

As was mentioned above, the LDDMM registration produces a properly defined structure of interrelation between two images. One of several possible ways to construct kernel matrix is to use the length of the path in the diffeomorphic space. But since we consider registration to on a particular template, the inner product of the vector space, where velocity fields defined, is a natural choice. This accounts for diffeomorphic space geometry and employs the possible simplification in the case of template-based registration.

The matrix of pairwise distances is considered as a kernel for the predictive model and constructed as follows. Let $x_i \in D$ be an image, which after registration to on a particular template J produces a corresponding velocity field and warping. The velocity field is constructed over time steps, denoted as $v_t^i = v^i(t, \phi(t, x))$ for each image $x_i, i = 1, \ldots, n$. Every vector field $v_1^i, i = 1, \ldots, n$ at time 1 is defined on the same tangent space at the identity transformation i.e., at the template J. Since this tangent space admits an inner product, the kernel is defined as $k(x_i, x_j) = <Lv_1^i, v_1^j>$. From here on, the time subscript will be omitted. As was mentioned above the meaning of such distance is a "slope" from source image to target image.

3   Metric Learning

In our work, we use Kernel Logistic Regression (KLR) as the base classifier. KLR is a flexible and tractable method that can be naturally used in the proposed method. Though a variety of classification and regression models admit kernels, KLR is among the simplest and most robust, making minimal assumptions about data distribution.

Let $D = \{(x_i, y_i)\}_{i=1}^{n}$ be a sample, where the target variable $y \in \{1, 0\}$ is a class label. KLR leads to the following optimization problem:

$$Loss(\beta) = -\sum_{i=0}^{n} \left(y_i \cdot \ln p_i + (1 - y_i) \cdot \ln(1 - p_i)\right) + C \cdot \|\beta\|_{L^2}^2$$

$$p_i = \frac{1}{1 + e^{-\beta^T k(x_i, x)}},$$

(4)

where $k(x_i, x)$ is a vector $(k(x_i, x_1), \dots, k(x_i, x_n))^T$ and C is a regularization coefficient.

3.1   Optimization Strategy

To address the registration parameter selection problem, we provide a gradient descent method as the strategy for optimizing the loss function (4) with respect to registration parameters (α, γ, J). The pipeline is shown in (Fig. 1) and an outline of the algorithm is given in Sect. 3.2. At the back propagation stage, we consider the solution of LDDMM and the classifier to be fixed, denoting both with a superscript (β^*, v^*).

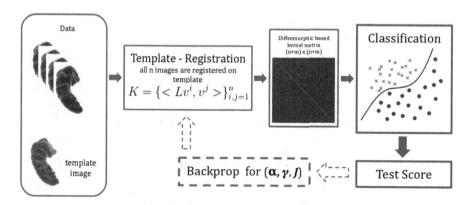

Fig. 1. Schematic visualization of registration-based optimization algorithm (v^i corresponds to optimal solution of LDDMM for subject i).

Briefly, the KLR and LDDMM optimization pipeline can be describe as follows. We initialize α, γ, J, compute the kernel, and find optimal KLR coefficients β. Next, we fix β^*, v^* and update α, γ, J with the gradient step of the loss function (4). The parameters β^* and v^* are the solutions of the optimization problem and depend on α, γ, J. Therefore the derivative of loss function (4) is a bi-level optimization problem. The solution of a general bi-level optimization problem is given in [9]. Below we provide step-by-step derivatives with respect to α, and explain the main differences in derivatives with respect to J.

Denoting the train and validation subsets of the data as $X_{train}, X_{val}, y_{train}, y_{val}$, we compute β^* as the argminimum of the loss function (4) on $\{X_{train}, y_{train}\}$. (Note that all unnecessary indices are again omitted.) The resulting gradients are computed on the validation set based on the following equations $(y_i, x_i \in \{X_{val}, y_{val}\})$:

$$\frac{dLoss(\beta^*)}{d\alpha} = -\sum_{i=1}^{n_{val}} \left(y_i \cdot \frac{d\ln p_i}{d\alpha} + (1-y_i) \cdot \frac{d\ln(1-p_i)}{d\alpha} \right) + 2C\beta^* \frac{d\beta^*}{d\alpha} \quad (5)$$

Expanding the mixed partial derivatives, we write:

$$\frac{\partial \ln p_i}{\partial \alpha} = -\frac{\partial \ln(1 + e^{-<\beta^*, k(x_i, x_{train})>})}{\partial \alpha}$$

$$= \frac{e^{-<\beta^*, k(x_i, x_{train})>}}{1 + e^{-<\beta^*, k(x_i, x_{train})>}} \cdot \left((\beta^*)^T \frac{\partial x_i}{\partial \alpha} + \frac{\partial(\beta^*)^T}{\partial \alpha} x_i \right)$$

$$= (1 - p_i) \left((\beta^*)^T \frac{\partial x_i}{\partial \alpha} + \frac{\partial(\beta^*)^T}{\partial \alpha} x_i \right); \quad (6)$$

$$\frac{\partial \ln(1 - p_i)}{\partial \alpha} = -p_i \left((\beta^*)^T \frac{\partial x_i}{\partial \alpha} + \frac{\partial(\beta^*)^T}{\partial \alpha} x_i \right)$$

$$\frac{\partial k(x_i, x_{train})}{\partial \alpha} = [k(x_i, x_{train}) = <Lv_i, v_{train}>]$$

$$= <\frac{\partial L}{\partial \alpha} v_i, v_{train}> + <L\frac{\partial v_i}{\partial \alpha}, v_{train}> + <Lv_i, \frac{\partial v_{train}}{\partial \alpha}> \quad (7)$$

The gradients below are also computed exclusively on $\{X_{train}, y_{train}\}$:

$$\frac{\partial \beta^*}{\partial \alpha} = \left[\beta^* = \underset{\beta}{\arg\min} \, Loss(\beta), (4), \textit{use formulae from} ([9]) \right]$$

$$\frac{\partial^2 Loss}{\partial \beta^2} = X^T B X + 2E \quad (8)$$

$$\frac{\partial}{\partial \alpha} \frac{\partial Loss}{\partial \beta} = \frac{\partial}{\partial \alpha} (X^T(p-y)) = \frac{\partial X^T}{\partial \alpha}(p-y) + X^T \frac{\partial p}{\partial \alpha},$$

where p and y correspond to the KLR probability vector and training labels, and the matrix B is diagonal with entries $p_i(1 - p_i)$.

We can see that all derivatives above include $\frac{dv^*}{d\alpha}$. To differentiate v^* w.r.t. the scalar parameters, we use the same bi-level optimization problem solution. We use the finite difference approach rather than calculating $\frac{\partial^2 E(v)}{\partial v^2}$ for scalar parameters such as α. In this work, we use the second order central finite difference. The same strategy can be used for γ. Also of note is that one of these parameters in 2 is redundant. It is the ratio of α, γ, σ^2 that is of import.

One of the possible ways to find the derivative of the template image J is to treat it like a scalar intensity function $J(x, y)$ defined on Ω. Each voxel's intensity is treated as independent from the rest. We suggest a combined approach to obtain the derivative $\frac{dv^*}{dJ}$ as in the bi-level problem [9]. The derivative $\frac{\partial^2 E(v)}{dJdv}$ is derived from the closed form of the full derivative [1]. As only the second term of $\frac{\partial E(v)}{dv}$ depends on the template image J and each voxel in J is independent, the final form of the derivative is substantially simplifed. Below, we describe the optimization strategy for 2-dimensional images. However, it can be easily expanded to higher dimensions. To obtain $\frac{\partial^2 E(v)}{\partial v^2}$ we use a forth order central finite difference scheme for unmixed second derivative and for mixed second derivatives. For computational reasons, this approximation uses two key assumptions: first, only the voxel's immediate neighbors are correlated; second, the entry v_y^{ij} does not interact with the entry v_x^{kl} if $i \neq k$ or $j \neq l$, where the superscript refers to the axis, i, j, k, l are the corresponding voxel coordinates, and v_x, v_y denote components of the velocity field.

3.2 Optimization Algorithm

To summarize the previous section, We have two loss functions $E(v)$ and $Loss(\beta)$, whose argminima v^*, β^* parameterize the optimization of the registration parameters (α, γ, J). In practice, we find that (1) the LDDMM kernel multiplication constant does not affect the solution of optimization task and only the ratio α/γ has effect on the loss, we do omit the optimization of γ. The complete algorithm consists of two main parts: the "forward pass" and "the backward pass".

Result: (α^*, J^*)
$\alpha = \alpha_0, J = J_0$;
for $i \leftarrow 0$ **to** N **do**
 | with fixed α_i, J_i forward pass:
 | {
 | calculate $v_i^* = \operatorname{argmin} E(v)$;
 | construct Kernels for train-val-test;
 | fit KLR on train;
 | evaluate metrics (ROC AUC) on val-test;
 | }
 | backward pass α, J:
 | {
 | calculate gradients $(\frac{dLoss}{d\alpha_i}, \frac{dLoss}{dJ_i})$ on val;
 | do gradient step:
 | $\alpha_{i+1} = \alpha_i - lr \cdot \frac{dLoss}{d\alpha}$
 | $J_{i+1} = J_i - lr \cdot \frac{dLoss}{dJ}$
 | }
end

Algorithm 1. Pipeline of the proposed algorithm

4   Experiments

In our initial experiments, we used synthetic data to sanity-check our approach and hippocampal shape data from the ShizConnect dataset [10]. In all experiments, we fixed $\sigma^2 = 10^3$ and $\gamma = 1$. As well as the step for finite differences $h = 0.1$.

4.1   Synthetic Data

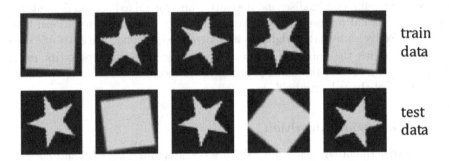

train data

test data

Fig. 2. Example of synthetic data: first row: train data, second row: test data (rectangle is labeled as 1 and star - 0.)

Our initial experiments were based on 200 synthetic images with two balanced classes: randomly rotated stars and rectangles (Fig. 2). This task is very simple from the classification perspective. The primary interest here is to assess the validity of our simplifying assumptions in computing the derivatives, especially w.r.t to the template image J. Here, we used 10-fold cross-validation, fitting the L2 regularization term in KLR independently.

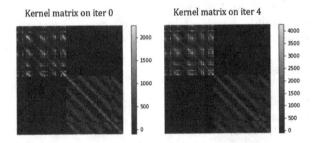

Fig. 3. Kernel matrix for the synthetic data set. The first half of the elements corresponds to data points labelled as stars, and the rest to rectangles

The result of template optimization is shown in (Fig. 4). First, we initialize template J as the mean image of the training set. Next, we make a gradient step on template J and update its initial value. We initialize $\alpha = 0.4$. As we can see, the template begins to look like a star. In this task, the classification-optimal template appears to be closer to one of the classes. After iteration step 4, the optimal template fluctuate around the template on 4 step. The distribution of distances is plotted in (Fig. 3). We note that the ROC area under the curve (AUC) for this experiment is 1, achieving perfect classification.

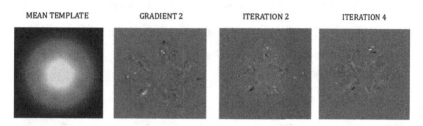

| MEAN TEMPLATE | GRADIENT 2 | ITERATION 2 | ITERATION 4 |

Fig. 4. 'MEAN TEMPLATE' image correspond to initialization of template as mean image of training set, 'GRADIENT 2' image is an example of derivative $\nabla_J Loss(\beta^*)$ on iteration step 2, 'ITERATION i' image is the template image J_i on at the i'th iteration

4.2 Subcortical Shapes

Our 3D hippocampal shape sample was derived from the SchizConnect brain MRI data set. We used right & left hippocampal segmentations extracted with FreeSurfer [11] from 227 Schizophrenia (SCZ) patients and 496 controls (CTL). All shapes were affinely registered to the ENIGMA hippocampal shape atlas [12], and their binary masks were computed from the transformed mesh model and used as the input data. Classes were balanced to reduce bias in classification and template reconstruction. We used down sampled images in 4 time steps to reduce computational time.

It's worth to notice that the same pipeline can be applied to other subcortical structures, such as amygdala or ventricles as well as the whole brain. Out method produce individual optimal parameters for each structure since it depends on geometry of image domain.

Our initial hippocampal experiments followed those for synthetic data, optimizing only the template. We modified slightly the full optimization as described above for (α, γ, J) as follows. First, we initialized all parameters. At each subsequent step, we optimized (α, γ) and every 5 steps we updated the template J. Initialization was analogous to what was done in synthetic experiments. We show the initial and final template in Fig. 5. To compare the results, we used a simple Logistic Regression on vectorized images and KLR with Radial Basis Function (RBF) kernel. RBF-KLR appears to overfit substantially, likely because the RBF embedding space is infinite-dimensional and not in regularized in any domain-specific sense. Though LDDMM embedding is also infinite-dimensional, the fact that it is derived from image-based regularization likely explains the improved classification accuracy. Linear LR performs much better than RBF-KLR, but is still inferior to LDDMM-KLR. ROC AUC scores of the models' performance are shown in Table 1.

Table 1. All results are rounded to 2 significant digits. The result is presented by the best ROCAUC score, counted on the same test set. LR was performed with a grid search to optimize the L2 regularization term weight. Registration-based model was derived as described in the experiments section, for 11 iterations.

	Left hippocampal	Right hippocampal
Logistic Regression (LR)	0.77	0.74
Registration-based Optimized	0.81	0.83

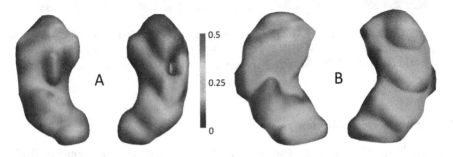

Fig. 5. Hippocampal templates. (a) Mean initial template; (2) LDDMM-KLR optimized template.

5   Conclusion

We have presented a novel method for diffeomorphic metric learning for image registration and predictive modeling. The unique contribution of the paper is to exploit the much-celebrated Riemannian structure of the LDDMM framework in the essence concise representation of the geometry of objects. To show the comprehensive view of our approach, we used a predictive task of practical utility. Though we have focused here on 2-class classification problems, the framework is general both with respect to the predictive modelling approach and the type of target variable. For example, rather than using diagnosis and logistic regression, we may as well have predicted the age of onset of Schizophrenia using kernel Support Vector Regression. Our only requirement is that the ML model admit kernels, and that the kernel optimization remains tractable for the given model.

A further improvement on previous work is the template optimization. Unlike previous work on template optimization [8], which focused on intrinsic statistical properties, we optimize a template with a specific predictive task in mind. In this way, we learn a metric that highlights the most essential deformations with respect to a specific biological question.

Acknowledgements. The research was conducted in the IITP RAS and solely supported by the Russian Science Foundation grant (project 17-11-01390).

References

1. Beg, M.F., Miller, M.I., Trouvé, A., Younes, L.: Computing large deformation metric mappings via geodesic flows of diffeomorphisms. Int. J. Comput. Vision **61**(2), 139–157 (2005)
2. Mussabayeva, A., et al.: Image registration and predictive modeling: learning the metric on the space of diffeomorphisms. In: Reuter, M., Wachinger, C., Lombaert, H., Paniagua, B., Lüthi, M., Egger, B. (eds.) ShapeMI 2018. LNCS, vol. 11167, pp. 160–168. Springer, Cham (2018). https://doi.org/10.1007/978-3-030-04747-4_15
3. Ceritoglu, C., et al.: Computational analysis of LDDMM for brain mapping. Front. Neurosci. **7**, 151 (2013)
4. Cho, Y., Saul, L.K.: Kernel methods for deep learning. In: Advances in Neural Information Processing Systems, pp. 342–350 (2009)
5. Ayat, N.-E., Cheriet, M., Suen, C.Y.: Optimization of the SVM kernels using an empirical error minimization scheme. In: Lee, S.-W., Verri, A. (eds.) SVM 2002. LNCS, vol. 2388, pp. 354–369. Springer, Heidelberg (2002). https://doi.org/10.1007/3-540-45665-1_28
6. Huang, J., Yuen, P.C., Chen, W.S., Lai, J.H.: Kernel subspace LDA with optimized kernel parameters on face recognition. In: Proceedings of Sixth IEEE International Conference on Automatic Face and Gesture Recognition, pp. 327–332. IEEE (2004)
7. Niethammer, M., Kwitt, R., Vialard, F.X.: Metric learning for image registration. In: The IEEE Conference on Computer Vision and Pattern Recognition (CVPR), June 2019
8. Zhang, M., Singh, N., Fletcher, P.T.: Bayesian estimation of regularization and atlas building in diffeomorphic image registration. In: Gee, J.C., Joshi, S., Pohl, K.M., Wells, W.M., Zöllei, L. (eds.) IPMI 2013. LNCS, vol. 7917, pp. 37–48. Springer, Heidelberg (2013). https://doi.org/10.1007/978-3-642-38868-2_4
9. Gould, S., Fernando, B., Cherian, A., Anderson, P., Cruz, R.S., Guo, E.: On differentiating parameterized argmin and argmax problems with application to bi-level optimization. arXiv preprint arXiv:1607.05447 (2016)
10. Wang, L., et al.: SchizConnect: mediating neuroimaging databases on schizophrenia and related disorders for large-scale integration. NeuroImage **124**, 1155–1167 (2016). Sharing the wealth: Brain Imaging Repositories in 2015
11. Fischl, B.: FreeSurfer. Neuroimage **62**(2), 774–781 (2012)
12. Roshchupkin, G.V., et al.: Heritability of the shape of subcortical brain structures in the general population. Nat. Commun. **7**, 13738 (2016)

3D Mapping of Serial Histology Sections with Anomalies Using a Novel Robust Deformable Registration Algorithm

Daniel Tward[1]([envelope]) [ORCID], Xu Li[2], Bingxing Huo[2], Brian Lee[1] [ORCID], Partha Mitra[2], and Michael Miller[1]

[1] Johns Hopkins University, Baltimore, MD 21218, USA
{dtward,leebc,mim}@cis.jhu.edu
[2] Cold Spring Harbor Laboratory, Cold Spring Harbor, NY 11724, USA
{xli,bhuo,mitra}@cshl.edu

Abstract. The neuroimaging field is moving toward micron scale and molecular features in digital pathology and animal models. These require mapping to common coordinates for annotation, statistical analysis, and collaboration. An important example, the BRAIN Initiative Cell Census Network, is generating 3D brain cell atlases in mouse, and ultimately primate and human.

We aim to establish RNAseq profiles from single neurons and nuclei across the mouse brain, mapped to Allen Common Coordinate Framework (CCF). Imaging includes $\sim$500 tape-transfer cut $20\,\mu$m thick Nissl-stained slices per brain. In key areas $100\,\mu$m thick slices with 0.5–2 mm diameter circular regions punched out for snRNAseq are imaged. These contain abnormalities including contrast changes and missing tissue, two challenges not jointly addressed in diffeomorphic image registration.

Existing methods for mapping 3D images to histology require manual steps unacceptable for high throughput, or are sensitive to damaged tissue. Our approach jointly: registers 3D CCF to 2D slices, models contrast changes, estimates abnormality locations. Our registration uses 4 unknown deformations: 3D diffeomorphism, 3D affine, 2D diffeomorphism per-slice, 2D rigid per-slice. Contrast changes are modeled using unknown cubic polynomials per-slice. Abnormalities are estimated using Gaussian mixture modeling. The Expectation Maximization algorithm is used iteratively, with E step: compute posterior probabilities of abnormality, M step: registration and intensity transformation minimizing posterior-weighted sum-of-square-error.

We produce per-slice anatomical labels using Allen Institute's ontology, and publicly distribute results online, with several typical and abnormal slices shown here. This work has further applications in digital pathology, and 3D brain mapping with stroke, multiple sclerosis, or other abnormalities.

Keywords: Neuroimaging · Image registration · Histology

© Springer Nature Switzerland AG 2019
D. Zhu et al. (Eds.): MBIA 2019/MFCA 2019, LNCS 11846, pp. 162–173, 2019.
https://doi.org/10.1007/978-3-030-33226-6_18

1   Introduction

The neuroimaging field is moving toward the micron scale, accelerated by modern imaging methods [14,31], cell labeling techniques [36], and a desire to understand the brain at the level of circuits [18]. This is impacting basic neuroscience research involving animal model organisms, as well as human digital pathology for understanding neurological disease. While some 3D modalities based on tissue clearing are becoming available such as CLARITY or iDISCO , two dimensional (2D) histological sections stained for relevant features and imaged with light microscopy are a gold standard for identification of anatomical regions [10], and making diagnoses in many neurodegenerative diseases [16]. To interpret this data, mapping to the common coordinates of a well characterized 3D atlas is required. This allows automatic labeling of anatomical regions for parsing experimental results, as well as the ability to combine data from different experiments or laboratories, facilitating a statistical understanding of neuroimaging.

The Brain Initiative Cell Census Network https://www.braininitiative.nih.gov/brain-programs/cell-census-network-biccn was created with the goal of mapping molecular, anatomical, and functional data into comprehensive brain cell atlases. This project is beginning with mouse imaging data in the Allen Common Coordinate Framework (CCF) [20], and building toward nonhuman primates and ultimately humans. To understand cell diversity via gene expression throughout the brain, one important contribution is to perform single neuron RNA sequencing (snRNA-seq) [21] at key locations throughout the mouse brain. The data associated to this analysis includes coronal images of $20\,\mu m$ thick serially sectioned Nissl stained tissue, allowing visualization of the location and density of neuron cell bodies with a blue/violet color. At indicated locations, tissue is cut to $100\,\mu m$ thick, and 0.5–2 mm diameter circular regions are punched out for RNA sequencing after slicing but before staining and imaging. These heavily processed sections present variable contrast profiles, missing tissue, and artifacts as seen in Fig. 1, posing serious challenges for existing registration techniques.

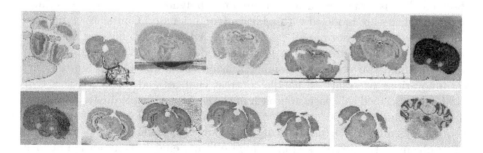

Fig. 1. Several Nissl stained coronal sections of the mouse brain are shown from anterior (top left) to posterior (bottom right).

The goal of this work is to develop an image registration algorithm using diffeomorphic techniques developed by the Computational Anatomy community, to accurately map the Allen Institute's CCF to our Nissl datasets. Because this community has largely studied mappings between pairs of images that are topologically equivalent, the fundamentally asymmetric nature of our 3D atlas as compared to sparsely sectioned 2D data requires a non standard approach.

Several approaches to registration with missing data or artifacts have been developed by the community. The simplest approach consists of manually defining binary masks that indicate data to be ignored by image similarity functions [9,35] before registration. A slightly more involved method is to use inpainting, where data in these regions is replaced by a specific image intensity or texture [33], a method included in ANTs [6,44] for registration in the presence of multiple sclerosis lesions. Anomalous data such as excised tissue tumors or other lesions [24–26,45] have been jointly estimated together with registration parameters using models for contrast changes. Others have used statistical approaches [11,27,40] based on Expectation Maximization (EM) algorithms [12] which is the approach we follow. In the presence of contrast differences this problem is more challenging. Image similarity functions designed for cross-modality registration, like normalized cross correlation [4,5,42], mutual information [22,23,30], or local structural information [7,15,41] cannot be used in an EM setting because they do not correspond to a data log likelihood.

The importance of mapping histology into 3D coordinates has long been recognized. A recent review [28] lists 30 different software packages attempting the task. While the review acknowledges that artifacts such as folds, tears, cracks and holes as important challenges, they are not adequately addressed by these methods. Modern approaches to solve the problem (e.g. [1–3,43]) tend to involve multiple preprocessing steps and stages of alignment, and carefully constructed metrics of image similarity. Instead, our approach follows statistical estimation within an intuitive generative model of the formation of 2D slice images from 3D atlases. Large 3D deformations of the atlas and 2D deformations of each slice are modeled via unknown diffeomorphisms using established techniques developed by the Computational Anatomy community, the contrast profile of each observed slice is estimated using an unknown polynomial transformation, and observed images are modeled with additive (conditionally) Gaussian white noise (conditioned on transformation parameters). Artifacts and missing tissue are accommodated through Gaussian mixture modeling (GMM) at each observed pixel. The final two parts, polynomial transformation and GMM, are the critical innovations necessary to handle contrast changes and missing tissue. Our group has described this basic approach in the context of single digital pathology images [39], and developed a simpler version for serial sections [19] (considering deformations only in 3D, without contrast changes or artifacts). Here we extend this problem to the serially sectioned mouse brain, enabling annotation of each pixel, and mapping of slices into standard 3D coordinates.

2   Algorithm

We first describe the generative model at the heart of our mapping algorithm, and then discuss its optimization via EM and gradient descent.

2.1   Generative Model

The generative model which predicts the shape and appearance of each 2D slice from our 3D atlas is shown schematically in Fig. 2, with transformation parameters summarized in Table 1. In this model the role of our 3D atlas and observed data are fundamentally asymmetric: slices can be generated from the atlas, but not vice versa. The motivation for the order of this scheme is to mimic the imaging process, where 3D transformations describe shape differences between an observed brain and a canonical atlas, and 2D transformations describe distortions that occur in the sectioning and imaging process. The steps below describe transformations that are all estimated jointly using a single cost (weighted sum of square error over all 2D slices), rather than simply connecting standard algorithms one after another in a pipeline. The final two steps, polynomial intensity transformation and posterior- weighted sum of square error using GMM, are novel in this work and critical for handling contrast variability and missing tissue. Below we describe each step in detail.

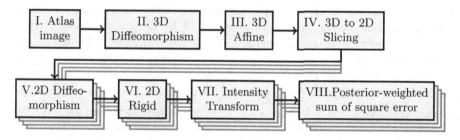

Fig. 2. A schematic of the transformations in our generative model are shown. The top row shows 3D transformations that affect all slices, while the bottom row shows transformations specific to each slice. Posterior weights estimate artifact and missing tissue locations via EM.

I. Atlas Image: We use the Nissl Allen atlas [13], denoted I, at 50 μm resolution in our studies with the 2017 anatomical labels, which is available publicly in nearly raw raster data (NRRD) format at http://download.alleninstitute.org/ informatics-archive/current-release/mouse_ccf/. This is a grayscale image, which we will align to red green blue (RGB) Nissl stained sections denoted J^i for $i \in \{1, \cdots, N\}$.

Table 1. Listed below are variables used in our transformation, as well as the number of degrees of freedom to be estimated (on each slice if applicable).

Name	Symbol	Each slice	Degrees of freedom
Atlas image	I	No	0
3D velocity field	v_t	No	$\sim 10^6$
3D diffeomorphism	$\varphi_1(x) = id + \int_0^1 v_t(\varphi_t)dt$	No	0
3D affine transform	A	No	12
2D velocity field	w_t^i	Yes	$\sim 10^4$
2D diffeomorphism	$\psi^i = id + \int_0^1 w_t^i(\psi_t^i)dt$	Yes	0
2D rigid transform	R^i	Yes	3
Polynomial coefficients	c^i	Yes	27
Polynomial function	f_c^i	Yes	0
Predicted slice image	$\hat{J}^i = f_{c^i}(R^i \cdot \psi^i \cdot [A \cdot \varphi \cdot I]_{z=z_i})$	Yes	0
Observed slice image	J^i	Yes	0
Artifact mean	μ_A^i	Yes	3
Background data mean	μ_B^i	Yes	3
Atlas image posterior	W_M^i	Yes	$\sim 10^4$
Artifact posterior	W_A^i	Yes	$\sim 10^4$
Background posterior	$W_B^i = 1 - W_M^i - W_A^i$	Yes	0

II. 3D Diffeomorphism: Diffeomorphisms are generated using the large deformation diffeomorphic metric mapping framework [8] by integrating smooth velocity fields numerically using the method of characteristics [34]. We denote our 3D smooth velocity field by v_t, and our 3D diffeomorphism by $\varphi = \varphi_1$ where $\dot{\varphi}_t = v_t(\varphi_t)$ and $\varphi_0 = $ identity. Smoothness is enforced using regularization penalty given by $E_{\text{reg}} = \frac{1}{2\sigma_R^2}\int_0^1 \int |Lv_t(x)|^2 dxdt$ with $L = (id - a^2\Delta)^2$ for id identity, Δ Laplacian, $a = 400\,\mu\text{m}$ a characteristic length scale, and $\sigma_R = 5 \times 10^4$ a parameter to control tradeoffs between regularization and accuracy. This time-integrated kinetic energy penalty is a standard approach to regularization in the computational anatomy community [8].

III. 3D Affine: We include linear changes in location and scale through a 4×4 affine matrix A with 12 degrees of freedom (9 linear and 3 translation).

IV. 3D to 2D Slicing: 2D images are generated by slicing the transformed 3D volume at N known locations z_i. Each slice is separated by $20\,\mu\text{m}$, with the exception of thick slices which are separated by $100\,\mu\text{m}$.

V. 2D Diffeomorphism: For each slice i a 2D diffeomorphism ψ^i is generated from a smooth velocity field w_t^i. This is generated using the same methods as in 3D, with a regularization scale $a_S = 400\,\mu\text{m}$ and weight $\sigma_{R_S} = 1 \times 10^3$, with penalty E_{reg}^i.

VI. 2D Rigid: For each slice a rigid transformation R^i is applied with 3 degrees of freedom (1 rotation and 2 translation). For identifiability, translations and rotations are constrained to be zero mean (averaged across each slice). We constrain the transformation to be rigid by parameterizing it as the exponential of an antisymmetric matrix.

VII. Intensity Transform: On each slice a cubic polynomial intensity transformation is applied to predict the observed Nissl stained data in a minimum weighted least squares sense. Since data consists of red-green-blue (RGB) images, this is 12 degrees of freedom, possibly nonmonotonic and flexible enough to permute the brightness order of background, gray matter, and white matter. We refer to the intensity transformed atlas corresponding to the ith slice as $\hat{J}^i$ (the "hat" notation is used to convey that this is an estimate of the shape and appearance of the observed image J^i).

VIII. Weighted Sum of Square Error: Each transformed atlas slice is compared to our observed Nissl slice using weighted sum of square error $E^i_{\text{match}} = \int \frac{1}{2\sigma_M^2} |\hat{J}^i(x,y) - J^i(x,y)|^2 W_M^i(x,y) dx$, where the weight W_M^i corresponds to the posterior probability that each pixel corresponds to some location in the atlas (to be estimated via EM algorithm), as opposed to being artifact or missing tissue. The constant σ_M represents the variance of Gaussian white noise in the image and is set to 0.05 (for an RGB image in the range [0,1]).

2.2   Optimization via Expectation Maximization

M step: Given a weight at each pixel, the M step corresponds to estimating unknown transformation parameters by minimizing the cost with a fixed W_M^i:

$$\text{Cost}_{W_M} = E_{\text{reg}} + \sum_{i=1}^N E^i_{\text{reg}} + E^i_{\text{match}}$$

All unknown deformation parameters are computed iteratively by gradient descent, with gradients backpropagated from each step to the previous. Rather than posing this as a sequential pipeline, optimization over each parameter is performed jointly. This mitigates negative effects in pipeline-based approaches such as poor initial affine alignment, and is consistent with the interpretation as joint maximum likelihood estimation.

Gradients for linear transformations are derived using standard calculus techniques. Gradients with respect to velocity fields were described originally in [8]. As shown in [38], gradients are backpropagated from the endpoint of a 3D diffeomorphic flow to time t via

$$(v_t \text{ gradient}) = \tfrac{1}{\sigma_R^2} v_t - K * \left[(\text{endpoint gradient}) \circ \varphi_{1t}^{-1} |D\varphi_{1t}^{-1}| \nabla (I \circ \varphi_{1t}^{-1}) \right]$$

where $K*$ is convolution with the Green's kernel of L^*L, $\nabla = \left(\frac{\partial}{\partial x}, \frac{\partial}{\partial x}, \frac{\partial}{\partial x}\right)^T$, and $\varphi_{1t} = \varphi_t \circ \varphi_1^{-1}$ (a transformation from the endpoint of the flow $t = 1$, to time t). The backpropagation for 2D diffeomorphisms is similar.

To simplify backpropagation of gradients from 3D to 2D, we interpret each slice as a 3D volume at the appropriate plane, using $J^i(x, y, z) \simeq \Delta(z - z_i)J^i(x, y)$, for Δ a triangle approximation to the Dirac δ with width given by the slice spacing, modeling the process of physically sectioning the tissue at known thickness. This allows our cost to be written entirely as an integral over 3D space, allowing the backpropagation with standard approaches.

All intensity transformation parameters are computed exactly at each iteration of gradient descent by weighted least squares. This includes unknown polynomial coefficients for the intensity transformations on each slice, and unknown means for (B)ackground pixels (missing tissue) or (A)rtifact (μ_B, μ_A).

E Step: Given an estimate of each of the transformation parameters, the E step corresponds to estimating the posterior probabilities that each pixel corresponds to the atlas, to missing tissue, or to artifact. This is computed at each pixel via Bayes theorem using a Gaussian model, by specifying a variance $\sigma_M^2 = \sigma_B^2 = \sigma_A^2/100$ for the image (M)atching, (B)ackground, and (A)rtifact. Additionally, we include a spatial prior with a Gaussian shape of standard deviation 3 mm, making missing tissue and artifacts more likely to occur near the edges of the image, a common feature of this dataset (e.g. streaks near the bottom of images in Fig. 1).

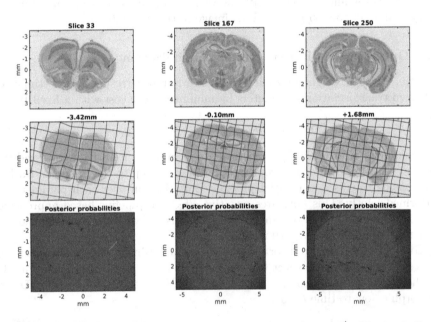

Fig. 3. Registration result for 3 typical slices i. Top: target image J^i with annotations overlayed. Middle: Transformed atlas image $\hat{J}^i$ predicting RGB contrast of observed Nissl images from grayscale atlas. Bottom: Posterior probabilities that each pixel corresponds to the deformed atlas (red), an artifact (green), or missing tissue (blue). (Color figure online)

3 Results

We demonstrate our algorithm by mapping onto 484 tissue slices from one mouse brain produced using a tape transfer technique [17,29,32]. Out of these, 460 were 20 μm thick and produced using a standard Nissl staining technique, and 24 were 100 μm thick for snRNA-seq analysis. On these slices, 2–12 punches of roughly 1 mm diameter were removed before tissue staining. The images J^i were resampled to 45 μm resolution, with a maximum size 864 × 1020 pixels, stored as RGB tiffs with a bit depth of 24 bits per pixel, for a total of approximately 500 MB. While we show results here for one brain, on the order of 50 samples are becoming available as part of the BICCN project. To avoid local minima, the registration procedure is performed at 3 resolutions (downsampled by 4, then 2, then native resolution) and takes approximately 24 h total using 4 cores on a Intel(R) Xeon(R) CPU E5-1650 v4 at 3.60 GHz. All our registered data is made available through http://mousebrainarchitecture.org, and the accuracy of our mapping techniques is verified by anatomists on each slice using a custom designed web interface.

The mapping accuracy for three typical slices is shown in Fig. 3. The top row shows our raw images with atlas labels superimposed. The second row shows our predicted image $\hat{J}^i$ for each corresponding slice, with a 1 mm grid overlayed showing the distortion of the atlas. The bottom row shows our estimates of missing tissue (blue) or artifact (green). Note that a large streak artifact in the left column is detected (green), as well as missing or torn tissue (blue or green).

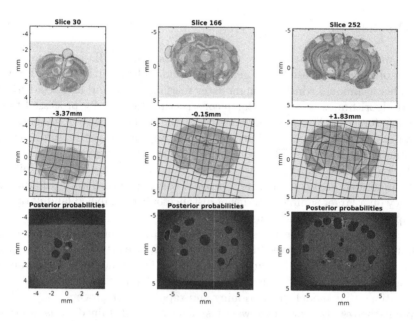

Fig. 4. Registration result for 3 thick cut slices. Layout as in Fig. 3.

Results for 3 nearby thick cut slices are shown in Fig. 4. Here we see that missing tissue is easily detected (blue) and does not interfere with registration accuracy. Other artifacts including smudges on microscope slides are also detected. In Fig. 5 we show registration results for the same slices, using a traditional approach without identifying abnormalities ($W_M^i = 1, W_A^i = W_B^i = 0$). One observes inaccurate registration and dramatic distortions of the atlas.

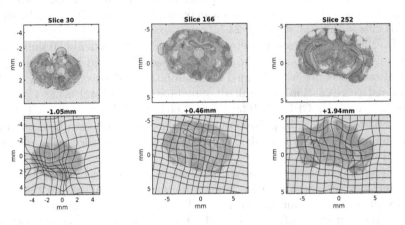

Fig. 5. Registration result on thick cut slices using a traditional algorithm (no EM). Layout as in Fig. 3 (top two rows).

4 Discussion

In this work we described a new method for mapping a 3D atlas image onto a series of 2D slices, based on a generative model of the image formation process. This technique, which accommodates missing tissue and artifacts through an EM algorithm, was essential for reconstructing the heavily processed tissue necessary for snRNA-seq. We demonstrated the accuracy of our method with several examples of typical and atypical slices, and illustrated its improvement over standard approaches. This work is enabling the BICCN's goal of quantifying cell diversity throughout the mouse brain in standard 3D coordinates. While the results presented here demonstrate a proof of concept, future work will quantify accuracy on a larger sample in terms of distance between labeled landmarks and overlap of manual segmentations.

This work departs from the standard random orbit model of Computational Anatomy, in that our observed 2D slices do not lie in the orbit of our 3D template under the action of the diffeomorphism group. This fundamental asymmetry between atlas and target images is addressed by using a realistic sequence of deformations that model the sectioning and tape transfer process.

While the results shown here were restricted to Nissl stained mouse sections, this algorithm has potential for larger impact. A common criticism of using brain mapping to understand medical neuroimages is its inability to function in the presence of abnormalities such as strokes, multiple sclerosis, or other lesions. This algorithm can be applied in these situations, automatically classifying abnormal regions and down-weighting the importance of intensity matching in these areas.

Acknowledgements. This work was supported by the National Institutes of Health P41EB015909, R01NS086888, R01EB020062, R01NS102670, U19AG033655, R01MH105660, U19MH114821, U01MH114824; National Science Foundation 16-569 NeuroNex contract 1707298; Computational Anatomy Science Gateway as part of the Extreme Science and Engineering Discovery Environment [37] (NSF ACI1548562); the Kavli Neuroscience Discovery Institute supported by the Kavli Foundation, the Crick-Clay Professorship, CSHL; and the H. N. Mahabala Chair, IIT Madras.

References

1. Adler, D.H., et al.: Histology-derived volumetric annotation of the human hippocampal subfields in postmortem mri. Neuroimage **84**, 505–523 (2014)
2. Agarwal, N., Xu, X., Gopi, M.: Geometry processing of conventionally produced mouse brain slice images. J. Neurosci. Meth. **306**, 45–56 (2018)
3. Ali, S., Wörz, S., Amunts, K., Eils, R., Axer, M., Rohr, K.: Rigid and non-rigid registration of polarized light imaging data for 3D reconstruction of the temporal lobe of the human brain at micrometer resolution. Neuroimage **181**, 235–251 (2018)
4. Avants, B.B., Grossman, M., Gee, J.C.: Symmetric diffeomorphic image registration: evaluating automated labeling of elderly and neurodegenerative cortex and frontal lobe. In: Pluim, J.P.W., Likar, B., Gerritsen, F.A. (eds.) WBIR 2006. LNCS, vol. 4057, pp. 50–57. Springer, Heidelberg (2006). https://doi.org/10.1007/11784012_7
5. Avants, B.B., Tustison, N.J., Song, G., Cook, P.A., Klein, A., Gee, J.C.: A reproducible evaluation of ants similarity metric performance in brain image registration. Neuroimage **54**(3), 2033–2044 (2011)
6. Avants, B.B., Tustison, N.J., Stauffer, M., Song, G., Wu, B., Gee, J.C.: The insight toolkit image registration framework. Front. Neuroinform. **8**, 44 (2014)
7. Bashiri, F., Baghaie, A., Rostami, R., Yu, Z., D'Souza, R.: Multi-modal medical image registration with full or partial data: a manifold learning approach. J. Imag. **5**(1), 5 (2019)
8. Beg, M.F., Miller, M.I., Trouvé, A., Younes, L.: Computing large deformation metric mappings via geodesic flows of diffeomorphisms. Int. J. Comput. Vis. **61**(2), 139–157 (2005)
9. Brett, M., Leff, A.P., Rorden, C., Ashburner, J.: Spatial normalization of brain images with focal lesions using cost function masking. Neuroimage **14**(2), 486–500 (2001)
10. Brodmann, K.: Vergleichende Lokalisationslehre der Grosshirnrinde in ihren Prinzipien dargestellt auf Grund des Zellenbaues. Barth (1909)
11. Chitphakdithai, N., Duncan, J.S.: Non-rigid registration with missing correspondences in preoperative and postresection brain images. In: Jiang, T., Navab, N., Pluim, J.P.W., Viergever, M.A. (eds.) MICCAI 2010. LNCS, vol. 6361, pp. 367–374. Springer, Heidelberg (2010). https://doi.org/10.1007/978-3-642-15705-9_45
12. Dempster, A.P., Laird, N.M., Rubin, D.B.: Maximum likelihood from incomplete data via the em algorithm. J. Royal Stat. Soc. Ser. B (Methodological) **39**(1), 1–38 (1977)

13. Dong, H.W.: The Allen Reference Atlas: A Digital Color Brain Atlas of the C57Bl/6J Male Mouse. John Wiley & Sons Inc, Hoboken (2008)

14. Hagmann, P., et al.: Mapping the structural core of human cerebral cortex. PLoS Biol. **6**(7), e159 (2008)

15. Heinrich, M.P., et al.: Mind: modality independent neighbourhood descriptor for multi-modal deformable registration. Med. image Anal. **16**(7), 1423–1435 (2012)

16. Hyman, B.T., et al.: National institute on aging-alzheimer's association guidelines for the neuropathologic assessment of alzheimer's disease. Alzheimer's Dement. **8**(1), 1–13 (2012)

17. Jiang, X., et al.: Histological analysis of gfp expression in murine bone. J. Histochem. Cytochem. **53**(5), 593–602 (2005)

18. Kasthuri, N., Lichtman, J.W.: The rise of the'projectome'. Nat. Meth. **4**(4), 307 (2007)

19. Lee, B.C., Tward, D.J., Mitra, P.P., Miller, M.I.: On variational solutions for whole brain serial-section histology using a Sobolev prior in the computational anatomy random orbit model. PLoS Comput. Biol. **14**(12), e1006610 (2018)

20. Lein, E.S., et al.: Genome-wide atlas of gene expression in the adult mouse brain. Nature **445**(7124), 168 (2007)

21. Macosko, E.Z., et al.: Highly parallel genome-wide expression profiling of individual cells using nanoliter droplets. Cell **161**(5), 1202–1214 (2015)

22. Maes, F., Collignon, A., Vandermeulen, D., Marchal, G., Suetens, P.: Multimodality image registration by maximization of mutual information. IEEE Trans. Med. Imag. **16**(2), 187–198 (1997)

23. Mattes, D., Haynor, D.R., Vesselle, H., Lewellen, T.K., Eubank, W.: Pet-ct image registration in the chest using free-form deformations. IEEE Trans. Med. Imag. **22**(1), 120–128 (2003)

24. Miller, M.I., Trouvé, A., Younes, L.: On the metrics and euler-lagrange equations of computational anatomy. Annu. Rev. Biomed. Eng. **4**(1), 375–405 (2002)

25. Niethammer, M., et al.: Geometric metamorphosis. In: Fichtinger, G., Martel, A., Peters, T. (eds.) MICCAI 2011. LNCS, vol. 6892, pp. 639–646. Springer, Heidelberg (2011). https://doi.org/10.1007/978-3-642-23629-7_78

26. Nithiananthan, S., et al.: Extra-dimensional demons: a method for incorporating missing tissue in deformable image registration. Med. Phys. **39**(9), 5718–5731 (2012)

27. Periaswamy, S., Farid, H.: Medical image registration with partial data. Med. Image Anal. **10**(3), 452–464 (2006)

28. Pichat, J., Iglesias, J.E., Yousry, T., Ourselin, S., Modat, M.: A survey of methods for 3D histology reconstruction. Med. Image Anal. **46**, 73–105 (2018)

29. Pinskiy, V., Jones, J., Tolpygo, A.S., Franciotti, N., Weber, K., Mitra, P.P.: High-throughput method of whole-brain sectioning, using the tape-transfer technique. PLoS One **10**(7), e0102363 (2015)

30. Pluim, J.P.W., Maintz, J.B.A., Viergever, M.A.: Mutual-information-based registration of medical images: a survey. IEEE Trans. Med. Imag. **22**(8), 986–1004 (2003). https://doi.org/10.1109/TMI.2003.815867

31. Rubinov, M., Sporns, O.: Complex network measures of brain connectivity: uses and interpretations. Neuroimage **52**(3), 1059–1069 (2010)

32. Salie, R., Li, H., Jiang, X., Rowe, D.W., Kalajzic, I., Susa, M.: A rapid, non-radioactive in situ hybridization technique for use on cryosectioned adult mouse bone. Calcified Tissue Int. **83**(3), 212–221 (2008)

33. Sdika, M., Pelletier, D.: Nonrigid registration of multiple sclerosis brain images using lesion inpainting for morphometry or lesion mapping. Hum. Brain Map. **30**(4), 1060–1067 (2009)

34. Staniforth, A., Côté, J.: Semi-lagrangian integration schemes for atmospheric models–a review. Mon. Weather Rev. **119**(9), 2206–2223 (1991)

35. Stefanescu, R., et al.: Non-rigid atlas to subject registration with pathologies for conformal brain radiotherapy. In: Barillot, C., Haynor, D.R., Hellier, P. (eds.) MIC-CAI 2004. LNCS, vol. 3216, pp. 704–711. Springer, Heidelberg (2004). https://doi.org/10.1007/978-3-540-30135-6_86

36. Taniguchi, H., et al.: A resource of cre driver lines for genetic targeting of gabaergic neurons in cerebral cortex. Neuron **71**(6), 995–1013 (2011)

37. Towns, J., et al.: Xsede: accelerating scientific discovery. Comput. Sci. Eng. **16**(5), 62–74 (2014)

38. Tward, D., Miller, M., Trouve, A., Younes, L.: Parametric surface diffeomorphometry for low dimensional embeddings of dense segmentations and imagery. IEEE Trans. Pattern Anal. Mach. Intell. **39**(6), 1195–1208 (2017)

39. Tward, D.J., et al.: Diffeomorphic registration with intensity transformation and missing data: Application to 3D digital pathology of Alzheimer's disease. BioRxiv, p. 494005 (2019)

40. Vidal, C., Hewitt, J., Davis, S., Younes, L., Jain, S., Jedynak, B.: Template registration with missing parts: application to the segmentation of m. tuberculosis infected lungs. In: 2009 IEEE International Symposium on Biomedical Imaging: From Nano to Macro, pp. 718–721. IEEE (2009)

41. Wachinger, C., Navab, N.: Entropy and laplacian images: structural representations for multi-modal registration. Med. Image Anal. **16**(1), 1–17 (2012)

42. Wu, J., Tang, X.: Fast diffeomorphic image registration via gpu-based parallel computing: an investigation of the matching cost function. In: Proceedings of SPIE Medical Imaging (SPIE-MI) (February 2018)

43. Xiong, J., Ren, J., Luo, L., Horowitz, M.: Mapping histological slice sequences to the allen mouse brain atlas without 3D reconstruction. Front. Neuroinform. **12**, 93 (2018)

44. Yoo, T.S., et al.: Engineering and algorithm design for an image processing api: a technical report on itk-the insight toolkit. Stud. Health Technol. Inform. **85**, 586–592 (2002)

45. Zacharaki, E.I., Shen, D., Lee, S.K., Davatzikos, C.: Orbit: a multiresolution framework for deformable registration of brain tumor images. IEEE Trans. Med. Imag. **27**(8), 1003–1017 (2008)

Spatiotemporal Modeling for Image Time Series with Appearance Change: Application to Early Brain Development

James Fishbaugh[1(✉)], Martin Styner[2,3], Karen Grewen[3], John Gilmore[3], and Guido Gerig[1]

[1] Department of Computer Science and Engineering, Tandon School of Engineering, NYU, New York, NY, UK
james.fishbaugh@nyu.edu
[2] Department of Computer Science, UNC Chapel Hill, Chapel Hill, NC, USA
[3] Department of Psychiatry, UNC School of Medicine, Chapel Hill, NC, USA

Abstract. There has been considerable research effort into image registration and regression, which address the problem of determining correspondence primarily through estimating models of structural change. There has been far less focus into methods which model both structural and intensity change. However, medical images often exhibit intensity changes over time. Of particular interest is MRI of the early developing brain, where such intensity change encodes rich information about development, such as rapidly increasing white matter intensity during the first years of life. In this paper, we develop a new spatiotemporal model which takes into account both structural and appearance changes jointly. This will not only lead to improved regression accuracy and data-matching in the presence of longitudinal intensity changes, but also facilitate the study of development by direct analysis of appearance change models. We propose to combine a diffeomorphic model of structural change with a Gompertz intensity model, which captures intensity trajectories with 3 intuitive parameters of asymptote, delay, and speed. We propose an optimization scheme which allows to control the balance between structural and intensity change via two data-matching terms. We show that Gompertz parameter maps show great promise to characterize regional patterns of development.

1 Introduction

Time series imaging data are commonly acquired in medical imaging studies. In the simplest form, changes are assessed between a baseline and follow-up scan. To facilitate comparison, image registration establishes voxel-wise correspondence so measurements can be directly compared between baseline and follow-up, or the registration deformation field can itself be studied as a description of change. When more than two scans are available, registration naturally gives way to regression, in order to model the inferred continuous image change.

© Springer Nature Switzerland AG 2019
D. Zhu et al. (Eds.): MBIA 2019/MFCA 2019, LNCS 11846, pp. 174–185, 2019.
https://doi.org/10.1007/978-3-030-33226-6_19

In either case, registration or regression, the problem is most often solved by a deformation of image structure; appearance changes are not explicitly modeled. Rather, differences in intensities between images are considered a hindrance to the estimation of accurate deformation fields. However, image intensity and local contrast may contain rich and valuable information. For example, the maturation process in the early developing brain manifests as rapidly increasing white matter intensity [1]. Recent work has demonstrated that MRI intensity and contrast measures quantify patterns of early brain development, showing a brain maturation rate difference between males and females [2]. In this paper, we similarly seek to quantify early brain development by explicitly modeling intensity change over time as part of an image regression framework.

There has been tremendous research effort into accurate registration schemes in the presence of appearance changes. However, as previously mentioned, appearance changes are rarely handled explicitly. Rather, image similarity metrics such as mutual information or normalized cross correlation are used to reduce sensitivity to intensity differences. In the case of appearance change due to pathology, registration methods often involve masking, and thus require prior segmentation to aid in registration [3].

An approach to image matching which combines structural and intensity changes was proposed as image metamorphosis [4], and was later integrated into a geodesic regression framework [5], though the baseline image was assumed to be fixed to the earliest observations, and experimentation appeared limited to 2D. In the metamorphosis approach, image intensity change is smoothly interpolated for exact matching. However, intensity change under the metamorphosis model does not have a clear interpretation to answer clinical questions about development. Importantly, the study of intensity change trajectories *themselves* as a representation of development has not yet been explored.

For clear interpretation and straightforward statistical analysis, parametric models of image intensity have been proposed. This includes linear intensity models for registration [6] and atlas building [7], and a logistic image intensity model for longitudinal registration [8]. However, the method [8] requires a tissue segmentation which itself requires non-linear registration as a preprocessing step. The method of [9] proposes a parametric pharmacokinetic intensity model to improve accuracy in atlas building, for motion correction of dynamic contrast-enhanced MRI. Ultimately, these methods are registration schemes, which are inherently limited to estimating a discrete set of deformations, one for each image, rather than a single time-varying flow of deformation which more naturally captures longitudinal changes. Nevertheless, our work takes the spirit of these previous methods when it comes to modeling appearance, as we favor the parametric approach for the power to distill down complex patterns of development into a small number of easy to understand parameters.

To summarize, there has been considerable work in addressing appearance change for registration and atlas building, though there has been limited work on image regression with appearance change. Furthermore, the study of the intensity trajectories, either as curves or as parameters of functions, is a relatively unexplored topic. In other words, modeling image appearance change is not only a mechanism to achieve more accurate registration; intensity trajectories themselves contain rich information about development and warrant further study. In this paper, we propose a spatiotemporal model for image time series which explicitly models both structural and appearance change. Image deformations are modeled by diffeomorphic flow with a flexible and non-parametric acceleration based method [10]. We favor this image deformation model for its flexibility, however, one could instead choose from a variety of models, such as geodesic [11] or higher order models [12,13]. Intensity changes are modeled by a Gompertz function, which has three intuitive parameters of asymptote, delay, and speed. The deformation and intensity change models are motivated by the driving application of modeling brain development from birth, which is characterized by early accelerated growth which saturates to an asymptote [14]. In contrast to previous work, our model requires no masking or prior segmentation, and simultaneously estimates *continuous* structural deformations along with parametric intensity change trajectories with a clear interpretation. Experimental validation on a synthetic image sequence as well as longitudinal MR images demonstrate that Gompertz parameter maps encode regional patterns of development using natural terms of speed and delay.

2   Methods

In this section, we describe the two main components of our proposed spatiotemporal model: the structural deformation model and the intensity change model. We then combine the two components and provide a least squares estimation procedure.

2.1   Structural Deformation Model

Here, we introduce the structural deformation model, first proposed in [15] for shape regression and more recently for image regression [10], with the main idea of parameterizing diffeomorphic flow by a time-varying function of acceleration. Acceleration is defined as

$$a(x,t) = \sum_{i=1}^{N_C} K^V(x, c_i(t))\alpha_i(t) \tag{1}$$

where an impulse vector field $\alpha_i(t)$ is attached to a sparse set of N_C control points $c_i(t)$ and smooth kernel operator K defining the reproducing kernel Hilbert space V (for example, a Gaussian with standard deviation σ_V^2). Given such a time-varying acceleration field, a flow of diffeomorphisms of the ambient space can be computed by solving:

$$\ddot{\phi}(x(t),t) = a(x(t),t) \tag{2}$$

given initial position $x_0 = x(t_0)$ and initial velocity $v_0 = v(t_0)$. Solving Eq. 2 generates a flow of diffeomorphisms starting from identity $\phi(0) = Id$, which defines the trajectory of a point starting from $x(t_0)$ and ending at $x(T)$. Starting from a given distribution of control points $c_i(0)$, the continuous path of control points $c_i(t)$ is computed by solving Eq. 2. Just as with control points, coordinates of image voxels also evolve according to Eq. 2, starting from a baseline image I_0. Therefore, given $\alpha_i(t)$, one can compute the continuous evolution of control points, and compute acceleration at physical image coordinates. This shows that the system can be parameterized by a finite number of parameters, given a time discretization of $\alpha_i(t)$.

From here on, let $\boldsymbol{\alpha}(t)$, $\boldsymbol{v}_0$, and $\boldsymbol{c}_0$ be the concatenation of the $\alpha_i(t)$'s, $v_i(0)$'s, and $c_i(0)$'s. Let a set of image observations in time range t_0 to T be written as $I_{t_i} = (I_{t_1}, I_{t_2}, ...I_{t_n})$. The acceleration controlled deformation model can be leveraged for image regression by estimating impulse vectors $\boldsymbol{\alpha}(t)$, control point locations $\boldsymbol{c}_0$, and baseline image I_0 which minimizes

$$E(\boldsymbol{\alpha}(t), \boldsymbol{c}_0, I_0) = \sum_{i=1}^{N} d(\phi_{t_i} \circ I_0, I_{t_i})^2 + \gamma_A \int_{t_0}^{T} ||\mathbf{a}(t)||_V^2 \, dt \qquad (3)$$

where d is a distance metric between images, γ_A weights the regularity of the time-varying acceleration $\mathbf{a}(t)$, and initial velocity $v_0 = 0$.

2.2 Gompertz Intensity Change Model

Motivated by the study of early brain development, we propose to model image appearance change with a Gompertz function. We believe the Gompertz function, which is a sigmoid curve, is a good fit for modeling early acceleration growth which eventually tapers off, which has been observed in MRI intensity of the developing brain [14]. The authors of [8] used similar reasoning to select a logistic appearance model, while the work of [16] found the Gompertz function to be an accurate model of diffusion measures during early development. The Gompertz function is written as: $g(t) = A \exp(-B \exp(-Ct))$ where $B > 0$ and $C > 0$.

One powerful feature of the Gompertz function is the straightforward interpretability of it's three parameters. The parameters A, B, and C, can be interpreted as asymptote, delay, and speed, respectively. This allows complex patterns of change to be communicated in simple terms that are naturally used to discuss development. We therefore propose the following Gompertz image appearance model:

$$\hat{I}(x, t) = g(x, t) = A(x) \exp(-B(x) \exp(-C(x)t)) \qquad (4)$$

which describes continuous image appearance change over time t at location x. Gompertz parameters A, B, and C vary spatially, and can be thought of as parameter *images*. Later we will see how these parameter images can be analysed to study regional patterns of development. We will denote the appearance model at time t as $\hat{\mathbf{I}}(t)$.

2.3 Spatiotemporal Model with Appearance Change

We now propose a combined spatiotemporal model which simultaneously estimates continuous structural image deformations along with appearance change.

The main difficulty in designing such a model is the inherent non-uniqueness in a solution which combines structural and appearance changes. As an example, consider an image of a white circle which grows isotropically over time, but does not change appearance. The progression could be described completed by image deformations which capture the change in scale of the circle, or alternatively, entirely by an appearance model which "paints" in additional pixels. To address this issue, we allow for control over the contribution of the deformation and appearance models. This is accomplished with two data-matching terms, one measuring fit via deformation only, and one measuring fit by intensity change only. While this doesn't provide a globally optimal solution, it does allow the user to control estimation based on domain knowledge or empirical observation. Together with regularity terms, the model criterion is written

$$E(\boldsymbol{\alpha}(t), \mathbf{c}_0, A, B, C) = \left[\sum_{i=1}^{N_{obs}} \lambda_D \ d(\phi_{t_i}(\hat{\mathbf{I}}(t_0)), I_{t_i})^2 + \lambda_A \ d(\hat{\mathbf{I}}(t_i), I_{t_i})^2 \right]$$
$$+ \lambda_R \int_{t_0}^{T} ||\mathbf{a}(t)||_V^2 dt + \lambda_{TV} \ \mathrm{TV}(A, B, C) \tag{5}$$

where the first two terms are data-matching by deformation only and intensity change only, the third term measures regularity of the time-varying deformation, and the last term is a total variation regularizer on the Gompertz parameters. We use an anisotropic version of total variation, which is differentiable. This term may be used promote regional consistency in asymptote, delay, and speed images, based on the assumption that tissue development is highly spatially correlated. For measuring image similarity d, we use sum-of-squared intensity difference. Weights λ allow to control the importance of each term in the overall cost. The final image sequence is then computed as $\phi_t(\hat{\mathbf{I}}(t))$ (Fig. 1).

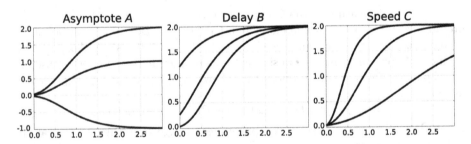

Fig. 1. The Gompertz function $g(t) = A \exp(-B \exp(-Ct))$ is parameterized by three intuitive values: asymptote, delay, and speed. In each plot, a range of values is plotted for each parameter while holding the other two fixed.

Alternatively, the model may be expressed with a single data term measuring fit between observations and the generative model as $d(\phi_t(\hat{\mathbf{I}}(t)), I_{t_i})^2$. In this case, the relative contribution of the deformation and intensity model would be controlled entirely by regularity terms and weights λ_R and λ_{TV}. While this model is not explored in this paper, research into this and other formulations remains ongoing work with the goal of developing a robust and intuitive model of structural and appearance change.

Model estimation consists in finding time varying impulse vectors $\alpha(t)$, location of control points c_0, and Gompertz appearance parameters A, B, and C which minimize (5). The algorithm is initialized with $\alpha(t) = \mathbf{0}$ (corresponding to no deformation), control points c_0 on a regular grid with user selected spacing, and Gompertz appearance parameters $A = B = C = \mathbf{0}$. We implement a gradient descent scheme with gradients computed using autograd in PyTorch [17]. We also use KeOps (http://www.kernel-operations.io), which provides memory efficiency on the GPU, enabling the use of 3D image volumes on a TITAN Xp. Our implementation is available at https://github.com/jamesfishbaugh/acceleration-diffeos.

3   Experimental Validation

3.1   Synthetic Bull's-Eye

We first validate our model on a synthetic image time series of a bull's-eye with both structural and appearance changes. The top row of Fig. 2 shows the observations of the bull's-eye images. The image sequence undergoes complex structural change, with the outer ring increasing in size over time according to an exponential, while the inner circle shrinks linearly. The outer ring is further characterized by two distinct patterns of appearance change. First, the bottom half shows a delay with respect to the top half. Second, intensity in the bottom half increases faster than intensity in the top region. The trajectory of change in the top half is given by a logistic function, while intensity in the bottom half changes linearly. The inner circle does not undergo any appearance change.

Figure 2(B) shows the model estimated with our proposed method. Here we show only several frames, though the model can alternatively be viewed as a continuous animation for more intuitive understanding. The estimated image sequence very closely matches the observations, effectively capturing complex patterns of structural and appearance changes simultaneously. The average structural similarity was 0.99 while the average mean square error was 1.5×10^{-4}. Furthermore, our method provides realistic trajectories *between* observation time points, with smooth and continuous trajectories of both structure and appearance. For longitudinal data, this is a more natural representation of image change compared to a discrete set of diffeomorphisms, one for each image, which must be cascaded as in longitudinal registration [8].

We also estimated an image trajectory with a deformation model only, shown in Fig. 2(C). Here, we measured average structural similarity of 0.81 and average mean square error of 0.05. Finally, we compare against a readily available baseline method, a geodesic model using the software package Deformetrica [18], shown in Fig. 2(C), with an average structural similarity of 0.83 and average mean square error of 0.04.

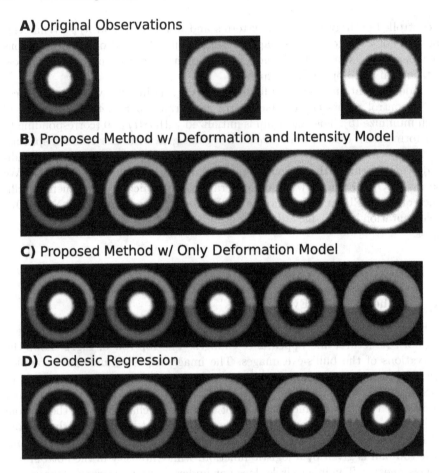

Fig. 2. (Top) Synthetic observations representing the progression of a bull's-eye undergoing both structural and appearance changes. The outer ring grows while the inner circle shrinks. The bottom half of the outer ring shows a delay with respect to the top half, along with a faster increase in intensity. The inner circle does not change in appearance. **(B) (C) (D)** Several frames from estimated continuous image trajectories under different models. Animation of our proposed method available at https://youtu.be/5OqmLZOjalw.

We can explore a statistical representation of the appearance changes by investigating the Gompertz parameter maps, which are themselves images of the same dimension as the observations, shown in Fig. 3. The delayed and accelerated intensity region in the lower half of the outer ring is well captured by the delay and speed image, while the asymptote has similar characteristics to the final image observation.

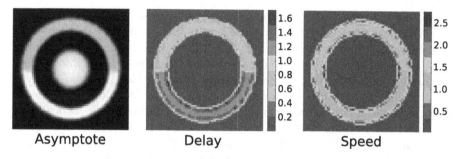

Fig. 3. Gompertz parameter images of asymptote A, delay B, and speed C for the synthetic bull's-eye progression from Fig. 2. The asymptote image most closely resembles the final image observation, representing intensity saturation. The lower half of the outer ring shows a significant delay with respect to the top half, as well as faster increase in intensity. The inner circle is not present in the delay and speed images, since the inner circle only undergoes structural changes.

3.2 Early Brain Development from Birth

Next, we seek to model structural and appearance change of the developing brain starting from birth. This is particularly challenging due to the rapid development and appearance changes observed in MR images during the first year of life. Imaging data consists of a longitudinal sequence of a healthy child scanned at birth, 1, 2, 4, and 6 years of age in the form of 3D T1W images of dimension

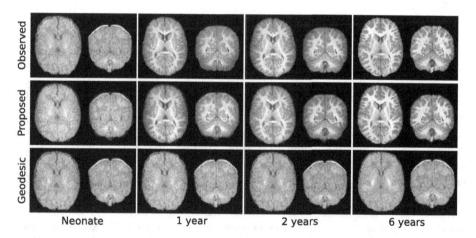

Fig. 4. (Top) Observed T1W image sequence at birth, 1, 2, and 6 years of age. **(Middle)** Images estimated by the proposed spatiotemporal model of structural and appearance change. Continuous evolution is better understood when viewed as an animation here: https://youtu.be/AWsai9_dkhU. **(Bottom)** Image sequence estimated by a baseline geodesic model with no appearance model, which results in a unrealistic sequence which always maintains the appearance of a neonate.

$196 \times 233 \times 159$ with $1 \times 1 \times 1$ voxel size. Images were skull stripped and affine aligned. Intensity values across the entire longitudinal sequence were normalized to be between 0 and 1 based on min and max values across the longitudinal sequence. This is a naive normalization procedure that doesn't take into account scanner differences or possible hyperintense areas such as blood vessels. Although this procedure is suitable for proof of concept of our spatiotemporal model, proper normalization will have to be addressed in future work, to deal with the impact of non-calibrated scans acquired at different sites and even different scanner generations. However, longitudinal normalization of MR images comes with many challenges which are beyond the scope of this work.

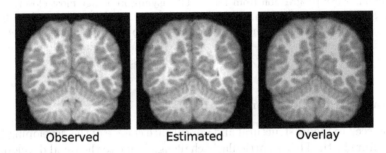

| Observed | Estimated | Overlay |

Fig. 5. Coronal slice from the 4 year old observation that was left out during model estimation, along with the image estimated by our model. The observed and estimated image are overlaid, with yellow indicating similar intensities, while red and green indicate intensity mismatch. (Color figure online)

To explore the impact of missing data, a model was estimated by excluding the year 4 observation. Figure 4 shows the original observations (top) and the estimated image sequence from our proposed model (middle). Qualitatively, the model closely matches the observed image sequence, well capturing the observed image progression. Figure 5 shows that the smooth and continuous trajectory estimated by our method generates realistic images between observations, as the estimated image at 4 years old closely resembles the true 4 year old observation, which was not included in model estimation. We measured a structural similarity index of 0.93 and a root-mean-square error of 0.004. We also note the added benefit of a reduction in skull stripping artifacts in the estimated image compared to the original observation. The bottom row of Fig. 4 shows an unrealistic trajectory estimated with a geodesic model without considering appearance changes. It is worth noting that the geodesic model may also be estimated backward in time starting from 6 years old, or alternatively, estimated in both directions starting in the middle. However, all such models appear artificial and unrealistic since they all carry the appearance of their starting image.

Gompertz parameter images are shown in Fig. 6, which capture regional patterns of development. There is a clear posterior to anterior pattern of development captured in the delay and speed images. The anterior region shows

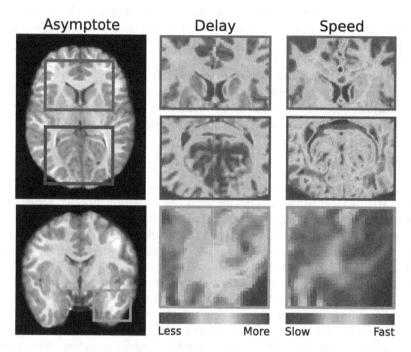

Fig. 6. (Top) Gompertz delay and speed images capture a posterior to anterior pattern of growth, with the posterior region developing earlier and faster. **(Bottom)** White matter development in the temporal lobe is delayed and progresses slowly compared to other regions.

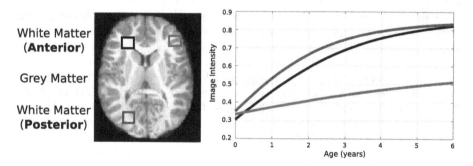

Fig. 7. (Left) Selected regions of white and grey matter overlaid on estimated scan at 6 years old. Colored boxes are shown enlarged for illustration purposes, true regions are slightly smaller homogeneous 3D regions. **(Right)** Regional averages of Gompertz parameters are shown from 0 to 6 years. We observe posterior white matter shows less delay than anterior white matter, but also undergoes accelerated development, reaching a shared asymptote quicker. Grey matter shows a more gradual linear increase in intensity over time.

increased delay and lower speed, while the posterior region is characterized by less delay and high speed. The temporal lobe also develops later, with relatively slow speed. These are all findings previously reported in pediatric radiology [1]. This can also been seen in Fig. 7 for selected regions of anterior white matter, posterior white matter, and also grey matter. It shows a pattern of delayed and slower white matter development in the anterior compared to the posterior, which starts at a higher value and also reaches the asymptote more quickly. Grey matter, on the other hand, undergoes a slow, nearly linear, increase in intensity.

4   Discussion

Brain maturation can be observed as a change of intensity and contrast over time in MR images. In this paper, we proposed a spatiotemporal model which explicitly accounts for intensity change through a Gompertz appearance model. Our method estimates continuous structural and appearance change jointly, for a comprehensive description of early brain development. To overcome the problem of solutions being non-unique, we introduced two data-matching terms to balance the contribution of structural and appearance change. The problem could also be approached with an alternative cost function formulation, which is currently being explored as ongoing work. Another solution would be to limit appearance changes to white matter regions via a segmentation mask, as in [8]. In addition to estimating a continuous image sequence that closely matches observations, we showed that Gompertz parameter images capture patterns of development in intuitive terms of asymptote, delay, and speed. Since MRI intensity values are uncalibrated, the most pressing future work is longitudinal as well as population wide normalization, as in [19]. Longitudinal imaging studies face the challenge of acquisitions from different technicians from a variety of physical locations, as well as changes in scanner technology over the lifetime of a study, which make direct comparison of MRI intensities an open challenge. Directly comparing intensity across sites and scanner generation requires careful harmonization and normalization procedures.

Acknowledgments. This work was supported by NIH grants NIBIB R01EB021391 (SlicerSALT), 1R01HD088125-01A1 (Down's Syndrome), 2R01HD055741-11 (ACE-IBIS), 1R01DA038215-01A1 (Cocaine Effects) and the New York Center for Advanced Technology in Telecommunications (CATT). HPC resources used for this research provided by grant NSF MRI-1229185.

References

1. Rutherford, M.A., Bydder, G.M.: MRI of the Neonatal Brain. WB Saunders, London (2002)
2. Vardhan, A., Fishbaugh, J., Vachet, C., Gerig, G.: Longitudinal modeling of multimodal image contrast reveals patterns of early brain growth. In: Descoteaux, M., Maier-Hein, L., Franz, A., Jannin, P., Collins, D.L., Duchesne, S. (eds.) MICCAI 2017. LNCS, vol. 10433, pp. 75–83. Springer, Cham (2017). https://doi.org/10.1007/978-3-319-66182-7_9

3. Niethammer, M., et al.: Geometric metamorphosis. In: Fichtinger, G., Martel, A., Peters, T. (eds.) MICCAI 2011. LNCS, vol. 6892, pp. 639–646. Springer, Heidelberg (2011). https://doi.org/10.1007/978-3-642-23629-7_78

4. Miller, M.I., Younes, L.: Group actions, homeomorphisms, and matching: a general framework. Int. J. Comput. Vis. **41**(1–2), 61–84 (2001)

5. Hong, Y., Joshi, S., Sanchez, M., Styner, M., Niethammer, M.: Metamorphic geodesic regression. In: Ayache, N., Delingette, H., Golland, P., Mori, K. (eds.) MICCAI 2012. LNCS, vol. 7512, pp. 197–205. Springer, Heidelberg (2012). https://doi.org/10.1007/978-3-642-33454-2_25

6. Periaswamy, S., Farid, H.: Elastic registration in the presence of intensity variations. IEEE Trans. Med. Imaging **22**(7), 865–874 (2003)

7. Gao, Y., Zhang, M., Grewen, K., Fletcher, P.T., Gerig, G.: Image registration and segmentation in longitudinal MRI using temporal appearance modeling. In: IEEE ISBI, pp. 629–632 (2016)

8. Csapo, I., Davis, B., Shi, Y., Sanchez, M., Styner, M., Niethammer, M.: Longitudinal image registration with temporally-dependent image similarity measure. IEEE Trans. Med. Imaging **32**(10), 1939–1951 (2013)

9. Bhushan, M., Schnabel, J.A., Risser, L., Heinrich, M.P., Brady, J.M., Jenkinson, M.: Motion correction and parameter estimation in dceMRI sequences: application to colorectal cancer. In: Fichtinger, G., Martel, A., Peters, T. (eds.) MICCAI 2011. LNCS, vol. 6891, pp. 476–483. Springer, Heidelberg (2011). https://doi.org/10.1007/978-3-642-23623-5_60

10. Fishbaugh, J., Gerig, G.: Acceleration controlled diffeomorphisms for nonparametric image regression. In: IEEE ISBI, pp. 1488–1491 (2019)

11. Niethammer, M., Huang, Y., Vialard, F.-X.: Geodesic regression for image time-series. In: Fichtinger, G., Martel, A., Peters, T. (eds.) MICCAI 2011. LNCS, vol. 6892, pp. 655–662. Springer, Heidelberg (2011). https://doi.org/10.1007/978-3-642-23629-7_80

12. Singh, N., Vialard, F.X., Niethammer, M.: Splines for diffeomorphisms. Med. Image Anal. **25**(1), 56–71 (2015)

13. Hinkle, J., Fletcher, P.T., Joshi, S.: Intrinsic polynomials for regression on riemannian manifolds. J. Math. Imaging Vis. **50**(1–2), 32–52 (2014)

14. Dobbing, J., Sands, J.: Quantitative growth and development of human brain. Arch. Dis. Child. **48**(10), 757–767 (1973)

15. Fishbaugh, J., Durrleman, S., Gerig, G.: Estimation of smooth growth trajectories with controlled acceleration from time series shape data. In: Fichtinger, G., Martel, A., Peters, T. (eds.) MICCAI 2011. LNCS, vol. 6892, pp. 401–408. Springer, Heidelberg (2011). https://doi.org/10.1007/978-3-642-23629-7_49

16. Sadeghi, N., Prastawa, M., Fletcher, P.T., Wolff, J., Gilmore, J.H., Gerig, G.: Regional characterization of longitudinal dt-mri to study white matter maturation of the early developing brain. Neuroimage **68**, 236–247 (2013)

17. Paszke, A., et al.: Automatic differentiation in pytorch (2017)

18. Bône, A., Louis, M., Martin, B., Durrleman, S.: Deformetrica 4: an open-source software for statistical shape analysis. In: Shape in Medical Imaging, pp. 3–13 (2018)

19. Sweeney, E., Shinohara, R., Shea, C., Reich, D., Crainiceanu, C.M.: Automatic lesion incidence estimation and detection in multiple sclerosis using multisequence longitudinal mri. Am. J. Neuroradiol. **34**(1), 68–73 (2013)

Surface Foliation Based Brain Morphometry Analysis

Chengfeng Wen[1], Na Lei[2], Ming Ma[1(✉)], Xin Qi[1], Wen Zhang[3], Yalin Wang[3],
and Xianfeng Gu[1]

[1] Department of Computer Science, Stony Brook University,
Stony Brook, NY 11794, USA
{chwen,minma,xinqi,gu}@cs.stonybrook.edu
[2] School of Software and Technology, Dalian University of Technology,
Dalian 116620, China
nalei@dlut.edu.cn
[3] School of Computing, Informatics, and Decision Systems Engineering,
Arizona State University, Tempe, AZ 85281, USA
{wzhan139,ylwang}@asu.edu

Abstract. Brain morphometry plays a fundamental role in neuroimaging research. In this work, we propose a novel method for brain surface morphometry analysis based on surface foliation theory. Given brain cortical surfaces with automatically extracted landmark curves, we first construct finite foliations on surfaces. A set of admissible curves and a height parameter for each loop are provided by users. The admissible curves cut the surface into a set of pairs of pants. A pants decomposition graph is then constructed. Strebel differential is obtained by computing a unique harmonic map from surface to pants decomposition graph. The critical trajectories of Strebel differential decompose the surface into topological cylinders. After conformally mapping those topological cylinders to standard cylinders, parameters of standard cylinders (height, circumference) are intrinsic geometric features of the original cortical surfaces and thus can be used for morphometry analysis purpose. In this work, we propose a set of novel surface features. To the best of our knowledge, this is the first work to make use of surface foliation theory for brain morphometry analysis. The features we computed are intrinsic and informative. The proposed method is rigorous, geometric, and automatic. Experimental results on classifying brain cortical surfaces between patients with Alzheimer's disease and healthy control subjects demonstrate the efficiency and efficacy of our method.

Keywords: Brain morphometry · Shape classification · Surface foliation · Alzheimer disease

1 Introduction

MRI based brain morphometry analysis has gained extensive interest in the past decades [17,20]. A lot of research works are focused on identifying very early signs

© Springer Nature Switzerland AG 2019
D. Zhu et al. (Eds.): MBIA 2019/MFCA 2019, LNCS 11846, pp. 186–195, 2019.
https://doi.org/10.1007/978-3-030-33226-6_20

of brain functional and structural changes for early identification and prevention of neurodegenerative diseases. Alzheimer's disease (AD), which is the sixth-
leading cause of death in the United States, and the fifth-leading cause of death
among those age 65 and older as reported by Alzheimer's Association in 2018 [1],
has obtained much interest from researchers around the world. Early detection
and prevention of AD can significantly impact treatment options, improve quality of life, and save considerable health care costs. As a non-invasive method,
brain imaging study has great potentials that will powerfully track disease progression and therapeutic efficacy in AD. For example, whole brain morphometry,
hippocampal and entorhinal cortex volumes are among most promising candidate biomarkers in structural MRI analysis. However, missing at this time is a
widely available, highly objective brain imaging biomarker capable of identifying
abnormal degrees of cerebral atrophy and accelerated rate of atrophy progression
in preclinical individuals at high risk for AD in who early intervention is most
needed.

Computational geometric methods are widely used in medical imaging fields
including virtual colonoscopy and brain morphometry analysis. Rooted in deep
geometry analysis research, computational geometric methods may provide rigorous and accurate quantification of abnormal brain development and thus hold
a potential to detect preclinical AD in presymptomatic subjects. Specifically,
surface morphometry techniques, such as conformal mapping and area preserving mapping, have shown to be feasible and powerful tools in brain morphometry
research.

To the best of our knowledge, this is the first work to propose the use of the
surface foliation theory for brain morphometry analysis. We validate our method
by classifying brain surfaces of patients with Alzheimer disease and healthy
control subjects. Experimental results indicate the efficiency and efficacy of our
proposed method. The main contributions are summarized as follows:

- A novel brain surface morphometry analysis method is proposed based on
  surface foliation theory.
- A set of new geometric features computed by pants decomposition and conformal mapping of topological cylinders are also proposed for surface indexing
  and classification.
- The proposed method is rigorous, geometric and automatic.

2   Previous Works

Brain morphometry analysis plays a fundamental role in medical imaging [11,
22,24]. Many research works have investigated the brain morphometry analysis
and shape classification. Thompson et al. [17] analyzed brain morphometry using
thickness features. Winkler et al. [20] proposed that the surface area could serve
as an important morphometry feature to study brain structural MRI images.
Besides, numerous methods have been presented in order to describe shapes,
including statistical methods [14], topology based methods [6], and geometry
based methods [12]. To solve real 3D shape problems, researchers have also

proposed many shape analysis and classification methods. Chaplot et al. [3] employed wavelets and neural network for classification of brain MR images. Zacharaki et al. [23] proposed the use of pattern classification methods for classifying different types of brain tumors. Recently, Su et al. [16] presented a shape classification method busing Wasserstein distance. The method computed a unique optimal mass transport map between two measures, and used Wasserstein distance to intrinsically measure the dissimilarities between shapes.

Foliation [15] is a generalization of vector field. In computer graphics field, Zhang et al. [25] invented a vector field design system which could help users create various vector fields with control over vector field topology. The technique can be used in some applications such as example-based texture synthesis, painterly rendering of images, and pencil sketch illustrations of smooth surfaces. Recently, Campen et al. [2] proposed a method for bijective parametrization of 2D and 3D objects based on simplicial foliations. The method decomposed a mesh into one-dimensional submanifolds, reducing the mapping problem to parametrization of a lower-dimensional manifold. It was proved that the resulting maps are bijective and continuous. In isogeometric analysis field, Lei et al. [9] presented a novel quadrilateral and hexahedral mesh generation method using foliation theory. A colorable quad-mesh method was employed to generate the quadrilateral mesh based on Strebel differentials, which then leads to the structured hexahedral mesh of the enclosed volume for high genus surfaces. Hsieh et al. [7] studied an elasticity model for shape evolution where the control is interpreted as the derivative of a body force density in the deforming volume, and a special case of the model decomposes the shapes into a family of layers called foliation.

3   Theoretic Foundation

We briefly review the basic concepts and theorems in conformal geometry. Detailed treatments can be found in [4,5,15].

A complex function $f : \mathbb{C} \to \mathbb{C}$, $(x,y) \to (u,v)$, satisfying the Cauchy-Riemann equation

$$u_x = v_y, u_y = -v_x,$$

is called a *holomorphic function*. If f is invertible, and f^{-1} is also holomorphic, then f is called a *bi-holomorphic function*. For a surface with a complex atlas $\mathcal{A}$, if all chart transition functions are bi-holomorphic, it is called a *Riemann surface*, the atlas $\mathcal{A}$ is called a *complex structure*. All oriented metric surfaces are Riemann surfaces.

Definition 1 (Holomorphic Quadratic Differentials). *Assume S is a Riemann surface. Let Φ be a complex differential form, such that on each local chart with the local complex parameter $\{z_\alpha\}$, $\Phi = \varphi_\alpha(z_\alpha)dz_\alpha^2$, in which $\varphi_\alpha(z_\alpha)$ is a holomorphic function. Then Φ is called a holomorphic quadratic differential.*

Based on the Riemann-Roch Theorem, the linear space of all holomorphic quadratic differentials is $3g - 3$ complex dimensional with the genus $g > 1$.

A point $z_i \in S$ is called a *zero* of Φ, if $\varphi(z_i)$ vanishes. A holomorphic quadratic differential has $4g - 4$ zeros. For any point away from zero, a local coordinates can be defined as follows:

$$\zeta(p) := \int^p \sqrt{\varphi(z)}dz. \tag{1}$$

which are so-called *natural coordinates* induced by Φ. The curves with constant real (imaginary) natural coordinates are called the *vertical (horizontal) trajectories*, and the trajectories through the zeros are called the *critical trajectories*.

Definition 2 (Strebel [15]). *If all of the horizontal trajectories of a holomorphic quadratic differential Φ on a Riemann surface S are finite, then Φ is called a Strebel differential.*

We say a holomorphic quadratic differential Φ is Strebel, if and only if its critical horizontal trajectories form a finite graph [15]. In the space of all holomorphic quadratic differentials, the Strebel differentials are dense. Given a holomorphic quadratic differential Φ, a flat metric with cone singularities (cone angles equal to $-\pi$), denoted as $|\Phi|$, is induced by the natural coordinates in Eq. 1. The following existence of a Strebel differential with prescribed type and heights was proved by Hubbard and Masur.

Theorem 1 (Hubbard and Masur [8]). *For non-intersecting simple loops $\Gamma = \{\gamma_1, \gamma_2, \cdots, \gamma_n\}$, and positive numbers $\{h_1, h_2, \cdots, h_n\}$, $n \leq 3g - 3$, there exists a unique holomorphic quadratic differential Φ, which satisfies the following:*

1. *A surface is partitioned by the critical graph of Φ into n cylinders which are denoted by $\{C_1, C_2, \cdots, C_n\}$, such that γ_k is the generator of C_k,*
2. *The height of each cylinder $(C_k, |\Phi|)$ is equal to h_k, $k = 1, 2, \cdots, n$.*

We give the geometric interpretation of above theorem as follows: under the flat metric $|\Phi|$, each cylinder C_k becomes a canonical flat cylinder with height h_k. Strebel's theorem allows for specifying the type of Φ and the height of each cylinder C_k.

Harmonic Map. Assume $G = \langle E, N \rangle$ is a graph, and $\mathbf{h} : E \rightarrow \mathbb{R}^+$ is an *edge weight* function. p and q denote two points on the graph, and $d_{\mathbf{h}}(p, q)$ represents the shortest distance between them. Suppose $(S, \mathbf{g})$ is a surface with a Riemannian metric $\mathbf{g}$. Given a map $f : (S, \mathbf{g}) \rightarrow (G, \mathbf{h})$, we say a point $p \in S$ is a *regular point*, if its image is not any node of G, otherwise it is a *critical point*. We denote the set of all critical points as Γ. For each regular point $p \in S$, a neighborhood U_p can be found and the restriction of the map on U_p can be treated as a normal function $f : U_p \rightarrow \mathbb{R}$. An *isothermal coordinates* (x, y) are selected on U_p, such that the metric has a special form $\mathbf{g} = e^{2\lambda(x,y)}(dx^2 + dy^2)$. Then the harmonic energy is represented by $E(f|_{U_p}) := \int_{U_p} |\nabla_{\mathbf{g}} f|^2 dA_{\mathbf{g}}$, where

$\nabla_{\mathbf{g}} = e^{-\lambda} \left(\frac{\partial}{\partial x}, \frac{\partial}{\partial y} \right)^T$, and the area element is $dA_{\mathbf{g}} = e^{2\lambda} dx dy$. The *harmonic energy* of the whole map is given as

$$E(f) := \int_{S \backslash \Gamma} |\nabla_{\mathbf{g}} f|^2 dA_{\mathbf{g}}.$$

The critical point of the harmonic energy is called a *harmonic map*. Wolf [21] proved the existence and the uniqueness of the harmonic map.

Theorem 2 (Wolf [21]). *The harmonic map $f : (S, \mathbf{g}) \to (G, \mathbf{h})$ exists and is unique in each homotopy class. Moreover, as induced by the harmonic map, the Hopf differential $\Phi = \langle f_z, f_z \rangle dz^2$ is a holomorphic quadratic differential, where $z = x + iy$ denotes the complex isothermal coordinates of $(S, \mathbf{g})$.*

Conformal Module. Let $(S, \mathbf{g})$ be a surface of genus $g > 1$. Given $3g - 3$ non-intersecting simple loops $\Gamma = \{\gamma_i\}$ and positive numbers $\{h_i\}$, the unique Strebel differential Φ based on Hubbard and Masur's theorem induces a flat metric $|\Phi|$ with cone singularities, and cylinders $\{C_i\}_{i=1}^{3g-3}$. The height and circumference for each cylinder $(C_k, |\Phi|)$ are denoted by (h_k, l_k). The set of all (h_k, l_k) are the conformal modules.

4   Algorithm

Pants Decomposition. Let S be a closed surface of genus g, represented by triangular mesh. Let $\Gamma = \{\gamma_i, i = 1, 2, ..., 3g - 3\}$ be a set of *admissible curves*, which can be generated automatically or manually specified. User also specifies a height parameter h_i for each admissible curve γ_i. These admissible curves decompose surface S to a set of *pants* $\mathcal{P} = \{P_i, i = 1, 2, ..., 2g - 2\}$. The pants decomposition graph G is then constructed in the following way:

- each pants P_i corresponds to a node in G;
- each admissible curve connecting two pants corresponds to an edge in G; two pants may be the same, in that case, the edge becomes a loop.

Figure 1 illustrates pants decomposition and pants decomposition graph.

Discrete Harmonic Map to Graph. We compute a unique harmonic map f from surface S to G. The harmonic energy is defined as

$$E(f) = \sum_{i,j,e_{ij} \in S} w_{ij} d^2(f(v_i), f(v_j))$$

where v_i are vertex on S, $f(v_i)$ on G, e_{ij} are edges, w_{ij} cotangent weight.

For each v_i, by moving $f(v_i)$ to the barycenter of its neighbors on graph G, the energy E will decrease monotonically, which is due to the following definition of barycenter. By iteratively doing so, energy E will attain its minimum value, at which point we obtain a harmonic map $f : S \to G$. Theorem 2 guarantees this

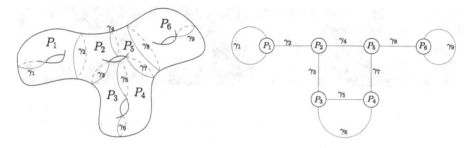

Fig. 1. Pants decomposition of surface (left) and pants decomposition graph (right)

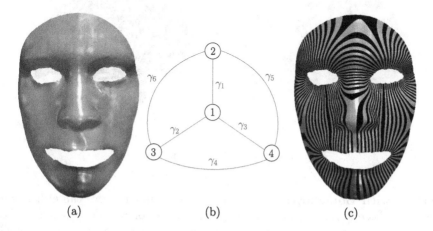

(a)   (b)   (c)

Fig. 2. Harmonic map from human face to pants decomposition graph and induced surface foliation

harmonic map we obtained is the unique one. Figure 2(a) illustrates harmonic map from a human face surface to its pants decomposition graph (b), (c) shows surface foliation, where color indicates vertices' target position on graph G.

The initial map f_0 should be specified in the same homotopy class as the final harmonic map f. Subgraph at a node consists of the node and all edges connecting to it. Then initial map can be obtained automatically in the following way: each pants P_i be mapped to the subgraph G_i at node i of G, then all pants maps are glued together to obtain f_0.

Calculate Barycenter. For each $f(v_i)$, we move $f(v_i)$ to the barycenter of its neighbors. Calculating barycenter is done by minimizing energy

$$f(v_i)^* = \arg\min_{f(v)} \sum_{j,e_{ij}\in S} w_{ij} d^2(f(v), f(v_j))$$

where the right are exactly the terms in E that involve $f(v_i)$. $d(f(v_i), f(v_j))$ can be calculated piecewisely. Then minimization of above energy boils down to minimum calculation of a set of quadratic functions.

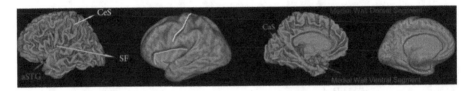

Fig. 3. A left cortical surface with six landmark curves, which are automatically labeled with Caret, showing in two different views on both the original and inflated surfaces.

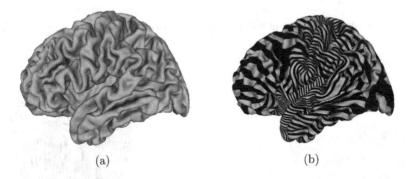

Fig. 4. A brain surface and its foliation.

Surface with Boundaries. For surfaces with boundaries, we can either double cover those surfaces to obtain a closed surface, or we can add boundaries to the set of admissible curves, such curves correspond to open edges on G. Computation of harmonic map remains same.

Extract Geometric Features. A holomorphic quadratic differential Φ can be induced from the harmonic map we obtained. Tracing the critical trajectories of Φ and slicing surface along them, we obtain a set of $3g - 3$ topological cylinders, each corresponds to an input admissible curve. The set of heights and circumferences of those cylinders are topological invariants, which we propose to use as geometric features for classification problems in next section.

5   Experiment

To evaluate the proposed method for brain morphometry study, we conducted experiments on a dataset of 60 brain cortical surfaces. Triangle mesh of each brain surface has around 100K triangles.

Data Preparation. The dataset used in our experiments includes images from 30 patients with Alzheimer disease and 30 healthy control subjects. The structural MRI images were from the Alzheimer's Disease Neuroimaging Initiative (ADNI) [13]. The brain cortical surfaces were reconstructed from the MRI images by FreeSurfer. Then, a set of 'Core 6' landmark curves, including the Central Sulcus (CeS), Anterior Half of the Superior Temporal Gyrus (aSTG), Sylvian

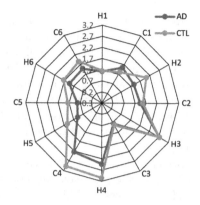

Fig. 5. Radar chart. (Color figure online)

Table 1. Classification accuracy comparison between our method and other methods.

Classification method	Correctness rate
Our method	**78.33%**
Brain surface area	56.67%
Brain mean curvature	55.00%

Fissure (SF), Calcarine Sulcus (CaS), Medial Wall Ventral Segment, and Medial Wall Dorsal Segment, are automatically traced on each cortical surface using the Caret package [19]. In Caret software, the PALS-B12 atlas is used to delineate the "core 6" landmarks, which are well-defined and geographically consistent, when compared with other gyral and sulcal features on human cortex. The stability and consistency of the six landmarks was validated in [18]. An illustration of the landmark curves on a left cortical surface is shown in Fig. 3 with two views. We show the landmarks with both the original and inflated cortical surfaces for clarity. A brain surface and its foliation are shown in Fig. 4(a) and (b), respectively.

Foliation Feature Visualization. We illustrate the difference of feature values between a pair of subjects with AD and healthy control subject (CTL) using radar chart. Radar chart displays multi-variate data in a two-dimensional chart where multiple variables are represented on axes starting from the same point. As shown in Fig. 5, six pairs of heights (H) and circumferences (C) corresponding to "core 6" landmarks, i.e., twelve features (labeled by 'H1', 'C1',..., 'H6', 'C6') are associated with twelve corners on the radar chart. We find that the pair of the H4 height and C4 circumference features associated to landmark curve of medial wall dorsal segment have the largest difference between these two subjects radar charts represented by a blue color line and an orange color line respectively. Although more validations are warranted, our research results may help discover AD related brain atrophy patterns.

Classification. We validated our method with brain surface classification on a dataset of brain cortical surfaces from 30 patients with Alzheimer disease and 30 healthy control subjects. The SVM method was employed as the classifier with 10-fold cross validation in our experiments. For each image, the input feature vector of the classifier includes 12 features. For comparison purpose, we also compute cortical surface area and cortical surface mean curvatures, two cortical surface features frequently adopted in prior structural MRI analyses [10]. We also applied SVM as the classifiers for these two features. Experimental results are shown in Table 1. Our proposed method achieved 78.33% correctness rate, which is better than the correctness rate 56.67% in the brain surface area based method and 55.00% in the brain surface mean curvature based method. Although multi-subject studies are clearly necessary, this experiment demonstrates that the foliation theory based geometric features may have the potential to quantify and measure AD related cortical surface changes.

6   Conclusion

In this paper, a novel brain surface classification method is proposed based on surface foliation theory. The method is rigorous, geometric, and automatic. In order to validate our proposed method, we applied our method on classifying brain cortical surfaces between patients with Alzheimer's disease and healthy control subjects, and the preliminary experimental results demonstrated the efficiency and efficacy of our method. In the future, we will employ our method to explore brain morphometry related to mild cognitive impairment (MCI) and other applications in the medical imaging field.

References

1. Alzheimer's Association: 2018 Alzheimer's disease facts and figures. Alzheimer's Dement. **14**(3), 367–429 (2018)
2. Campen, M., Silva, C., Zorin, D.: Bijective maps from simplicial foliations. ACM Trans. Graph. **35**(4), 7 (2016, to appear)
3. Chaplot, S., Patnaik, L., Jagannathan, N.: Classification of magnetic resonance brain images using wavelets as input to support vector machine and neural network. Biomed. Signal Process. Control **1**(1), 86–92 (2006)
4. Farkas, H., Kra, I.: Riemann Surfaces. Springer, New York (1992). https://doi.org/10.1007/978-1-4612-2034-3
5. Gu, X., Yau, S.-T.: Computational Conformal Geometry. International Press, Somerville (2008)
6. Hilaga, M., et al.: Topology matching for fully automatic similarity estimation of 3d shapes. In: Proceedings of the 28th Annual Conference on Computer Graphics and Interactive Techniques, pp. 203–212. ACM (2001)
7. Hsieh, D.-N., Arguillère, S., Charon, N., Miller, M.I., Younes, L.: A model for elastic evolution on foliated shapes. In: Chung, A.C.S., Gee, J.C., Yushkevich, P.A., Bao, S. (eds.) IPMI 2019. LNCS, vol. 11492, pp. 644–655. Springer, Cham (2019). https://doi.org/10.1007/978-3-030-20351-1_50

8. Hubbard, J., Masur, H.: Quadratic differentials and foliations. Acta Mathematica **142**(1), 221–274 (1979)

9. Lei, N., Zheng, X., Jiang, J., Lin, Y., Gu, X.: Quadrilateral and hexahedral mesh generation based on surfacefoliation theory. Comput. Methods Appl. Mech. Eng. **316**, 758–781 (2016)

10. Li, S., et al.: Abnormal changes of multidimensional surface features using multivariate pattern classification in amnestic mild cognitive impairment patients. J. Neurosci. **34**(32), 10541–10553 (2014)

11. Luders, E., et al.: Positive correlations between corpus callosum thickness and intelligence. Neuroimage **37**(4), 1457–1464 (2007)

12. Mahmoudi, M., Sapiro, G.: Three-dimensional point cloud recognition via distributions of geometric distances. Graph. Model. **71**(1), 22–31 (2009)

13. Mueller, S., et al.: The Alzheimer's disease neuroimaging initiative. Neuroimaging Clin. N. Am. **15**(4), 869–877 (2005)

14. Osada, R., Funkhouser, T., Chazelle, B., Dobkin, D.: Shape distributions. ACM Trans. Graph. (TOG) **21**(4), 807–832 (2002)

15. Strebel, K.: Quadratic Differentials. Springer, Heidelberg (1984). https://doi.org/10.1007/978-3-662-02414-0

16. Su, Z., Zeng, W., Wang, Y., Lu, Z.-L., Gu, X.: Shape classification using wasserstein distance for brain morphometry analysis. In: Ourselin, S., Alexander, D.C., Westin, C.-F., Cardoso, M.J. (eds.) IPMI 2015. LNCS, vol. 9123, pp. 411–423. Springer, Cham (2015). https://doi.org/10.1007/978-3-319-19992-4_32

17. Thompson, P., et al.: Dynamics of gray matter loss in Alzheimer's disease. J. Neurosci. **23**(3), 994–1005 (2003)

18. Van Essen, D.C.: A Population-Average, Landmark- and Surface-based (PALS) atlas of human cerebral cortex. Neuroimage **28**(3), 635–662 (2005)

19. Van Essen, D., et al.: An integrated software suite for surface-based analyses of cerebral cortex. J. Am. Med. Inform. Assoc. **8**(5), 443–459 (2001)

20. Winkler, A., et al.: Measuring and comparing brain cortical surface area and other areal quantities. Neuroimage **61**(4), 1428–1443 (2012)

21. Wolf, M.: On realizing measured foliations via quadratic differentials of harmonic maps tor-trees. Journal D'Analyse Mathematique **68**(1), 107–120 (1996)

22. Yang, J.-J., et al.: Prediction for human intelligence using morphometric characteristics of cortical surface: partial least square analysis. Neuroscience **246**, 351–361 (2013)

23. Zacharaki, E., et al.: Classification of brain tumor type and grade using MRI texture and shape in a machine learning scheme. Magn. Reson. Med. **62**(6), 1609–1618 (2009)

24. Zeng, W., et al.: Teichmüller shape descriptor and its application to Alzheimer's disease study. Int. J. Comput. Vis. **105**(2), 155–170 (2013)

25. Zhang, E., Mischaikow, K., Turk, G.: Vector field design on surfaces. ACM Trans. Graph. (ToG) **25**(4), 1294–1326 (2006)

Mixture Probabilistic Principal Geodesic Analysis

Youshan Zhang[1(✉)], Jiarui Xing[2], and Miaomiao Zhang[2,3]

[1] Computer Science and Engineering, Lehigh University, Bethlehem, USA
`yoz217@lehigh.edu`
[2] Electrical and Computer Engineering, University of Virginia, Charlottesville, USA
[3] Computer Science, University of Virginia, Charlottesville, USA
`{jx8fh,mz8rr}@virginia.edu`

Abstract. Dimensionality reduction on Riemannian manifolds is challenging due to the complex nonlinear data structures. While probabilistic principal geodesic analysis (PPGA) has been proposed to generalize conventional principal component analysis (PCA) onto manifolds, its effectiveness is limited to data with a single modality. In this paper, we present a novel Gaussian latent variable model that provides a unique way to integrate multiple PGA models into a maximum-likelihood framework. This leads to a well-defined mixture model of probabilistic principal geodesic analysis (MPPGA) on sub-populations, where parameters of the principal subspaces are automatically estimated by employing an Expectation Maximization algorithm. We further develop a mixture Bayesian PGA (MBPGA) model that automatically reduces data dimensionality by suppressing irrelevant principal geodesics. We demonstrate the advantages of our model in the contexts of clustering and statistical shape analysis, using synthetic sphere data, real corpus callosum, and mandible data from human brain magnetic resonance (MR) and CT images.

1 Introduction

PCA has been widely used to analyze high-dimensional data due to its effectiveness in finding the most important principal modes for data representation [12]. Motivated by the nice properties of probabilistic modeling, a latent variable model of PCA for factor analysis was presented [18,23]. Later, different variants of probabilistic PCA including Bayesian PCA [2] and mixture models of PCA [4] were developed for automatic data dimensionality reduction and clustering, respectively. It is important to extend all these models from flat Euclidean spaces to general Riemannian manifolds, where the data is typically equipped with smooth constraints. For instance, an appropriate representation of directional data, i.e., vectors of unit length in R^n, is the sphere S^{n-1} [16]. Another important example of manifold data is in shape analysis, where the definition of the shape of an object should not depend on its position, orientation, or scale, i.e., Kendall shape space [14]. Other examples of manifold data include geometric transformations such as rotations and translations, symmetric positive-definite tensors [10,25], Grassmannian manifolds (a set of m-dimensional linear

© Springer Nature Switzerland AG 2019
D. Zhu et al. (Eds.): MBIA 2019/MFCA 2019, LNCS 11846, pp. 196–208, 2019.
https://doi.org/10.1007/978-3-030-33226-6_21

subspaces of R^n), and Stiefel manifolds (the set of orthonormal m-frames in R^n) [24].

Data dimensionality reduction on manifolds is challenging due to the commonly used linear operations violate the natural constraints of manifold-valued data. In addition, basic statistical terms such as distance metrics, or data distributions vary on different types of manifolds [14,17,24]. A groundbreaking work, known as principal geodesic analysis (PGA), was the first to generalize PCA to nonlinear manifolds [10]. This method describes the geometric variability of manifold data by finding lower-dimensional geodesic subspaces that minimize the residual sum-of-squared geodesic distances to the data. Later on, an exact solution to PGA [19,20] and a robust formulation for estimating the output results [1] were developed. The probabilistic interpretation of PGA was firstly introduced in [26], which paved a way for factor analysis on manifolds. Since PPGA only defines a single projection of the data, the scope of its application is limited to uni-modal distributions. A more natural and motivating solution is to model the multi-modal data structure with a collection or mixture of local sub-models. Current mixture models on a specific manifold generally employ a two-stage procedure: a clustering of the data projected in Euclidean space followed by performing PCA within each cluster [6]. None of these algorithms define a probability density.

In this paper, we derive a mixture of PGA models as a natural extension of PPGA [26], where all model parameters including the low-dimensional factors for each data cluster is estimated through the maximization of a single likelihood function. The theoretical foundation of developing generative models of principal geodesic analysis for multi-population studies on general manifolds is brand new. In addition, the algorithmic inference of our proposed method is nontrivial due to the complicated geometry of manifold-valued data and numerical issues. Compared to previous methods, the major advantages of our model are: (i) it leads to a unified algorithm that well integrates soft data clustering and principal subspaces estimation on general Riemannian manifolds; (ii) in contrast to the two-stage approach mentioned above, our model explicitly considers the reconstruction error of principal modes as a criterion for clustering tasks; and (iii) it provides a more powerful way to learn features from data in non-Euclidean spaces with multiple subpopulations. We showcase our model advantages from two distinct perspectives: automatic data clustering and dimensionality reduction for analyzing shape variability. In order to validate the effectiveness of the proposed algorithm, we compare its performance with the state-of-the-art methods on both synthetic and real datasets. We also briefly discuss a Bayesian version of our mixture PPGA model that equips with the functionality of automatic dimensionality selection on general manifold data.

2   Background: Riemannian Geometry and PPGA

In this section, we briefly review PPGA [26] defined on a smooth Riemannian manifold M, which is a generalization of PPCA [23] in Euclidean space.

Before introducing the model, we first recap a few basic concepts of Riemannian geometry (more details are provided in [7]).

Covariant Derivative. The covariant derivative is a generalization of the Euclidean directional derivative to the manifold setting. Consider a curve $c(t) : [0,1] \to M$ and let $\dot{c} = dc/dt$ be its velocity. Given a vector field $V(t)$ defined along c, we can define the covariant derivative of V to be $\frac{DV}{dt} = \nabla_{\dot{c}} V$ that reflects the change of the vector field $\dot{c}$ in the V direction. A vector field is called parallel if the covariant derivative along the curve c is zero. A curve c is geodesic if it satisfies the equation $\nabla_{\dot{c}} \dot{c} = 0$.

Exponential Map. For any point $p \in M$ and tangent vector $v \in T_p M$ (also known as the tangent space of M at p), there exists a unique geodesic curve c with initial conditions $c(0) = p$ and $\dot{c}(0) = v$. This geodesic is only guaranteed to exist locally. The Riemannian exponential map at p is defined as $\mathrm{Exp}_p(v) = c(1)$. In other words, the exponential map takes a position and velocity as input and returns the point at time $t = 1$ along the geodesic with certain initial conditions. Notice that the exponential map is simply an addition in Euclidean space, i.e., $\mathrm{Exp}_p(v) = p + v$.

Logarithmic Map. The exponential map is locally diffeomorphic onto a neighborhood of p. Let $V(p)$ be the largest such neighborhood, the Riemannian log map, $\mathrm{Log}_p : V(p) \to T_p M$, is an inverse of the exponential map within $V(p)$. For any point $q \in V(p)$, the Riemannian distance function is given by $\mathrm{Dist}(p, q) = \|\mathrm{Log}_p(q)\|$. Similar to the exponential map, this logarithmic map is a subtraction in Euclidean space, i.e., $\mathrm{Log}_p(q) = q - p$.

2.1 PPGA

Given an d-dimensional random variable $y \in M$, the main idea of PPGA [26] is to model y as

$$y = \mathrm{Exp}\left(\mathrm{Exp}\left(\mu, Bx\right), \epsilon\right), \quad B = W\Lambda, \tag{1}$$

where μ is a base point on M, $x \in \mathbb{R}^q$ is a q-dimensional latent variable, with $x \sim N(0, I)$, B is an $d \times q$ factor matrix that relates x and y, and ϵ represents error. We will find it is convenient to model the factors as $B = W\Lambda$, where W is a matrix with q columns of mutually orthogonal tangent vectors in $T_\mu M$, Λ is a $q \times q$ diagonal matrix of scale factors for the columns of W. This removes the rotation ambiguity of the latent factors and makes them analogous to the eigenvectors and eigenvalues of standard PCA (there is still of course an ambiguity of the ordering of the factors).

The likelihood of PPGA is defined by a generalization of the normal distribution $\mathcal{N}(\mu, \tau^{-1})$, called Riemannian normal distribution, with its precision parameter τ. Therefore, we have

$$p(y|\mu, \tau) = \frac{1}{C(\mu, \tau)} \exp\left(-\frac{\tau}{2}\mathrm{Dist}(y, \mu)^2\right), \quad \text{with}$$

$$C(\mu, \tau) = \int_M \exp\left(-\frac{\tau}{2}\mathrm{Dist}(y, \mu)^2\right) dy. \tag{2}$$

This distribution is applicable to any Riemannian manifold, and the value of C in Eq. 2 does not depend on μ. It reduces to a multivariate normal distribution with isotropic covariance when $M = \mathbb{R}^n$ (see [9] for details). Note that this noise model could be replaced with other different distributions according to different types of applications.

Now, the PPGA model for a random variable y in Eq. (1) can be defined as

$$y \sim \mathcal{N}\left(\mathrm{Exp}\left(\mu, s\right), \tau^{-1}\right), \; s = W\Lambda x. \tag{3}$$

3   Our Model: Mixture Probability Principal Geodesic Analysis (MPPGA)

We now introduce a mixture model of PPGA (MPPGA) that provides a tempting prospect of being able to model complex multi-modal data structures. This formulation allows all model parameters to be estimated from maximum-likelihood, where both an appropriate data clustering and the associated principal modes are jointly optimized.

Consider observed data $y_n \in \{y_1, \cdots, y_N\}$ generated from K clusters on M (as shown in Fig. 1). We first introduce a K-dimensional binary random variable z_n with its k-th element $z_{nk} \in \{0,1\}$ as an indicator for n-th data point that belongs to cluster k, where $k \in \{1, \cdots, K\}$. This indicates that $z_{nk} = 1$ with other value being zero if the data y_n is in cluster k. The probability of each random variable z_n is

$$p(z_n) = \prod_{k=1}^{K} \pi_k^{z_{nk}}, \tag{4}$$

where $\pi_k \in [0,1]$ is the model mixing coefficient that satisfies $\sum_{k=1}^{K} \pi_k = 1$.

Analogous to PPGA in Eq. (1), the likelihood of each observed data y_n is

$$p(y_n \mid z_n) = \prod_{k=1}^{K} \mathcal{N}(y_n \mid \mathrm{Exp}\left(\mu_k, s_{nk}\right), \tau_k^{-1})^{z_{nk}}, \quad \text{with}$$

$$s_{nk} = W_k \Lambda_k x_{nk}, \tag{5}$$

where $x_{nk} \sim \mathcal{N}(0, I)$ is a latent random variable in $\mathbb{R}^q$, μ_k is a base point for each cluster k, W_k is a matrix with each columns representing the mutually orthogonal tangent vectors in $T_{\mu_k} M$, and Λ_k is a diagonal matrix of scale factors for the columns of W_k.

Combining Eq. (4) with Eq. (5), we obtain the complete data likelihood

$$p(y, z) = \prod_{n=1}^{N} p(y_n \mid z_n) p(z_n) p(x_n)$$

$$= \prod_{n,k=1}^{N,K} [\pi_k p(y_n \mid \mathrm{Exp}\left(\mu_k, s_{nk}\right), \tau_k^{-1}) p(x_{nk})]^{z_{nk}}. \tag{6}$$

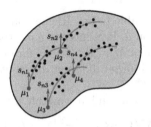

Fig. 1. Example MPPGA model with four clusters.

The log of the data likelihood in Eq. (6) can be computed as

$$\mathcal{L} \triangleq \ln p(y,z) = -\sum_{n,k=1}^{N,K} z_{nk} \ln\{\pi_k p(y_n \mid \text{Exp}\,(\mu_k, s_{nk}), \tau_k^{-1})p(x_{nk})\}. \quad (7)$$

3.1 Inference

We employ a maximum likelihood expectation maximization (EM) method to estimate model parameters $\theta = (\pi_k, \mu_k, W_k, \Lambda_k, \tau_k, x_{nk})$ and latent variables z_{nk}. This scheme includes two main steps:

E-step. To treat the binary indicator z_{nk} fully as latent random variables, we integrate them out from the distribution defined in Eq. (6). Similar to typical Gaussian mixture models, the expectation value of the complete-data log likelihood function is

$$\mathbb{E}[\mathcal{L}] = -\sum_{n,k=1}^{N,K} \mathbb{E}[z_{nk}]\,\{\ln p(y_n \mid \text{Exp}\,(\mu_k, s_{nk}), \tau_k^{-1}) + \ln p(x_{nk}) + \ln \pi_k\}. \quad (8)$$

The expected value of the latent variable z_{nk}, also known as the responsibility of component k for data point y_n [3], is then computed by its posterior distribution as

$$\mathbb{E}[z_{nk}] = p(z_{nk}|y_n) = \frac{p(y_n|z_{nk})p(z_{nk})}{\sum_{k=1}^{K} p(y_n|z_{nk})p(z_{nk})}$$

$$= \frac{\pi_k p(y_n|\text{Exp}\,(\mu_k, z_{nk}), \tau_k^{-1})}{\sum_{k=1}^{K} \pi_k p(y_n|\text{Exp}\,(\mu_k, z_{nk}), \tau_k^{-1})}. \quad (9)$$

Recall that the Rimannian distance function $\text{Dist}\,(p,q) = \|\text{Log}\,_p(q)\|$. We let $\gamma_{nk} \triangleq \mathbb{E}[z_{nk}]$ and rewrite Eq. (8) as

$$\mathbb{E}[\mathcal{L}] = -\sum_{n,k=1}^{N,K} \gamma_{nk}\{\frac{\tau_k}{2}\,\text{Log}\,(\text{Exp}\,(\mu_k, s_{nk}), y_n)^2 + \ln C + \ln \pi_k + \frac{\|x_{nk}\|^2}{2}\}, \quad (10)$$

where C is a normalizing constant.

M-step. We use gradient ascent to maximize the expectation function $\mathbb{E}[\mathcal{L}]$ and update parameters θ. Since the maximization of the mixing coefficient π_k is the same as Gaussian mixture model [3], we only give its final close-form update here as $\tilde{\pi}_k = \sum_{n=1}^N \gamma_{nk}/N$.

The computation of the gradient term requires we compute the derivative operator (Jacobian matrix) of the exponential map, i.e., $d_{\mu_k}\mathrm{Exp}\,(\mu_k, s_{nk})$, or $d_{s_{nk}}\mathrm{Exp}\,(\mu_k, s_{nk})$. Next, we briefly review the computations of derivatives w.r.t. the mean point μ and the tangent vector s separately. Closed-form formulations of these derivatives in the space of sphere, or 2D Kendall shape space are provided in [11,26].

For Derivative w.r.t. μ. Consider a variation of geodesics, e.g., $c(h,t) = \mathrm{Exp}\,(\mathrm{Exp}\,(\mu, hu), ts(h))$, where $u \in T_\mu M$ and $s(h)$ comes from parallel translating s along the geodesic $\mathrm{Exp}\,(\mu, hu)$. The derivative of this variation results in a Jacobi field: $J_\mu(t) = dc/dh(0,t)$. This gives an expression for the exponential map derivative as $d_\mu\mathrm{Exp}\,(\mu, s) = J_\mu(1)$ (as shown on the left panel of Fig. 2).

For Derivative w.r.t. s. Consider a variation of geodesics, e.g., $c(h,t) = \mathrm{Exp}\,(\mu, hu + ts)$. Again, the derivative of the exponential map is given by a Jacobi field satisfying $J_s(t) = dc/dh(0,t)$, and we have $d_s\mathrm{Exp}\,(\mu, s)u = J_s(1)$ (as shown on the right panel of Fig. 2).

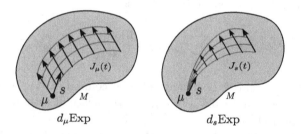

Fig. 2. Jacobi fields

Now we are ready to derive all gradient terms of $\mathbb{E}[\mathcal{L}]$ in Eq. 10 w.r.t. the parameters θ. For purpose of better readability, we simplify the notation by defining $\mathrm{Log}\,(\cdot) \triangleq \mathrm{Log}\,(\mathrm{Exp}\,(\mu_k, s_{nk}), y_n)$ in remaining sections.

Gradient for μ_k: the gradient of updating μ_k is

$$\nabla_{\mu_k}\mathbb{E}[\mathcal{L}] = \sum_{n,k=1}^{N,K} \gamma_{nk}\,\tau_k\,d_{\mu_k}\mathrm{Exp}\,(\mu_k, s_{nk})^\dagger\mathrm{Log}\,(\cdot), \qquad (11)$$

where $\dagger$ represents adjoint operator, i.e., for any tangent vectors $\hat{u}$ and $\hat{v}$,

$$\langle d_{\mu_k}\mathrm{Exp}\,(\mu_k, s_{nk})\hat{u}, \hat{v}\rangle = \langle \hat{u}, d_{\mu_k}\mathrm{Exp}\,(\mu_k, s_{nk})^\dagger\hat{v}\rangle.$$

Gradient for τ_k: the gradient of τ_k is computed as

$$\nabla_{\tau_k}\mathbb{E}[\mathcal{L}] = \sum_{n,k=1}^{N,K} \gamma_{nk}\frac{1}{C(\tau)}A_{n-1}\int_0^R \frac{r^2}{2}\mathrm{Exp}(-\frac{\tau}{2}r^2)\cdot$$

$$\prod_{\kappa=2}^n \kappa_\kappa^{-1/2}f_\kappa(\sqrt{\kappa_\kappa}r)dr - \frac{1}{2}\mathrm{Log}\,(\cdot)^2dr, \tag{12}$$

where A_{n-1} is the surface area of $n-1$ hypershpere. r is radius, κ_κ is the sectional curvature. Here $R = \min_v R(v)$, where $R(v)$ is the maximum distance of $\mathrm{Exp}(\mu_k, rv)$ with v being a point of unit sphere $S^{n-1} \subset T_{\mu_k}M$. While this formula is only valid for simple connected symmetric spaces, other spaces should be changed according to different definitions of the probability density function in Eq. (2).

To derive the gradient w.r.t. W_k, Λ_k and x_{nk}, we need to compute $d(\mathrm{Log}\,(\cdot)^2)/ds_{nk}$ first. Analogous to Eq. 11, we have

$$\frac{d(\mathrm{Log}\,(\cdot)^2)}{ds_{nk}} = 2\left(d_{s_{nk}}\mathrm{Exp}\,(\mu_k, s_{nk})^\dagger\mathrm{Log}\,(\cdot)\right). \tag{13}$$

After applying chain rule, we finally get all gradient terms as following:

Gradient for W_k: the gradient term of W_k is

$$\nabla_{W_k}\mathbb{E}[\mathcal{L}] = \sum_{n,k=1}^{N,K} \gamma_{nk}\frac{\tau_k}{2}\cdot\frac{d(\mathrm{Log}\,(\cdot)^2)}{ds_{nk}}\cdot x_{nk}^T\Lambda_k. \tag{14}$$

To maintain the mutual orthogonality of each column of W_k, we consider W_k as a point in Stiefel manifold $V_q(T_\mu M)$, i.e., the space of orthonormal q-frames in $T_\mu M$, and project the gradient of Eq. 14 into tangent space $T_{W_k}V_q(T_\mu M)$. We then update W_k by taking a small step along the geodesic in the projected gradient direction. For details on Stiefel manifold, see [8].

Gradient for Λ_k^a: the gradient term of each a-th diagonal element of Λ_k is:

$$\nabla_{\Lambda_k^a}\mathbb{E}[\mathcal{L}] = \sum_{n,k=1}^{N,K} \gamma_{nk}\tau_k(W_k^a x_{nk}^a)^T\cdot\frac{d(\mathrm{Log}\,(\cdot)^2)}{ds_{nk}}, \tag{15}$$

where W_k^a is the ath column of W_k and x_{nk}^a is the ath component of x_{nk}.

Gradient for x_{nk}: the gradient w.r.t. each x_{nk} is

$$\nabla_{x_{nk}}\mathbb{E}[\mathcal{L}] = -\sum_{n,k=1}^{N,K} \gamma_{nk}\{x_{nk} - \frac{\tau_k}{2}\Lambda_k W_k^T\cdot\frac{d(\mathrm{Log}\,(\cdot)^2)}{ds_{nk}}\}. \tag{16}$$

In this section, we further develop a Bayesian variant of MPPGA that equips with the functionality of automatic data dimensionality reduction. A critical issue in maximum likelihood estimate of principal geodesic analysis is the choice of the number of principal geodesic to be retained. This also could be problematic in our proposed MPPGA model since we assume each cluster has different dimensions of principal subspaces, and an exhaustive search over the parameter space can become computationally intractable.

To address this issue, we develop a Bayesian mixture principal geodesic analysis (MBPGA) model that determines the number of principal modes automatically to avoid adhoc parameter tuning. We carefully introduces an automatic relevance determination (ARD) prior [3] on each ath diagonal element of the eigenvalue matrix Λ as

$$p(\Lambda|\beta) = \prod_{i=1}^{d-1} (\frac{\beta^a}{2\pi})^{d/2} e^{-\frac{1}{2}\beta^a \|\Lambda^a\|^2}. \tag{17}$$

Each hyper-parameter β^a controls the inverse variance of its corresponding principal geodesic W^a, which is the ath column of W matrix. This indicates that if β^a is particularly large, the corresponding W^a will tend to be small and will be effectively eliminated.

Incorporating this ARD prior into our MPPGA model defined in Eq. 7, we arrive at a log posterior distribution of Λ as

$$\ln p(\Lambda|Y) = \mathcal{L} - \frac{1}{2} \sum_{i=1}^{d-1} \beta^a \|\Lambda^a\|^2 + \text{const.}. \tag{18}$$

Analogous to the EM algorithm introduced in Sect. 3.1, we maximize over Λ^a in M-step by using the following gradient:

$$\nabla_{\Lambda^a} \mathbb{E}[\mathcal{L}] = \sum_{n,k=1}^{N,K} \gamma_{nk} \tau_k (W_k^a x_{nk}^a)^T \cdot \frac{d(\text{Log}(\cdot)^2)}{ds_{nk}} - \beta^a \Lambda^a. \tag{19}$$

Similar to the ARD prior discussed in [2], the hyper-parameter β^a can be effectively estimated by $\beta^a = d/\|\Lambda^a\|^2$, where d is the dimension of the original data space.

4   Evaluation

We demonstrate the effectiveness of our MPPGA and MBPGA model by using both synthetic data and real data, and compare with two baseline methods K-means-PCA [6] and MPPCA [22] designed for multimodal Euclidean data. The geometry background of specific sphere and Kendall shape space including the computations of Riemannian exponential map, log map, and Jacobi fields can be found in [9, 26].

4.1 Data

Sphere. Using the generative model for PGA, we simulate a random sample of 764 data points on the unit sphere S^2 with known parameters W, Λ, τ, and π (see Table 1). All data points consist three clusters (Green: 200; Blue: 289; Black: 275). Note that our ground truth μ is generated from random uniform points on the sphere. The W is generated from a random Gaussian matrix, to which we then apply the Gram-Schmidt algorithm to ensure its columns are orthonormal.

Corpus Callosum Shape. The corpus callosum data are derived from public released Open Access Series of Imaging Studies (OASIS) database www.oasis-brains.org. It includes 32 magnetic resonance imaging scans of human brain subjects, with age from 19 to 90. The corpus callosum is segmented in a midsagittal slice using the ITK SNAP program www.itksnap.org. The boundaries of these segmentations are sampled with 64 points. This algorithm generates a sampling of a set of shape boundaries while enforcing correspondences between different point models within the population.

Mandible Shape. The mandible data is extracted from a collection of CT scans of human mandibles, with 77 subjects (36 female vs. 41 male) aged from 0 to 19. We sample 2×400 points on the boundaries.

4.2 Experiments

We first run our EM algorithm estimation of both MPPGA and MBPGA to test whether we could recover the model parameters. To initialize the model parameters (e.g., the cluster mean μ, principal eigenvector matrix W, and eigenvalue Λ), we use the output of K-means algorithm followed by performing linear PCA within each cluster. We uniformly distribute the weight to each mixing coefficient, i.e., $\pi_k = 1/K$. The initialization of all precision parameters $\{\tau_k\}$ is 0.01. We compare our model with two existing algorithms - mixture probabilistic principal components (MPPCA) [22] and K-means-PCA [6] performed in Euclidean space. For fair comparison, we keep the number of clusters the same across all algorithms.

To further investigate the applicability of our model MPPGA to real data, we test on 2D shapes of corpus callosum to study brain degeneration. The idea is to identify shape differences between two sub-populations: healthy vs. control group by analyzing their shape variability. We also run the extended Bayesian version of our model MBPGA to automatically select a compact set of principal geodesics to represent data variability. We perform similar experiments on the 2D mandible shape data to study group differences across genders, as well as within-group shape variability that reflects localized regions of growth.

4.3 Results

Figure 3 compares the estimated results of our model MPPGA/MBPGA with two baseline methods K-means-PCA and MPPCA. For the purpose of visualization, we project the estimated principle modes of K-means-PCA and MPPCA model from Euclidean space onto the sphere. Our model automatically separates the sphere data into three groups, which aligns fairly well with the ground truth (Green: 200; Blue: 289; Black: 275). For geodesics in each cluster (ground truth in yellow and model estimate in red), our results overlap better with the ground truth than others. This also indicates that our model can recover the parameters closer to the truth (as shown in Table 1). In particular, the MBPGA model is able to automatically select an effective dimension of the principal subspaces to represent data variability.

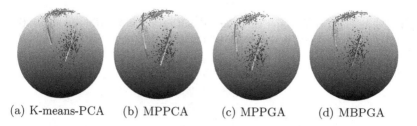

(a) K-means-PCA   (b) MPPCA   (c) MPPGA   (d) MBPGA

Fig. 3. The comparison of our model MPPGA/MBPGA with K-means-PCA and MPPCA (after being projected from Euclidean space onto the sphere). We have three clusters marked in green, blue, and black. Yellow lines: ground truth geodesics; Red lines: estimated geodesics. (Color figure online)

Table 1. Comparison between ground truth parameters $\{\lambda_k, \pi_k, \tau_k\}$ and the estimation of our model and baseline algorithms.

	$\lambda_{k=1,2,3}$	$\pi_{k=1,2,3}$	$\tau_{k=1,2,3}$
Ground truth	(0.2, 0.01, 0)	(0.2618, 0.3783, 0.3599)	(277.7778, 123.4568, 69.4444)
K-means-PCA	(0.1843, 0.0177, 0)	(0.2500, 0.3927, 0.3573)	NA
MPPCA	(0.5439, 0.0450, 0)	(0.2585, 0.3586, 0.3829)	(163.9344, 107.5269, 101.0101)
MPPGA	(0.1901, 0.0099, 0)	(0.2618, 0.3783, 0.3599)	(211.8783, 137.7593, 94.8111)
MBPGA	(0.1905, 0, 0)	(0.2618, 0.3783, 0.3599)	(212.4965, 140.0511, 96.1169)

Figure 4 demonstrates result of shape variations estimated by our model MPPGA and MBPGA. The corpus callosum shapes are automatically clustered into two different groups: healthy vs. control. An example of a segmented corpus callosum from brain MRI is shown in Fig. 4(a). Figure 4(b)–(e) show shape variations generated from points along the first principal geodesic: $\mathrm{Exp}\,(\mu, \alpha w^a)$, where $\alpha = -2, -1, 0, 1, 2 \times \sqrt{\lambda}$), for $a = 1$. It is shown that the corpus callosum from healthy group is significantly larger than control group. Meanwhile, the anterior and posterior ends of the corpus callosum show larger variation than the mid-caudate, which is consistent with previous studies.

Figure 5 shows fairly close eigenvalues estimated by MPPGA and MBPGA on corpus callosum data. Since the ARD prior introduced in MBPGA automatically

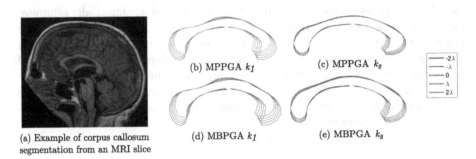

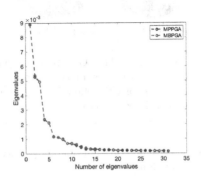

Fig. 4. Corpus callosum shape variations (healthy k_1 vs. control k_2) along the first principal geodesic $(-2, -1, 0, 1, 2) \times \sqrt{\lambda}$ estimated by our model MPPGA and MBPGA.

Fig. 5. Eigenvalues estimated by MPPGA/ MBPGA on corpus callosum data.

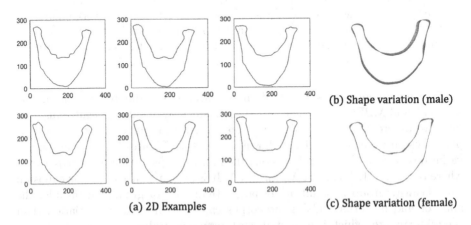

Fig. 6. 2D examples of mandible shape data and shape variations (male vs. female) along the first principal geodesic $(-2, -1, 0, 1, 2) \times \sqrt{\lambda}$ estimated by MBPGA model.

suppresses irrelevant principal geodesics to zero, we have 15 selected out of 128 in total.

We validate our MBPGA model to analyze the the mandible shape data (visualization of 2D examples are shown in Fig. 6(a)) since MBPGA produces fairly close results as MPPGA, but with the functionality of automatic data dimensionality reduction. The MBPGA model reduces the original data dimension from $d = 800$ to $d = 70$. Figure 6(b)(c) displays shape variations of mandibles from both male and female group. It clearly shows that generally male mandibles have larger variations than female mandibles, which is consistent with previous studies [5]. In particular, male mandibles have a larger variation in the temporal crest and the base of mandible.

5   Conclusion and Future Work

We presented a mixture model of PGA (MPPGA) on general Riemannian manifolds. We developed an Expectation Maximization for maximum likelihood estimation of parameters including the underlying principal subspaces and automatic data clustering results. This work takes the first step to generalize mixture models of principal mode analysis to Riemannian manifolds. A Bayesian variant of MPPGA (MBPGA) was also discussed in this paper for automatic dimensionality reduction. This model is particularly useful, as it avoids singularities that are associated with maximum likelihood estimations by suppressing the irrelevant information, e.g., outliers or noises. Our proposed model also paves a way for new tasks on manifolds such as hierarchical clustering and classification. Notice that all experiments conducted in this paper are with the number of clusters k being determined (e.g., healthy vs. control in corpus callosum data, or male vs. female in mandible data). For datasets with completely unknown clusters, current methods such as Elbow [15], Silhouhette [13], and Gap statistic methods [21] can be performed to determine the optimal number of clusters. This will be further investigated in our future work.

References

1. Banerjee, M., Jian, B., Vemuri, B.C.: Robust Fréchet mean and PGA on riemannian manifolds with applications to neuroimaging. In: Niethammer, M., et al. (eds.) IPMI 2017. LNCS, vol. 10265, pp. 3–15. Springer, Cham (2017). https://doi.org/10.1007/978-3-319-59050-9_1
2. Bishop, C.M.: Bayesian PCA. In: Advances in Neural Information Processing Systems, pp. 382–388 (1999)
3. Bishop, C.M.: Pattern recognition and machine learning, pp. 500–600 (2006)
4. Chen, J., Liu, J.: Mixture principal component analysis models for process monitoring. Ind. Eng. Chem. Res. 38(4), 1478–1488 (1999)
5. Chung, M.K., Qiu, A., Seo, S., Vorperian, H.K.: Unified heat kernel regression for diffusion, kernel smoothing and wavelets on manifolds and its application to mandible growth modeling in ct images. Med. Image Anal. 22(1), 63–76 (2015)

6. Cootes, T.F., Taylor, C.J.: A mixture model for representing shape variation. Image Vis. Comput. **17**(8), 567–573 (1999)
7. Do Carmo, M.: Riemannian Geometry. Birkhauser (1992)
8. Edelman, A., Arias, T.A., Smith, S.T.: The geometry of algorithms with orthogonality constraints. SIAM J. Matrix Anal. Appl. **20**(2), 303–353 (1998)
9. Fletcher, P.T.: Geodesic regression and the theory of least squares on riemannian manifolds. Int. J. Comput. Vis. **105**(2), 171–185 (2013)
10. Fletcher, P.T., Lu, C., Pizer, S.M., Joshi, S.: Principal geodesic analysis for the study of nonlinear statistics of shape. IEEE Trans. Med. Imaging **23**(8), 995–1005 (2004)
11. Fletcher, P.T., Zhang, M.: Probabilistic geodesic models for regression and dimensionality reduction on riemannian manifolds. In: Turaga, P.K., Srivastava, A. (eds.) Riemannian Computing in Computer Vision, pp. 101–121. Springer, Cham (2016). https://doi.org/10.1007/978-3-319-22957-7_5
12. Jolliffe, I.T.: Principal component analysis and factor analysis. In: Jolliffe, I.T. (ed.) Principal Component Analysis. Springer Series in Statistics, pp. 115–128. Springer, New York (1986). https://doi.org/10.1007/978-1-4757-1904-8_7
13. Kaufman, L., Rousseeuw, P.J.: Partitioning around medoids (program PAM). In: Finding Groups in Data: An Introduction to Cluster Analysis, pp. 68–125 (1990)
14. Kendall, D.G.: Shape manifolds, procrustean metrics, and complex projective spaces. Bull. Lond. Math. Soc. **16**(2), 81–121 (1984)
15. Ketchen, D.J., Shook, C.L.: The application of cluster analysis in strategic management research: an analysis and critique. Strat. Manag. J. **17**(6), 441–458 (1996)
16. Mardia, K.V., Jupp, P.E.: Directional Statistics, vol. 494. Wiley, Hoboken (2009)
17. Obata, M.: Certain conditions for a Riemannian manifold to be isometric with a sphere. J. Math. Soc. Jpn. **14**(3), 333–340 (1962)
18. Roweis, S.T.: EM algorithms for PCA and SPCA. In: Advances in Neural Information Processing Systems, pp. 626–632 (1998)
19. Sommer, S., Lauze, F., Hauberg, S., Nielsen, M.: Manifold valued statistics, exact principal geodesic analysis and the effect of linear approximations. In: Daniilidis, K., Maragos, P., Paragios, N. (eds.) ECCV 2010. LNCS, vol. 6316, pp. 43–56. Springer, Heidelberg (2010). https://doi.org/10.1007/978-3-642-15567-3_4
20. Sommer, S., Lauze, F., Nielsen, M.: Optimization over geodesics for exact principal geodesic analysis. Adv. Comput. Math. **40**(2), 283–313 (2014)
21. Tibshirani, R., Walther, G., Hastie, T.: Estimating the number of clusters in a data set via the gap statistic. J. R. Stat. Soc. Ser. B (Stat. Methodol.) **63**(2), 411–423 (2001)
22. Tipping, M.E., Bishop, C.M.: Mixtures of probabilistic principal component analyzers. Neural Comput. **11**(2), 443–482 (1999)
23. Tipping, M.E., Bishop, C.M.: Probabilistic principal component analysis. J. R. Stat. Soc. Ser. B (Stat. Methodol.) **61**(3), 611–622 (1999)
24. Turaga, P., Veeraraghavan, A., Srivastava, A., Chellappa, R.: Statistical computations on grassmann and stiefel manifolds for image and video-based recognition. IEEE Trans. Pattern Anal. Mach. Intell. **33**(11), 2273–2286 (2011)
25. Tuzel, O., Porikli, F., Meer, P.: Pedestrian detection via classification on riemannian manifolds. IEEE Trans. Pattern Anal. Mach. Intell. **30**(10), 1713–1727 (2008)
26. Zhang, M., Fletcher, P.T.: Probabilistic principal geodesic analysis. In: Advances in Neural Information Processing Systems, pp. 1178–1186 (2013)

A Geodesic Mixed Effects Model
in Kendall's Shape Space

Esfandiar Nava-Yazdani$^{(\boxtimes)}$ ⓘ, Hans-Christian Hege ⓘ,
and Christoph von Tycowicz ⓘ

Zuse Institute Berlin, Takustraße 7, 14195 Berlin, Germany
{navayazdani,hege,vontycowicz}@zib.de

Abstract. In many applications, geodesic hierarchical models are adequate for the study of temporal observations. We employ such a model
derived for manifold-valued data to Kendall's shape space. In particular,
instead of the Sasaki metric, we adapt a functional-based metric, which
increases the computational efficiency and does not require the implementation of the curvature tensor. We propose the corresponding variational time discretization of geodesics and apply the approach for the
estimation of group trends and statistical testing of 3D shapes derived
from an open access longitudinal imaging study on osteoarthritis.

Keywords: Longitudinal modeling · Shape trajectory · Riemannian
metric · Geodesic regression · Parallel transport · Kendall's shape space

1 Introduction

Analysis of time-dependent shape data has become increasingly important for
a wide range of applications. For individual biological changes, subject-specific
smooth regression models are adequate. The obtained trajectories provide the
possibility to estimate data values at unobserved times and to compare trends
even with unbalanced data. Due to the non-linear structure of Kendall's shape
space, common statistical tools derived for Euclidean spaces are not applicable. Within the previous years, many novel approaches have been presented for
the statistical analysis of time-dependent manifold-valued data [2,8,11,15]. The
derived schemes benefit from a compact encoding of constraints and exhibit a
superior consistency as compared to their Euclidean counterparts.

In this work, we employ the generative hierarchical approach, based on
geodesic analysis, introduced in [3] and [11] with some modifications. In the first
stage, inner-individual changes are modeled as geodesic trends, which in the
second phase are considered as disturbances of a population-averaged geodesic
trend. For an introduction and overview over longitudinal analysis based on
mixed effects models we refer to [5].

We use the approach, to approximate the observed temporal shape data
by geodesics in the shape space and to estimate the overall trends within the

© Springer Nature Switzerland AG 2019
D. Zhu et al. (Eds.): MBIA 2019/MFCA 2019, LNCS 11846, pp. 209–218, 2019.
https://doi.org/10.1007/978-3-030-33226-6_22

groups on this basis. Geodesic models are attractive because they have a compact representation and enable computational efficiency. Moreover inconsistencies, e.g. due to acquisition noise and reconstruction errors, are minimized via geodesic regression.

Analysis of geodesic trends requires a notion of distance that is consistent with the Riemannian metric of shape space. State-of-the-art approaches parametrize geodesics as points in the tangent bundle of the shape space [11]. While the Sasaki metric is a natural metric on the tangent bundle, its geodesic computations require time-discrete approximation schemes involving the Riemannian curvature tensor. This not only incurs high computational costs but also impacts numerical stability. We consider a novel approach that overcomes these shortcomings. To this end, we identify elements of the tangent bundle with vector fields along the geodesic trend. This provides a notion of a canonical metric that is motivated from a functional view of parameterized curves in the shape space [16]. Considering the space of the geodesics as a submanifold in the space of shape trajectories, this allows in particular the use of a naturally induced distance. The corresponding shortest path, log map and average geodesic, can be computed by variational time-discretization. Remarkably, the underlying energy function allows for fast and simple evaluation increasing computational efficiency. In particular, it neither requires curvature computation nor decomposition in horizontal and vertical components.

The main challenge in the first stage, viz. geodesic regression, is to determine parallel transport and Jacobi fields in Kendall's shape space. While these important geometric quantities are not given by closed form expressions, efficient approximation schemes have been presented [9,10,12].

Using the derived metric for geodesic trends, we obtain a notion of mean, covariance, and Mahalanobis distance. This allowed us to develop a statistical hypothesis test for comparing the group-wise mean trends. Non-parametric permutation tests are applied to test for significance of estimated differences in group trends. We perform this in terms of a manifold-valued Hotelling t^2 statistic described in [3] by applying it to the tangent bundle. As example application we demonstrate the methodology on the long term study of incident knee osteoarthritis (OA).

This paper is organized as follows. In Sect. 2, after a short overview of Kendall's shape space, we present main mathematical tools corresponding to the geometry of the shape space and its tangent bundle, particularly parallel transport, geodesic regression and mean geodesic. Essential for these considerations is to encode the geometry of the shape space via computations in the pre-shape space. In Sect. 3 we present the application of our approach to femur data from an epidemiological longitudinal study dealing with osteoarthritis and discuss the numerical results.

2   Kendall's Shape Space

In the following we present a brief overview of Kendall's shape space and its tangent bundle as well as main quantities which will be employed for geodesic analysis and statistics.

2.1   Preliminaries

For a comprehensive introduction to Kendall's shape space and details on the subjects of this section, we refer to [7] and [12]. For the relevant tools from Riemannian geometry, we refer to [4] and [13].

Let $M(m, k)$ denote the space of real $m \times k$ matrices endowed with its canonical scalar product given by $\langle x, y \rangle = \text{trace}(xy^t)$, and $\| \cdot \|$ the induced Frobenius norm. We call the set of k-ad of landmarks in $\mathbb{R}^m$ after removing translations and scaling the pre-shape space and identify it with $\mathcal{S}_m^k := \{x \in M(m, k) : \sum_{i=1}^k x_i = 0, \|x\| = 1\}$ endowed with the spherical Procrustes metric $d(x, y) = \arccos(\langle x, y \rangle)$. A shape is a pre-shape with rotations removed. More precisely, the left action of SO_m on $\mathcal{S}_m^k$ given by $(R, x) \mapsto Rx$ defines an equivalence relation given by $x \sim y$ if and only if $y = Rx$ for some $R \in \text{SO}_m$. Kendall's shape space is defined as $\Sigma_m^k = \mathcal{S}_m^k / \sim$. Now, denoting the canonical projection of $\sim$ by π, the induced distance between any two shapes $\pi(x)$ and $\pi(y)$ is given by

$$d_\Sigma(x, y) = \min_{R \in \text{SO}_m} d(x, Ry) = \arccos \sum_{i=1}^m \lambda_i,$$

where $\lambda_1 \geq \cdots \geq \lambda_{m-1} \geq |\lambda_m|$ denote the pseudo-singular values of yx^t. Note that for simplicity of notation, we have identified shapes and their representing pre-shapes in the definition of d_Σ. Moreover, for $k \geq 3$, the shape space Σ_1^k (resp. Σ_2^k) is isometric to the sphere (resp. projective space). We call $x, y \in \mathcal{S}_m^k$ well positioned and write $x \overset{\omega}{\sim} y$ if and only if yx^t is symmetric and $d(x, y) = d_\Sigma(x, y)$. For each $x, y \in \mathcal{S}_m^k$, there exists an optimal rotation $R \in \text{SO}_m$ such that $x \overset{\omega}{\sim} Ry$. Due to [7] the horizontal and vertical spaces at $x \in \mathcal{S}_m^k$ read

$$\text{Hor}_x = \{u \in M(m, k-1) : ux^t = xu^t \text{ and } \langle x, u \rangle = 0\},$$
$$\text{Ver}_x = \{Ax : A + A^t = 0\}.$$

A smooth curve is called horizontal if and only if its tangent field is horizontal. Geodesics in the shape space are equivalence classes of horizontal geodesics. Now, let exp and log denote the exponential and log map of the pre-shape sphere. For $x \overset{\omega}{\sim} y$ the geodesic from x to y given by

$$\Phi(x, y, t) := \exp_x(t \log_x y) = \frac{\sin((1-t)\varphi)}{\sin \varphi} x + \frac{\sin(t\varphi)}{\sin \varphi} y \qquad (1)$$

with $\varphi = \arccos(\langle x, y \rangle)$, $0 \leq t \leq 1$, is horizontal. Hence Φ realizes the minimizing geodesic from $\pi(x)$ to $\pi(y)$. We recall, that pre-shapes with rank $\geq m - 1$, denoted by $\mathcal{S}$, constitute an open and dense subset of $\mathcal{S}_m^k$ and the restriction of the quotient map π to $\mathcal{S}$ is a Riemannian submersion with respect to the metric induced by the ambient Euclidean space. Key quantities of the shape space geometry such as parallel transport, Jacobi fields and Fréchet mean can be computed by horizontal lifting to $\mathcal{S}$ (and extension to $\mathcal{S}_m^k$). We refer the reader to [12] for corresponding results.

2.2   Geodesic Regression

The first stage of the employed model is geodesic regression, which we summarize below. We recall that diameter of Σ_m^k is $\pi/2$. Now, let Ω_x be a neighborhood of $x \in \mathcal{S}_m^k$ with radius smaller then $\pi/4$ and such that for any $y \in \Omega_x$, denoting the pseudo-singular values of yx^t by λ_i, $\lambda_{m-1} + \lambda_m > 0$ holds. Then, due to [7, 6.6], for $y \in \Omega_x$ the optimal rotation R with $x \overset{\omega}{\sim} Ry$ is unique. Hence the function $\Omega_x \ni y \mapsto \omega(x, y) := Ry$ is well-defined.

Now, consider scalars $0 = t_1 < t_2 < \cdots < t_N = 1$ and distinct pre-shapes $q_1, \cdots, q_N$. Geodesic regression aims at finding a geodesic curve in shape space that best fits the data $\pi(q_i)$ at t_i in a least-squares sense. Computationally, we employ the parametrization given by (1) to determine the corresponding horizontal geodesic $\Phi(x^*, y^*, .)$, where $(x^*, y^*) := \arg \min F$ and

$$F(x, y) := \sum_{i=1}^{N} d^2(q_i, \omega(q_i, \Phi(x, y, t_i,))), \ x \overset{\omega}{\sim} y,$$

with $(q_1, \omega(q_1, q_N))$ as initial guess.

We recall that the significance of the regression model can be measured by coefficient of determination denoted R^2. To compute it, let $F_{min} := F(x^*, y^*)$ and denote the minimum of $G(x) := \sum_{i=1}^{N} d^2(q_i, \omega(x, q_i))$ by G_{min}. Then $R^2 = 1 - \frac{F_{min}}{G_{min}}$.

2.3   Tangent Bundle and Mean Geodesic

Geodesic mixed effects models and particularly mean geodesic (group trend) require a notion of distance for the tangent bundle consistent with the Riemannian metric of the shape space. In the following, we present a brief introduction to a natural choice for such a distance provided by the Sasaki metric employed in [11]. Then, we propose an alternative L^2-type approach and induced variational time-discrete geodesics.

In the sequel, $I := [0, 1]$. Let (M, g) be an μ-dimensional Riemannian manifold and δ a Riemannian metric on the tangent bundle TM with the canonical projection τ. Identifying a geodesic γ with $(\gamma(0), \dot{\gamma}(0))$, mean of geodesics is determined by δ. A prominent natural choice for δ is the Sasaki metric. It is uniquely determined by the following properties (cf. [14]): (a) τ becomes a Riemannian submersion. (b) The restriction of δ to any tangent space coincides with g. (c) Parallel vector fields along arbitrary curves in M are orthogonal to their fibers, i.e., for any curve γ and parallel vector field v along it, $\dot{\gamma} \perp T_\gamma M$.

Let $\eta := (p, u) : I \to TM$ be a curve. τ being a Riemannian submersion, $T_\eta TM$ enjoys an orthogonal decomposition in vertical (viz. kernel of $d_\eta \tau$) and horizontal subspaces, both μ-dimensional. Identifying each of them with $T_p M$, the Sasaki metric at η is induced by the quadratic form $\|v\|^2 + \|w\|^2$, where $v = p'$ and $w = u'$. Denoting the covariant derivative and curvature tensor of g by ∇ and R, Sasaki geodesics are given by

$$\nabla_v v = -R(u, w, v),$$
$$\nabla_v w = 0.$$

Algorithms for the computation of the exponential and log map as well as mean geodesic with respect to Sasaki metric, and also an application to corpus callosum longitudinal data as trajectories in Kendall's shape space are given in [11]. In this case $m = 2$ (planar shapes), the shape space can be identified with the complex projective space and the Riemannian curvature tensor is explicitly given in terms of the canonical complex structure and the curvature tensor of the pre-shape space. For $m \geq 3$, computation of R is more delicate.

Next, we present the proposed approach to employ a metric on the tangent bundle. Fix $s \in I$ and let $\gamma_s : J \to M$ be the geodesic emerging from $p(s)$ with initial velocity $u(s) = \dot\gamma_s(0)$. Note that γ_s is horizontal. Now, let ξ_s be a vector field along γ_s. Then by $\int_J g(\xi_s(t), \xi_s(t)) \, dt$ a quadratic form at $(p(s), u(s))$ is given, which in turn defines a metric, again denoted by δ in the space of geodesics. Let $H = H(s, t)$ be a path in TM with $\alpha := H(0, .)$ and $\beta := H(1, .)$ arc length parametrized geodesics. The energy of H induced by the above quadratic form reads $E(H) = \frac{1}{2} \int_0^1 \int_0^1 g(H'(s, t), H'(s, t)) \, dt \, ds$ ($\xi_s = H'(s, .)$). Let H^* denote the minimizer of E restricted to paths through geodesics, i.e. $H(s, .)$ geodesic for all $s \in I$. Next, we construct time-discrete paths H_n to approximate H^*. E achieves its minimum over all paths connecting α to β in M if $H(., t)$ is a geodesic for all t (for a proof, we refer the reader to [16, Theorem 3.2]). Now, suppose that α and β are close enough, and let Φ denote the arc length parametrized geodesic from x to y and (x_n^*, y_n^*) the minimizer of

$$E(x, y) := \sum_{i=0}^{n-1} \int_0^1 d^2(\Phi(x_i, y_i, t), \Phi(x_{i+1}, y_{i+1}, t)) \, dt \tag{2}$$

over $M^n \times M^n$, where $x_0 = \alpha(0), y_0 = \alpha(1), x_n = \beta(0), y_n = \beta(1)$. A natural choice for the initial values x^0 and y^0 is given by the equidistant partition $x_i^0 = \Phi(x_0, x_n, t_i), y_i^0 = \Phi(y_0, y_n, t_i)$ with $t_i = \frac{i}{n}$. Then, the desired discrete shortest path reads $H_n = (\Phi(x_0^*, y_0^*, .), \cdots, \Phi(x_n^*, y_n^*, .))$.

Notion and computation of the corresponding tangent bundle's log map is immediate and its linearization ($n = 1$) reads $\mathrm{Log}_\alpha \beta$. Similarly, the induced mean of n dense enough geodesics $\gamma_i : I \to M$ is the geodesic with initial- and endpoints x and y minimizing

$$E(x, y) = \sum_i^n \int_0^1 d^2(\Phi(x, y, t), \Phi(x_i, y_i, t)) \, dt \tag{3}$$

over M^2, where $x_i = \gamma(0)$ and $y_i = \gamma(1)$. A natural choice for the initial value is given by the point-wise mean, viz. $(x^0, y^0) :=$ mean of (x_i, y_i), $i = 1, \cdots, n$. In the sequel, we call δ the functional-based L^2-metric.

Figure 1 shows a geodesic in TS^2 as shortest path connecting two S^2-geodesics for the Sasaki- and the proposed functional-based metric. For none of them footpoint curves constitute geodesics. However, the functional-based one is closer to the more intuitive shortest path given by the simple point-wise construction $H(s, t) = \Phi(\alpha(t), \beta(t), s)$.

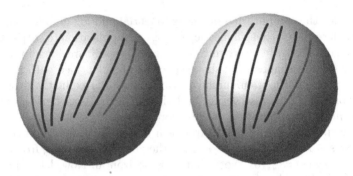

Fig. 1. Minimal geodesic in the tangent bundle identified as shortest path connecting two geodesics (red) with respect to Sasaki (left) and functional-based L^2-metric (right). (Color figure online)

Note that computations of the log map and mean with respect to δ neither involve the curvature tensor nor decomposition in horizontal and vertical components.

Figure 2 shows the result of an experiment with synthetic spherical data. Geodesics were generated by randomly sampling endpoints following a normal distribution. Computed Sasaki- and functional-mean geodesics consistently provide adequate approximations of the true mean geodesic.

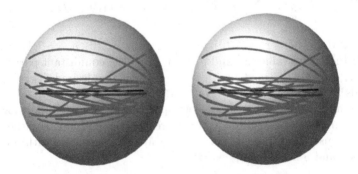

Fig. 2. Red geodesics are generated by randomly perturbing the endpoints of the black one. Their mean geodesic with respect to Sasaki (left) and functional-based L^2-metric (right) are blue. (Color figure online)

3 Application

In this section, we present the input data, our approach for the estimation of group-wise trends based on regression model, the Hotelling T^2 test for group differences, and numerical results (Fig. 3).

3.1 Data Description

We apply the derived scheme to the analysis of group differences in longitudinal femur shapes of subjects with incident and developing osteoarthritis (OA) versus normal controls. The dataset is derived from the Osteoarthritis Initiative (OAI), which is a longitudinal study of knee osteoarthritis maintaining (among others) clinical evaluation data and radiological images from 4,796 men and women of age 45–79. The data are available for public access at http://www.oai.ucsf.edu/. From the OAI database, we determined three groups of shapes trajectories: HH (healthy, i.e. no OA), HD (healthy to diseased, i.e. onset and progression to severe OA), and DD (diseased, i.e. OA at baseline) according to the Kellgren–Lawrence score [6] of grade 0 for all visits, an increase of at least 3 grades over the course of the study, and grade 3 or 4 for all visits, respectively. We extracted surfaces of the distal femora from the respective 3D weDESS MR images (0.37×0.37 mm matrix, 0.7 mm slice thickness) using a state-of-the-art automatic segmentation approach [1]. For each group, we collected 22 trajectories (all available data for group DD minus a record that exhibited inconsistencies, and the same number for groups HD and HH, randomly selected), each of which comprises shapes of all acquired MR images, i.e. at baseline, the 1-, 2-, 3-, 4- and 6-year visits. In a supervised post-process, the quality of segmentations as well as the correspondence of the resulting meshes (8,988 vertices) were ensured.

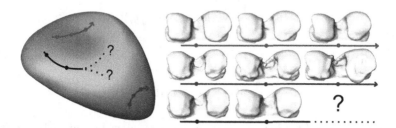

Fig. 3. Longitudinal femoral data are divided in groups based on Kellgren–Lawrence score (right). Temporal observations are mapped to trajectories in the shape space (left). An important task is to estimate overall trends within groups.

3.2 Numerical Results

We applied the geodesic regression approach to the femoral trajectories described above and represented in Kendall's shape space. For details and computational

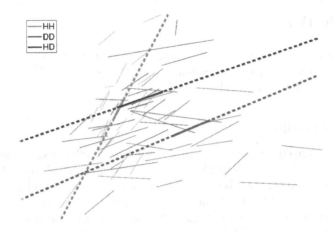

Fig. 4. Principal components for Group-wise trends estimated as means of fitted geodesics.

aspects, we refer to [12]. Note that geodesic representation provides a less cluttered visualization of the trajectory population making it easier to identify trends within as well as across groups. For the statistical testing of group differences, we employ the manifold-valued Hotelling T^2 test described in [11] and present the formulas used therein for the convenience of the reader. Let $x = x_1, \cdots, x_{n_1}$ and $y = y_1, \cdots, y_{n_2}$ two samples with corresponding Fréchet means $\bar{x}$ and $\bar{y}$, $v_x = \log_{\bar{x}} \bar{y}$, $v_y = \log_{\bar{y}} \bar{x}$. Then the individual group covariances are given by

$$W_x = \frac{1}{n_1} \sum_{i=1}^{n_1} (\log_{\bar{x}} x_i)(\log_{\bar{x}} x_i)^t$$

$$W_y = \frac{1}{n_2} \sum_{i=1}^{n_2} (\log_{\bar{y}} y_i)(\log_{\bar{y}} y_i)^t$$

and the sample T^2 statistic reads

$$t^2 = \frac{1}{2}(v_x^t W_x^{-1} v_x + v_y^t W_y^{-1} v_y).$$

For the estimations of the log map and mean, we employed (2) and (3). We found t^2-values 0.0012, 0.000703 and 0.000591 for HH vs. DD, DD vs. HD and HH vs. HD with corresponding p-values 0, 0.011 and 0.033. For the computation of the statistical significance, i.e. p-values, we randomly permuted group memberships of the subject-specific geodesic trends, each identified with its (initial-, end-point), 1,000 times. The results reveal clear differences between the group-wise average geodesics demonstrating the descriptiveness of the proposed approach. In particular, the results confirm the obvious differences in group-average trends depicted in the low-dimensional visualization in Fig. 4.

4   Conclusion

We presented a modification of the geodesic hierarchical model introduced in [3] and [11] by employing a discrete geodesic for the tangent bundle of the shape space instead of Sasaki geodesics. Our approach does not involve the Riemannian curvature tensor and provides an efficient approximation. Moreover, we estimated average geodesics and group trends for the example application of femoral longitudinal data incorporating Kendall's shape space. Furthermore, we employed a manifold-valued Hotelling t^2 test confirming that the model well distinguishes the group differences. There are several potential direction for future work. First, it would be interesting to perform the computations utilizing the Sasaki metric and to compare with our numerical result. Second, we would like to extend our approach to independently test for systematic differences in intercept and slope of the trends. Finally, an extension of the approach to higher-dimensional parameters would allow to take further effects into account providing more insight on more complex phenomena.

Acknowledgments. We are grateful for the open-access OAI dataset of the Osteoarthritis Initiative, that is a public-private partnership comprised of five contracts (N01-AR-2-2258; N01-AR-2-2259; N01-AR-2-2260; N01-AR-2-2261; N01-AR-2-2262) funded by the National Institutes of Health, a branch of the Department of Health and Human Services, and conducted by the OAI Study Investigators. Private funding partners include Merck Research Laboratories; Novartis Pharmaceuticals Corporation, GlaxoSmithKline; and Pfizer, Inc. Private sector funding for the OAI is managed by the Foundation for the National Institutes of Health. This manuscript was prepared using an OAI public use data set and does not necessarily reflect the opinions or views of the OAI investigators, the NIH, or the private funding partners.

References

1. Ambellan, F., Tack, A., Ehlke, M., Zachow, S.: Automated segmentation of knee bone and cartilage combining statistical shape knowledge and convolutional neural networks: Data from the Osteoarthritis Initiative. In: Medical Imaging with Deep Learning (2018). https://openreview.net/pdf?id=SJ_-Nx3jz
2. Bône, A., Colliot, O., Durrleman, S.: Learning distributions of shape trajectories from longitudinal datasets: a hierarchical model on a manifold of diffeomorphisms. In: Proceedings of the IEEE Conference on Computer Vision and Pattern Recognition, pp. 9271–9280 (2018)
3. Fletcher, P.T.: Geodesic regression and the theory of least squares on Riemannian manifolds. Int. J. Comput. Vis. **105**(2), 171–185 (2013)
4. Gallot, S., Hulin, D., Lafontaine, J.: Riemannian Geometry, 3rd edn. Springer, Heidelberg (2005). https://doi.org/10.1007/978-3-642-18855-8
5. Gerig, G., Fishbaugh, J., Sadeghi, N.: Longitudinal modeling of appearance and shape and its potential for clinical use. Med. Imag. Anal. **33**, 114–121 (2016). https://doi.org/10.1016/j.media.2016.06.014
6. Kellgren, J., Lawrence, J.: Radiological assessment of osteo-arthrosis. Ann. Rheum. Diseases **16**(4), 494 (1957)

7. Kendall, D.G., Barden, D., Carne, T.K., Le, H.: Shape and Shape Theory. Wiley, Chichester (1999)
8. Kim, H.J., Adluru, N., Suri, H., Vemuri, B.C., Johnson, S.C., Singh, V.: Riemannian nonlinear mixed effects models: analyzing longitudinal deformations in neuroimaging. In: Proceedings of the IEEE Conference on Computer Vision and Pattern Recognition, pp. 2540–2549 (2017)
9. Lorenzi, M., Ayache, N., Pennec, X.: Schild's ladder for the parallel transport of deformations in time series of images. In: Székely, G., Hahn, H.K. (eds.) IPMI 2011. LNCS, vol. 6801, pp. 463–474. Springer, Heidelberg (2011). https://doi.org/10.1007/978-3-642-22092-0_38
10. Louis, M., Charlier, B., Jusselin, P., Pal, S., Durrleman, S.: A fanning scheme for the parallel transport along geodesics on Riemannian manifolds. SIAM J. Num. Anal. **56**(4), 2563–2584 (2018)
11. Muralidharan, P., Fletcher, P.T.: Sasaki metrics for analysis of longitudinal data on manifolds. In: 2012 IEEE Conference on Computer Vision and Pattern Recognition, Providence, RI, USA, June 16–21, 2012. pp. 1027–1034 (2012). https://doi.org/10.1109/CVPR.2012.6247780
12. Nava-Yazdani, E., Hege, H.C., Sullivan, T.J., von Tycowicz, C.: Geodesic analysis in kendall's shape space with epidemiological applications Manuscript submitted for publication, 2018. Preprint https://arxiv.org/abs/1906.11950
13. O'Neill, B.: The fundamental equations of a submersion. Mich. Math. J. **13**(4), 459–469 (1966)
14. Sasaki, S.: On the differential geometry of tangent bundles of riemannian manifolds. Tohoku Math. J. (2) **10**(3), 338–354 (1958). https://doi.org/10.2748/tmj/1178244668
15. Singh, N., Hinkle, J., Joshi, S., Fletcher, P.T.: A hierarchical geodesic model for diffeomorphic longitudinal shape analysis. In: Gee, J.C., Joshi, S., Pohl, K.M., Wells, W.M., Zöllei, L. (eds.) IPMI 2013. LNCS, vol. 7917, pp. 560–571. Springer, Heidelberg (2013). https://doi.org/10.1007/978-3-642-38868-2_47
16. Srivastava, A., Klassen, E.P.: Functional and Shape Data Analysis. SSS. Springer, New York (2016). https://doi.org/10.1007/978-1-4939-4020-2

An As-Invariant-As-Possible $GL^+(3)$-Based Statistical Shape Model

Felix Ambellan$^{(\boxtimes)}$ (iD), Stefan Zachow (iD), and Christoph von Tycowicz (iD)

Therapy Planning Group, Zuse Institute Berlin, Berlin, Germany
{ambellan,zachow,vontycowicz}@zib.de

Abstract. We describe a novel nonlinear statistical shape model based on differential coordinates viewed as elements of $GL^+(3)$. We adopt an as-invariant-as possible framework comprising a bi-invariant Lie group mean and a tangent principal component analysis based on a unique $GL^+(3)$-left-invariant, O(3)-right-invariant metric. Contrary to earlier work that equips the coordinates with a specifically constructed group structure, our method employs the inherent geometric structure of the group-valued data and therefore features an improved statistical power in identifying shape differences. We demonstrate this in experiments on two anatomical datasets including comparison to the standard Euclidean as well as recent state-of-the-art nonlinear approaches to statistical shape modeling.

Keywords: Statistical shape analysis · Tangent principal component analysis · Lie groups · Classification · Manifold valued statistics

1 Introduction

Changes in the shape of anatomies are often early indicators of specific diseases. For example, musculoskeletal disorders affecting large proportions of the adult population such as Osteoarthritis (OA) [17] are associated with morphological changes. The overall socio-economic burden [6] associated with these diseases provides a strong impetus to develop novel computational approaches for the support of treatment and prevention strategies. Statistical models of shape have been established as one of the most successful methods for understanding the geometric variability of anatomical structures [1]. Given a set of samples from an object class under study, statistical shape models estimate the distribution of the underlying population in terms of a mean shape and a hierarchy of principle modes encoding the variation of the samples around that mean. Moreover, representing the samples within the basis of principle modes provides a concise and highly discriminative description that is susceptible for analysis and inference algorithms. In particular, descriptors based on statistical shape modeling have proven effective for predicting the onset and progression of OA [5,20,22,23].

© Springer Nature Switzerland AG 2019
D. Zhu et al. (Eds.): MBIA 2019/MFCA 2019, LNCS 11846, pp. 219–228, 2019.
https://doi.org/10.1007/978-3-030-33226-6_23

While linear approaches like the *point distribution model* (PDM) [7] are still the most widely used in applied morphometrics, they fail to fully capture the inherent nonlinearity in biological shape variation [8]. Many exciting ideas to account for this nonlinearity have been presented ranging from the large deformation framework [19] based on diffeomorphisms of the ambient space to modeling the variability of surfaces employing concepts from shell theory [4,14,25]. However, due to the inherent complexity of the involved nonlinear estimation problems the practical applicability especially in time-critical applications is limited. To address this challenge, one line of work encodes shapes using differential coordinates that provide a local description of the geometry rather than absolute positions [3,10,12,13,24]. In particular, statistical shape models based on differential coordinates have recently been successfully employed for classification of radiographic OA significantly outperforming the linear PDM [3,24]. Typically differential coordinates are derived from the (deformation) gradient of the map that encodes the shape relative to a reference and, hence, naturally belong to the group of orientation preserving linear transformations $GL^+(3)$. However, to the best of our knowledge, previous work does not account for the rich geometric structure inherent to $GL^+(3)$. On the one hand, approaches like [27] based on the Riemannian framework are not stable according to group operations (composition and inversion) due to the lack of bi-invariant metrics for $GL^+(3)$. Anyhow, consistency with group operations is desirable as it provides invariance w.r.t. changes of reference and data coordinate systems and, thus, prevents bias due to arbitrary choices thereof. On the other hand, equipping $GL^+(3)$ with an alternative group structure as done for the *differential coordinates model* (DCM) in [24] provides bi-invariance but ignores its original, canonical structure. Furthermore, while Woods [26] proposes a similar approach for image deformation, he employs a surface representation that is not group-valued.

In this work, we derive a novel statistical shape model based on linear differential coordinates that is as-invariant-as-possible and, hence, promises increased consistency and reduced bias. To this end, we adapt the notion of bi-invariant mean as proposed in [21] employing an affine connection structure on $GL^+(3)$. Furthermore, we perform second-order statistics based on a family of Riemannian metrics providing the most possible invariance, viz. $GL^+(3)$-left-invariance and $O(3)$-right-invariance. We evaluate the performance of the derived model in terms of shape-based classification of pathological malformations of the human knee demonstrating superior accuracy over state-of-the-art [3,24] approaches.

2   Differential Coordinates

In this section, we provide a concise introduction to linear differential coordinates and refer the reader to [24] for further details. We consider shapes to be instances of a class of anatomical objects that are topologically consistent, s.t. they can be represented as a left-acting deformation ϕ of a common reference $\bar{S}$. We further, assume that $\bar{S}$ is discretized as a simplicial surface mesh with k vertices and m triangles. In order to perform analysis on local geometric details rather than absolute coordinates of a shape $S = \phi(\bar{S})$, we can employ a differential representation given by the deformation gradient $\nabla\phi$, i.e. the 3×3 matrix of partial derivatives of ϕ. Let ϕ be orientation-preserving and affine on each triangle $\bar{T}_i \in \bar{S}$, then the derivatives are constant on each triangle with $\nabla\phi|_{\bar{T}_i} \equiv D_i \in \mathrm{GL}^+(3)$. Note, that the deformation of a triangle fully specifies an affine map of $\mathrm{I\!R}^3$ if we assume that triangle normals are mapped onto each other (cf. Kirchhoff–Love kinematic assumptions). Accordingly, a representation of a shape S in linear differential coordinates is given by $\xi = (D_1, \ldots, D_m)^T$.

A key feature of this representation is that the inverse problem of mapping differential coordinates back to a deformation ϕ leads to the well-known Poisson equation

$$\Delta\phi = \nabla \cdot \xi, \tag{1}$$

where $\Delta \in \mathrm{I\!R}^{k \times k}$ and $\nabla \cdot \in \mathrm{I\!R}^{k \times 3m}$ denote the discrete Laplacian and divergence operator, respectively. Note, as (1) is a linear differential equation it can be solved very efficiently. Furthermore, the solutions are unique up to translations of each connected component of $\bar{S}$.

3   Geometric Statistics in GL$^+$(3)

In order to derive information of our geometric data we perform element-wise geometric statistics on it. Let $\{\xi^j = (D_1^j, \ldots, D_m^j)^T\}_{j=1}^n$ be the set of all input shapes represented in differential coordinates. The essential components to set up a statistical shape model are a mean value and a tangent Principal Component Analysis (tPCA) [9] to analyze the input as deviations thereof.

3.1   Bi-Invariant Mean

Since $\mathrm{GL}^+(3)$ does not admit a bi-invariant metric there can not exist a bi-invariant *Riemannian* mean. Nevertheless, due to the Lie group structure there exists a naturally bi-invariant candidate for the mean in terms of the group exponential barycenter called *bi-invariant mean*. We follow hereby the work of Pennec and Arsigny [21] who delivered a comprehensive characterization and analysis on this topic. The bi-invariant mean M_i is defined through:

$$\sum_{j=1}^n \log\left(D_i^j \cdot M_i^{-1}\right) = 0, \tag{2}$$

where log denotes the group logarithm. To solve for the unknown M_i we apply an iterative fixed point scheme:

$$M_i^{k+1} = \exp\left(\sum_{j=1}^n \log\left(D_i^j \cdot (M_i^k)^{-1}\right)\right) \cdot M_i^k, \tag{3}$$

where exp denotes the group exponential.

The local existence and uniqueness of the bi-invariant mean have been proven for data with small enough dispersion, i.e. if the data lies within a sufficiently small normal convex neighborhood of some point of the Lie group. Furthermore, the algorithm given by Eq. (3) always converges to M_i at least with linear speed provided that the initialization is chosen sufficiently close to the data.

From Eq. (3) we see that the group logarithm and exponential of $GL^+(3)$ are essential operations required to determine the mean shape as well as for the statistical analysis in its tangent space (Sect. 3.2). However, it should be emphasized that there does not exist a *real* logarithm for every element in $GL^+(3)$. We can classify such elements by investigating the underlying eigenvalue structure. Let D be an arbitrary element in $GL^+(3)$. It is known that there always exists a *real* Jordan-Decomposition [11] $D = V \cdot E \cdot V^{-1}$ s.t. E belongs (modulo permutation) to one of the following three types:

$$A: \begin{pmatrix} \lambda_1 & 0 & 0 \\ 0 & \lambda_2 & 0 \\ 0 & 0 & \lambda_3 \end{pmatrix}, \qquad \text{where } \lambda_i \in \mathbb{R}^+,$$

$$B: \begin{pmatrix} -\lambda_1 & 0 & 0 \\ 0 & -\lambda_2 & 0 \\ 0 & 0 & \lambda_3 \end{pmatrix}, \qquad \text{where } \lambda_i \in \mathbb{R}^+, \lambda_1 \neq \lambda_2,$$

$$C: \begin{pmatrix} \lambda_1 & \mu & 0 \\ -\mu & \lambda_1 & 0 \\ 0 & 0 & \lambda_2 \end{pmatrix}, \qquad \text{where } \lambda_1 + i\mu \in \mathbb{C} \setminus \mathbb{R}_0^+, \lambda_2 \in \mathbb{R}^+.$$

As the logarithm is compatible with a change of basis it is enough to consider only matrices of the above form. Both cases A and C admit a real logarithm, contrasting case B that does not allow for its existence. This raises the question what deformation gradients could feature such an eigenvalue configuration and whether it is likely to appear. If we take a closer look at case B we see that it encodes an anisotropic scale with two negative weights. Since the respective deformation is orientation preserving it must invert two edges of a triangle and change their lengths in a non-uniform fashion. This seems to be a rather unlikely deformation, if we consider data to be aligned and without artifacts such as local overfolds. In particular, the two real word datasets we performed our experiments on (Sect. 4) did not admit any element in any input shape that came across with a deformation gradient of this structure. Neither during calculation of the mean nor during analysis.

However, in order to do statistics in $GL^+(3)$ that are robust to such extreme cases we require an alternative strategy. To this end, we propose to perform a *pseudo* logarithm operation. Let D be an element of $GL^+(3)$ with no logarithm. We define its pseudo logarithm *plog* employing polar decomposition as follows:

$$\text{plog}(D) = \text{plog}(RU) := \log(R) + \log(U)$$

In case a real $\log(D)$ exists this formula can be seen as first order (commutator free) approximation in terms of the Baker–Campbell–Hausdorff formula and for commutating R, U this formula would be even exact. This can additionally be interpreted as a fallback to the product structure of the DCM [24]. Contrary to the logarithm, the matrix exponential always exists and can efficiently be calculated using the scaling-and-squaring method together with Padé approximations [15].

3.2 Tangent Principal Component Analysis

In the previous section we were able to circumvent the absence of a bi-invariant metric but this is no longer possible if we want to perform higher-order analysis using tPCA. While there is no bi-GL$^+$(3)-invariant metric, we are interested in metrics that yield at least invariance under orthogonal transformations, i.e. metrics that are invariant with respect to a change of coordinates obtained by rotating or mirroring the data. Indeed, there exists exactly one family of metrics that is GL$^+$(3)-left-invariant and O(3)-right-invariant and uniquely determined up to three positive real constants [18]. We define the metric as usual via the inner product on the respective Lie algebra.

Let $X, Y \in \mathfrak{gl}(3) = \mathbb{R}^{3 \times 3}$ and $\mu, \nu, \kappa \in \mathbb{R}^+$:

$$\langle X, Y \rangle_{\mu, \nu, \kappa} := \mu \langle \operatorname{dev} \operatorname{sym} X, \operatorname{dev} \operatorname{sym} Y \rangle + \nu \langle \operatorname{skew} X, \operatorname{skew} Y \rangle + \frac{\kappa}{3} \operatorname{tr}(X) \operatorname{tr}(Y),$$

where we have used the following notation:

$$\langle X, Y \rangle = \langle X, Y \rangle_2 = \operatorname{tr}\left(X^T Y\right) \quad \text{(standard inner product)},$$
$$\operatorname{sym} X = \frac{1}{2}(X + X^T) \quad \text{(symmetric part of } X),$$
$$\operatorname{skew} X = \frac{1}{2}(X - X^T) \quad \text{(skew-symmetric part of } X),$$
$$\operatorname{dev} X = X - \frac{\operatorname{tr} X}{3} I_3 \quad \text{(deviator of } X).$$

If we consider X as *infinitesimal transformation* the above terms admit certain geometric interpretations: skew$X$ represents the rotational part and sym$X$ the distortion part. While the trace tr quantifies volume changes, the deviator dev represents the trace-free part and, hence, devsym$X$ describes the shearing (volume-preserving distortion) part of X. Furthermore, the above inner product features two interesting properties:

$$\langle X, Y \rangle_{1,1,1} = \langle X, Y \rangle \quad \text{for all } X, Y \in \mathfrak{gl}(3),$$
$$\langle X, Y \rangle_{\mu, \nu, \kappa} = 0 \quad X \in \mathfrak{so}(3), Y \text{ symmetric}.$$

Hence, this family of metrics can be seen as natural generalization of the standard metric arising from the standard inner product for matrices. Let us assume to have n input shapes with m triangles each, then we perform tPCA in the tagent space $T_M(\mathrm{GL}^+(3))^m$ at the differential coordinates of the mean shape $M = (M^1, \ldots, M^m)$. The $(p+1)$-th mode of variation is hereby given as:

$$v_{p+1} = \underset{g_{\mu,\nu,\kappa}^M(v,v)=1}{\arg\max} \sum_{i=1}^{n} \sum_{l=1}^{p} g_{\mu,\nu,\kappa}^M(v_l, \log(D_i))^2 + g_{\mu,\nu,\kappa}^M(v, \log(D_i))^2, \quad (4)$$

where $D_i = (D_i^1, \ldots, D_i^m)$, log is applied component-wise and $g_{\mu,\nu,\kappa}^M = \sum g_{\mu,\nu,\kappa}^{M^j}$ is the metric emerging from $\langle \cdot, \cdot \rangle_{\mu,\nu,\kappa}$.

4   Experiments and Results

The following experiments are performed utilizing (rounded) metric parameters $\mu = 0.1$, $\nu = 29.42$, $\kappa = 1.3$ that have been found conducting *hyper parameter optimization* (HPO) w.r.t. best performance in our classification experiment. HPO was carried out within the Scikit-Optimize[1] python framework performing a sequential optimization using decision trees (forest_minimize) on the cubical domain $[0.05, 1000]^3$.

Data. We employ two datasets:

(i) Distal femora (see Fig. 2) from the Osteoarthritis Initiative (OAI) for 58 severely diseased and 58 healthy subjects that were also used for evaluation in [3,24] and are publicly available as segmentations[2] [2]. For a detailed list of the exact subjects that are included in the experiment as well as their disease state we refer to the supplemental material of [3]. We used the surface meshes as provided by the authors (in particular the correspondences) and we refer to [24] for further details on the creation of the dataset.

(ii) Skeletal human hand (see Fig. 3) taken from the publicly available data[3] of [16] that is based on data of the Large Geometric Models Archive from the Georgia Institute of Technology.

Knee Osteoarthritis Classification. OA is i.a. characterized by changes of the shape of bones composing the knee. With this experiment we want to investigate the proposed $\mathrm{GL}^+(3)$ model's sensitivity w.r.t. pathological shape changes and thus its ability to classify knee OA for the OAI dataset of distal femora. To achieve this, we utilize a simple support vector machine (SVM) with linear kernel directly on the 115-dimensional space of shape weights. These weights are the vectors of coefficients w.r.t. the principal modes for each shape. The weights serve as input features to the SVM. The classifier is trained on a balanced set (healthy/diseased) of feature vectors for different shares of randomly chosen data varying from 10% to 90% whereas the testing is performed on the respective

---

[1] https://scikit-optimize.github.io.
[2] https://doi.org/10.12752/4.ATEZ.1.0.
[3] http://graphics.stanford.edu/~niloy/research/shape_space/shape_space_sig_07.html.

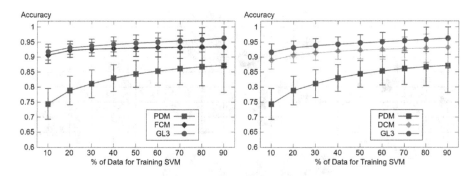

Fig. 1. OA classification experiment for the proposed GL$^+$(3) model, PDM [7] and the recent FCM [3] (left) and the related DCM [24] (right). The accuracy of the GL$^+$(3) model ranges from 91.6% (at 10% training) to 96.3% (at 90% training).

complement. Since we have some randomness in our experimental design we carry out the experiment 10000 times for each partition and consider the mean accuracy and the standard deviation. We compare our method to the PDM [7] as well as to the in a way related DCM [24] and the recent *fundamental coordinate model* (FCM) [3], which both achieved highly accurate classification results. To this end, we employ the above outlined classifier setup using the respective model specific shape weights.

Figure 1 shows the results in terms of average accuracy and standard deviation. The accuracy of the GL$^+$(3) model ranges from 91.6% (at 10% training) to 96.3% (at 90% training). Note that solely the proposed GL$^+$(3) method achieves an accuracy of over 91% in case of sparse (10%) training data.

Qualitative Evaluation. We perform two qualitative experiments.

(i) A comparison of the mean shape of the OAI dataset as determined by the DCM as well as the proposed GL$^+$(3) model. To achieve this we align both shapes and calculate the surface distance between them. Both mean shapes are highly similar as can be seen in Fig. 2.

(ii) An analysis of the skeletal hand dataset. We calculate the mean shape of the two input poses, perform tPCA and (visually) investigate the resulting trajectory connecting the two input shapes through the mean w.r.t. plausibility. As shown in Fig. 3 the principal mode shows natural nonlinear deformation characteristics.

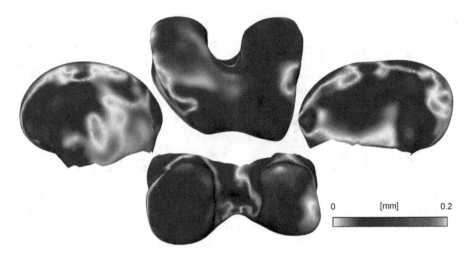

Fig. 2. Deviations of mean distal femur shape as calculated with the proposed $GL^+(3)$ model and the DCM [24]. Absolute values of the surface distance are plotted color-coded on the DCM mean shape.

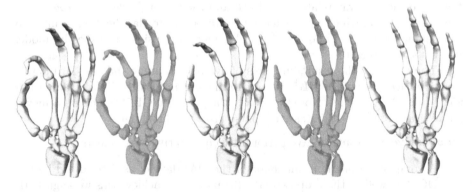

Fig. 3. Trajectory as calculated with the proposed $GL^+(3)$ model connecting the input shapes (left, right) via the exponential mean (center) showing natural deformation characteristics.

5   Conclusion and Future Work

In this work, we presented a novel nonlinear statistical shape model based on $GL^+(3)$. The model utilized the bi-invariant Lie group mean and a tangent principal component analysis employing a $GL^+(3)$-left-invariant, $O(3)$-right-invariant metric in $GL^+(3)$. It can thus be considered as as-invariant-as-possible w.r.t. the canonical $GL^+(3)$ structure of the deformation gradient. We have shown that the proposed model possesses a high descriptiveness w.r.t. natural biological differences in shape. In order to determine the parameters of the metric we applied a hyper parameter optimization targeting classification accuracy.

In particular, we conducted experiments on OA classification achieving results that are superior to those of the state-of-the-art models [3,24].

We consider it valuable and interesting to also investigate the purely Riemannian perspective associated with the above metric and compare it to our present work. Although geodesics can be evaluated in closed form for a given direction and the existence of a shortest geodesic connecting two arbitrary points is theoretically guaranteed, no closed form solution to determine the direction of one (and not necessarily the shortest) connecting geodesic is known [18].

Acknowledgments. The authors are funded by the Deutsche Forschungsgemeinschaft (DFG, German Research Foundation) under Germany's Excellence Strategy – The Berlin Mathematics Research Center MATH+ (EXC-2046/1, project ID: 390685689). Furthermore, we are grateful for the open-access OAI dataset of the Osteoarthritis Initiative, that is a public-private partnership comprised of five contracts (N01-AR-2-2258; N01-AR-2-2259; N01-AR-2-2260; N01-AR-2-2261; N01-AR-2-2262) funded by the National Institutes of Health, a branch of the Department of Health and Human Services, and conducted by the OAI Study Investigators. Private funding partners include Merck Research Laboratories; Novartis Pharmaceuticals Corporation, GlaxoSmithKline; and Pfizer, Inc. Private sector funding for the OAI is managed by the Foundation for the National Institutes of Health. This manuscript was prepared using an OAI public use data set and does not necessarily reflect the opinions or views of the OAI investigators, the NIH, or the private funding partners.

References

1. Ambellan, F., Lamecker, H., von Tycowicz, C., Zachow, S.: Statistical shape models: understanding and mastering variation in anatomy. In: Rea, P.M. (ed.) Biomedical Visualisation. AEMB, vol. 1156, 1st edn, pp. 67–84. Springer, Cham (2019). https://doi.org/10.1007/978-3-030-19385-0_5
2. Ambellan, F., Tack, A., Ehlke, M., Zachow, S.: Automated segmentation of knee bone and cartilage combining statistical shape knowledge and convolutional neural networks. Med. Image Anal. **52**, 109–118 (2019)
3. Ambellan, F., Zachow, S., von Tycowicz, C.: A surface-theoretic approach for statistical shape modeling. In: Proceedings of Medical Image Computing and Computer Assisted Intervention (MICCAI) (2019, accepted for publication)
4. Brandt, C., von Tycowicz, C., Hildebrandt, K.: Geometric flows of curves in shape space for processing motion of deformable objects. Comput. Graph Forum **35**(2), 295–305 (2016)
5. Bredbenner, T.L., Eliason, T.D., Potter, R.S., Mason, R.L., Havill, L.M., Nicolella, D.P.: Statistical shape modeling describes variation in tibia and femur surface geometry between control and incidence groups from the osteoarthritis initiative database. J. Biomech. **43**(9), 1780–1786 (2010)
6. Conaghan, P.G., Kloppenburg, M., Schett, G., Bijlsma, J.W., et al.: Osteoarthritis research priorities: a report from a eular ad hoc expert committee. Ann. Rheum. Dis. **73**(8), 1442–1445 (2014)
7. Cootes, T.F., Taylor, C.J., Cooper, D.H., Graham, J.: Active shape models-their training and application. Comput. Vis. Image Underst. **61**(1), 38–59 (1995)
8. Davis, B.C., Fletcher, P.T., Bullitt, E., Joshi, S.: Population shape regression from random design data. Int. J. Comput. Vis. **90**(2), 255–266 (2010)

9. Fletcher, P., Lu, C., Pizer, S., Joshi, S.: Principal geodesic analysis for the study of nonlinear statistics of shape. IEEE. Trans. Med. Imaging **23**(8), 995–1005 (2004)
10. Freifeld, O., Black, M.J.: Lie bodies: a manifold representation of 3D human shape. In: Fitzgibbon, A., Lazebnik, S., Perona, P., Sato, Y., Schmid, C. (eds.) ECCV 2012. LNCS, vol. 7572, pp. 1–14. Springer, Heidelberg (2012). https://doi.org/10.1007/978-3-642-33718-5_1
11. Gallier, J.: Logarithms and square roots of real matrices existence, uniqueness and applications in medical imaging. arXiv preprint arXiv:0805.0245 (2018)
12. Gao, L., Lai, Y.K., Liang, D., Chen, S.Y., Xia, S.: Efficient and flexible deformation representation for data-driven surface modeling. ACM Trans. Graph **35**(5), 158 (2016)
13. Hasler, N., Stoll, C., Sunkel, M., Rosenhahn, B., Seidel, H.P.: A statistical model of human pose and body shape. Comput. Graph Forum **28**(2), 337–346 (2009)
14. Heeren, B., Zhang, C., Rumpf, M., Smith, W.: Principal geodesic analysis in the space of discrete shells. Comput. Graph Forum **37**(5), 173–184 (2018)
15. Higham, N.J.: The scaling and squaring method for the matrix exponential revisited. SIAM J. Matrix Anal. Appl. **26**(4), 1179–1193 (2005)
16. Kilian, M., Mitra, N.J., Pottmann, H.: Geometric modeling in shape space. ACM Trans. Graph. (SIGGRAPH) **26**(3), #64, 1–8 (2007)
17. Lawrence, R.C., et al.: Estimates of the prevalence of arthritis and other rheumatic conditions in the united states: part II. Arthritis Rheumatol. **58**(1), 26–35 (2008)
18. Martin, R.J., Neff, P.: Minimal geodesics on GL(n) for left-invariant, right-O(n)-invariant Riemannian metrics. J. Geom. Mech. **8**(3), 323–357 (2016)
19. Miller, M.I., Trouvé, A., Younes, L.: Hamiltonian systems and optimal control in computational anatomy: 100 years since d'arcy thompson. Annu. Rev. Biomed. Eng. **17**, 447–509 (2015)
20. Neogi, T., et al.: Magnetic resonance imaging-based three-dimensional bone shape of the knee predicts onset of knee osteoarthritis. Arthritis Rheum. **65**(8), 2048–2058 (2013)
21. Pennec, X., Arsigny, V.: Exponential barycenters of the canonical Cartan connection and invariant means on Lie groups. In: Nielsen, F., Bhatia, R. (eds.) Matrix Information Geometry, pp. 123–166. Springer, Heidelberg (2013). https://doi.org/10.1007/978-3-642-30232-9_7
22. Thomson, J., O'Neill, T., Felson, D., Cootes, T.: Automated shape and texture analysis for detection of osteoarthritis from radiographs of the knee. In: Navab, N., Hornegger, J., Wells, W.M., Frangi, A.F. (eds.) MICCAI 2015. LNCS, vol. 9350, pp. 127–134. Springer, Cham (2015). https://doi.org/10.1007/978-3-319-24571-3_16
23. Thomson, J., O'Neill, T., Felson, D., Cootes, T.: Detecting osteophytes in radiographs of the knee to diagnose osteoarthritis. In: Wang, L., Adeli, E., Wang, Q., Shi, Y., Suk, H.-I. (eds.) MLMI 2016. LNCS, vol. 10019, pp. 45–52. Springer, Cham (2016). https://doi.org/10.1007/978-3-319-47157-0_6
24. von Tycowicz, C., Ambellan, F., Mukhopadhyay, A., Zachow, S.: An efficient Riemannian statistical shape model using differential coordinates. Med. Image Anal. **43**, 1–9 (2018)
25. von Tycowicz, C., Schulz, C., Seidel, H.P., Hildebrandt, K.: Real-time nonlinear shape interpolation. ACM Trans. Graph **34**(3), 34:1–34:10 (2015)
26. Woods, R.P.: Characterizing volume and surface deformations in an atlas framework: theory, applications, and implementation. NeuroImage **18**(3), 769–788 (2003)
27. Zacur, E., Bossa, M., Olmos, S.: Multivariate tensor-based morphometry with a right-invariant riemannian distance on GL+(n). J. Math. Imaging Vis. **50**(1–2), 18–31 (2014)

Author Index

Printed in the United States
By Bookmasters